Emily Chappell became a cycle courier after various stints as an academic and a financial editor. More recently she has cycled across Asia, fatbiked through Alaska and Canada in winter and taken up ultra-distance racing. As well as writing an award-winning blog about her travels, she has contributed to the *Guardian*, the *Independent*, *Vogue* and various cycling media. This is her first book

Further praise for *What Goes Aroun*

'Chappell really will tell you all that you need to know, and several things that you perhaps didn't realise you wanted to know . . . The result is a joy to read as she describes the highs and lows of the job.' Nick Young, *Times Literary Supplement*

'Chappell's never-ending awe of London's intricacies, smells, heartbreaks, triumphs, nooks and crannies is beautifully and vividly put across. Even the most committed hater of the capital would surely book a train ticket having read only a few chapters . . . The book is so well written that you can feel tired when you hear of the long days, and happy as you hear about summer blossom falling onto the road.' *Pedalicious*

'With remarkably intricate and evocative detail, Chappell takes us through her journey from wide-eyed new girl to hardened veteran. She combines fascinating insight into the job with raw personal experience and passion. It feels a privilege to cycling

mean you don't have to be at all interested in actual courier work to find this absorbing.' *Urban Cyclist*

'Chappell is a marvellous writer, and the book reads rather like a bike ride with its succession of turns and unexpected discoveries . . . The joy of cycling is at its heart, however; if any book could make you consider chucking in your desk job and throwing on some Lycra, this could be it.' *Diva*

'A very well-written, compelling read. This book brings to life London cycling in a way that is relevant and interesting to anyone who gets on a bike . . . An unpretentious, well-woven story of self-discovery that could be applicable to many regardless of age or station in life.' *London Cyclist*

'Delivers the goods in style . . . Chappell is a gifted storyteller. She deftly weaves in a plotted history of couriering, from the explosion of the industry in the late 1980s . . . through to its gentle decline at the hand of email attachments, file sharing and electronic signatures.' Rob Penn, *Observer*

'For any young city dweller stuck in limbo while finding a job, *What Goes Around* provides a refreshing solution on how to jump out the rat race while staying in employment . . . Chappell recounts the unbridled joy she found cycling around London – dancing through traffic, and overcoming mental and physical barriers.' *Jocks and Nerds*

What Goes Around
A London Cycle Courier's Story

EMILY CHAPPELL

First published in 2016
by Guardian Books, Kings Place,
90 York Way, London N1 9GU
and Faber & Faber Limited,
Bloomsbury House,
74–77 Great Russell Street,
London WC1B 3DA
This paperback edition first published in 2017

Typeset by Faber & Faber Limited
Printed and bound by CPI Group (UK) Ltd, Croydon, CR0 4YY

A CIP record for this book
is available from the British Library

ISBN 978–1–78335–054–4

2 4 6 8 10 9 7 5 3 1

This book is dedicated to the couriers of London,
with love and with gratitude.

Prologue

I knew as soon as I arrived in Tokyo that I was going to go home, although it took me several more weeks to admit to myself that my journey was – for now – at an end. It was the couriers that did it. As I rolled into Shibuya, trailing behind me an imaginary line that led all the way back to London, a lean and unmistakable silhouette flashed past me and my heart clenched with recognition. For over a year I had been riding out into the unknown – I'd left England's white cliffs behind me, pedalled through the apple-picking, log-piling hinterlands of central Europe and the Balkans, shivered in my tent through the fearsome winters of Turkey and Iran, crossed the mountains from Pakistan into China, and ridden further and faster than I ever thought was possible, to haul myself, my bicycle and fifty kilos of luggage to the farthest end of the landmass, thinking that from there I'd carry on, and on, and on, chasing an endlessly retreating horizon, always yearning to be somewhere new, until I'd made it the whole way around the world.

But here, among the bright lights and seething junctions of Tokyo's central districts, I seemed already to have come full circle, back to what I knew, and to what I thought I had left far behind. The traffic felt similar to London – the Japanese drive on the left, and it was a distressing sign of how long I had been away from home that it took me several days to get used to this after I stepped off the ferry from South Korea. The drivers follow the rules (unlike the Koreans, who see a red light as more of a guideline than a prohibition), and are used to seeing cyclists on the road. The traffic began to thicken a few days before I reached Tokyo – one of the world's largest metropolitan areas – and for the final few days I clawed my way through grey urban sprawl, past car dealerships and convenience stores, camping in parking lots at night and queuing at traffic lights during the day. I was surprisingly contented, just as much in love with the road when it's at its worst as when it's at its most beautiful and seductive. I rediscovered the simultaneous thrill and satisfaction of wriggling my way through stationary or slow-moving traffic, of handing over control to my sixth sense, no longer worrying about the proximity of trucks and buses, because my instincts knew far better than I did how to avoid them.

And as I neared the centre of the city, I found myself shaking with what I assumed to be exhaustion, but which might also have been excitement, my mind humming with the strange conceit that I was actually riding back into London. The rhythms of the traffic were so similar to what I'd left behind that it was like hearing a familiar voice speaking a foreign language. I noticed that I'd unconsciously changed my riding style, and was throwing my ponderous touring bike around the same way I would my skinny inner-city fixie, steering from the hips and waist, flicking the bike back and forth between the lanes of traffic, cornering so tightly at times that I knew I was in danger of overbalancing entirely. My excitement was tempered with a calm, glowing comfortable sense of familiarity, of coming home.

A pair of couriers whistled past me, one to my left, following the line of the gutter, and one to my right, skimming the outer edge of the crawling traffic, and then darting through a momentary gap just ahead of me to follow the narrow lane between the two lines of vehicles. They were riding together, I could tell, exchanging a few words here and there, across the roofs of the cars, dancing through the snarling city, like a pair of overexcited swallows just before sundown in the heady days of early summer, drunk on their own speed and beauty. This must be the last hour of their working day, I thought, and remembered my own surges of energy at around four o'clock, when sometimes rather than feeling tired I'd instead find a sweet spot where my body became so attuned to the bike and road that all resistance seemed to melt away, nothing hurt or jarred or dragged any more, and I would float through the city, knowing that I was riding faster than ever, but also experiencing a strange sense of stillness, as though I had gone so far into motion that I had reached its centre, and gone beyond it, and now the whole of the city pivoted around my wheels.

For a few seconds longer I watched the muscular calves of the courier in front of me, one of them with a few threads of fraying denim flapping against it as he frantically pedalled, and then with a tiny jump he skidded his back wheel to slow himself down, and cut through the traffic to his left with a sudden magnificent swoop, following the other courier down a side street. As I recall it, they both whooped with delight as they rode off, but I have every suspicion that my memory has written this in after the event, that the whooping was really my own, because how could you not whoop when witnessing such beauty, speed, skill and exhilaration, such joy in motion and moment?

A minute later I saw another courier. This one was at the side of the road, resting astride her bike, one hand on the bars, one hand on the button, head cocked towards the radio on her chest, oversized bag like a turtle's shell strapped to her back. To my great surprise, I felt my eyes swell with tears. Visually, this courier was so familiar that it was as if I'd spotted one of my brothers or sisters across a crowded room. But I also knew her posture intimately from the inside, having stood that way so often that I could still feel the residue of it in my bones and muscles – the left foot on the ground, the right foot on the pedal, the top tube pressing against my inner thigh, my right hand squeezing the radio and muttering 'one-four, one-four . . . roger-rodge', before swinging the weight back onto my right foot, pressing the bike into motion, and whirling off into the traffic with the nonchalance of one who is entirely in her element.

A couple of months later I was back on the streets of London, and it was as if I'd never left.

1

'Vauxhall, Lambeth, Waterloo. Umm . . . Southwark? No, Blackfriars. Then Southwark, right?'

Ash nodded, not taking her eyes off the A–Z she was holding up in front of her like a hand of cards.

'Go on.'

But I was lost. Further down the river was Tower Bridge, I knew that. But whatever lay between that and Blackfriars was a mystery. Were there any other bridges? What about Chelsea Bridge? Where did that come in? Wasn't there a railway bridge somewhere? And was there anything beyond Tower Bridge?

'Can I have a quick look?'

Ash handed me back the A–Z and I swept my eyes along the river again, west to east, noticing that Blackfriars did indeed come before Southwark, and that between them lay the Millennium footbridge, which I'd forgotten. And just to the north lay the tangle of the City, radiating out from the Bank junction, where eight roads meet, and where I had never successfully ridden through without taking a wrong turn and ending up in a very different place from what I had planned.

'I'm never going to learn all this!' I exclaimed despairingly.

'You don't need to learn all of it now,' Ash reassured me. 'Alex said they'll test you on things like the bridges, and the routes through Soho, and you can just pick up the rest of it on the job.'

I let myself be comforted by this, even though Ash probably had no better idea than I did about how these things worked. She had only been my girlfriend a few weeks, and we had found each other at similar stages of life: her at the end of a web-developer contract; me at the end of a master's degree; both of us without a plan or a purpose, thinking that couriering might be an enjoyable alternative to the responsibilities we had recently abdicated.

Had I not met someone with the same ambition, my own might well have continued to lie dormant – like many other paths in life I've pondered at length, idly or actively, but not taken. Becoming a cycle courier seemed just as likely as becoming a surgeon or a firefighter – by no means impossible, but so far removed from my narrow rounds of temp jobs and postgrad applications that it might as well have been. Until a couple of years before I started couriering, I didn't even know there was such an occupation, and planned to make my living using my mind rather than my legs. And when I first strapped the radio to my bag in 2008, I envisaged the job as a short adventure rather than a career – something I'd do for six months or so, and which would give me a good story to tell in years to come, when I'd rejoined the real world, and found a sensible, responsible way of earning my money.

My first encounter with a courier was shortly after I left university, and didn't feel particularly fateful. I had moved to London for no particularly good reason and was working as a part-time receptionist in Camden, struggling to stay afloat, and to make sense of the expanse of the city after the small market town I'd lived in for the past four years. Once, I'd innocently decided to stroll into the city centre for the evening (I was living in Ealing at the time, and had noticed that if I followed the Uxbridge Road east for long enough it would turn into Oxford Street), and been shocked when it took me over three hours.

If I tried walking in the opposite direction, I never managed to find the point at which the city met the fields, a line that in smaller towns is much more clearly demarcated – the final row of houses will overlook the countryside, and that's that. It wasn't that I was entirely unused to large cities – I'd spent summers in Vancouver and Barcelona, and found their noise and bustle and profusion exhilarating, rather than intimidating, after my quiet childhood in rural Wales – but London was of a different order of magnitude. My flat, my various jobs, and the few friends I had all seemed to be at least an hour's tube ride apart from each other, far too scattered for any sense of neighbourhood, and I travelled to job interviews in mysterious, far-flung places like Colindale and Dulwich, confidently following the different-coloured tube lines, but often with only the faintest idea of where I would actually end up, and of how these places fitted into the maddening sprawl that was London.

One afternoon, I was sitting at my reception desk, as usual, watching the world go by with alternating fascination and boredom. Although I was getting used to the repetitiveness of my working day, the thrill of being part of it all hadn't quite worn off. I still felt a little as if I was play-acting when I rubbed shoulders with the other commuters on the tube, and joined the chorus line queuing to buy morning coffee.

I drank in all the different people who passed through reception, noticing what they wore, how they acted, how they expected to be treated; not yet knowing how I wanted to live my own life, and wondering if I'd want to live theirs.

I watched the women in suits being escorted upstairs for a meeting; the van drivers who wheeled in boxes of stationery and cleaning products on trolleys; the cheerful young men who delivered sandwiches from bicycle trailers. And then a girl of about my own age appeared on a sleek black bicycle. She was blond and petite, and wearing frayed cut-off jeans over her cycling shorts. She leaned her bike against the plate-glass window without even locking it, strode through the revolving doors, briskly handed me an envelope, held out her clipboard for me to sign, and within seconds was back on the bike, standing tall on the pedals for a couple of strokes, and then swooping off towards Oval Road.

I remember very clearly how I felt as I watched her disappear round the corner. *If only I was the sort of person who could do that!* I imagined us as opposites – I was sitting placidly behind reception; she was outside riding her bike around the city. It was a novelty to me that you *could* ride a bike in a city. I wondered how different I would need to be, to be able to live my life the way she must live hers; what different turns I would have had to take in my teens and my childhood to have the courage to cycle through heavy traffic, the ingenuity to find my way through the city and fix the bike when it went wrong, the resilience to live what looked as if it must be an exhilarating but also a chaotic and precarious life. It wouldn't occur to me for another three years that I could, in fact, cast off the pinstripes and go and join her.

[4]

I was, of course, by no means the first person to be swept away by the romance of the cycle courier. As I began commuting by bike and making friends with other cyclists, I discovered that couriers were, for many, the heroes of the scene; that I wasn't the only one who rode the seven miles to work and wished that I could just carry on all day. I noticed them more and more, shooting through the traffic ahead of me, radios crackling. Sometimes I'd try to keep up with one, following his lines between the cars, copying his hesitations and accelerations and the way he balanced his bike through the curves, mustering the confidence to ride through smaller and smaller gaps when I saw that he made it through them just fine. Usually, he (they were always men) would lose me when we got to a red light, where I'd stop and he'd race straight across the junction, a split second before the traffic surged in. Whenever a courier delivered to an office where I was working, I'd gaze at him like an awestruck schoolgirl, desperate to identify myself as a fellow cyclist, and to ask him about his job, but too shy to puncture his surly mystique. Couriers are splendidly anachronistic figures – in an age where almost everything is mechanised and digitised, where the vast majority of our communications are sent electronically, and where navigating a capital city involves sitting in taxis in traffic jams, or paying money to use London's highly sophisticated public transport infrastructure, seeing actual human beings on bicycles darting among the traffic to deliver packages seemed almost equivalent to spotting Roman chariots racing between the buses on the Euston Road.

Part of the courier's romance, I realised, came from this incongruity. He was, manifestly, a human body among machines – but he was also, apparently, the equal of these machines, and therefore quite possibly superhuman, as well as a heartening reminder that, despite the advances of technology, there will always be a place for, and a need for, flesh and bone and muscle. Couriers seemed to me at once to have sidestepped society, and yet to be ubiquitously visible within it, striding sweatily into my reception with a package, pedalling alongside the bus for a moment before disappearing into the traffic jam ahead, sitting at the tables outside my habitual sandwich shop, radios blaring – a constant reminder to disillusioned wage slaves like me that there is another side to the desk, and a whole world outside the office.

I still hadn't quite memorised the bridges when I turned up at the Pink Express offices near Vauxhall Bridge, masking my nervousness with a layer of calm bravado.

But there was no test, and no interview. I'd been told to ask for Derrick, who was the fleet manager, though no one had bothered to tell me that. He was a jovial, steel-haired man, a few years off retirement, with tattoos on his forearms, and a paternal air that I was later told could turn very nasty, given the wrong provocation. His office was tiny and windowless, screened off from the main warehouse by plastic partitions, and, apart from his desk, contained nothing but a large filing cabinet, a set of coat hooks, hung with assorted scruffy courier paraphernalia, and a calendar with a picture of a red motorbike. He took down my bank details and National Insurance number, and explained that the deposit for my radio and Xda would be deducted from my first payslip, and a weekly equipment hire charge from all subsequent ones. Then he took me out to the yard next to the railway arches where the vans were parked and showed me how to call in on the radio, explained that 'POB' stood for package on board, and that 'empty' was what you said when you'd delivered all the packages in your bag and were ready for more; introduced me to the men in the control room (whose names I immediately forgot); told me to call in at eight the next morning, warned me to 'take it easy for the first couple of days', and dismissed me with a fatherly wink.

By far my strongest memory of those first few weeks on the road is the exhaustion, which flavours, obscures and crowds out most of the others. I wasn't entirely unprepared for the rigours of courier life – I'd spent the previous summer avoiding my master's thesis by going out on very long bike rides – but even so, I had failed to anticipate falling asleep into my dinner and being in bed by nine every evening, having abandoned the unequal struggle with my drooping eyelids. And if falling asleep was all too easy, getting up became much, much harder. I had always been an early riser; now it felt as if an unusually strong gravitational force were pinning me to the bed. Thursday, I learned, is the real killer. You already have three days of hard riding in your legs, and your body's crying out for a rest day, and unless you've been scrupulous in getting yourself to bed early (once you've over-come the exhaustion of the first month, it becomes just as easy to stay up till 1 a.m. as it always was, though you'll regret it far more the following day), you're also vague and dizzy with sleep deprivation. Friday is somehow never quite so bad, infused as it is with the adrenalin of everyone else's last-minute deadlines, and the promise of a whole weekend's rest in just a few hours' time.

I started couriering on a Thursday, grateful that I had to survive only two days before reaching the sanctuary of the weekend, but the following week stretched out ahead of me like a pit of hot coals – the end so distant, and the challenge so daunting, that even to contemplate an ending seemed pointless, since it seemed impossible that I'd survive what lay before. That Thursday morning, my second on the road, I hauled myself up the slope that leads onto Waterloo Bridge, my legs sore and slow and aching, remembering how, when this was part of my seven-mile commute into Bloomsbury, I'd dart up onto the bridge with legs like springs, overtaking men on road bikes, and watching my speedometer climb to the 20 mph I'd set myself as a daily challenge to reach at that point. Today, I had the same legs, and the same bicycle between them, and yet I could barely move. It was not a kind October: the sky was grey, and a cold wind whipped crisp packets and stray leaves in and out of the harsh concrete blocks of the South Bank Centre and the National Theatre. My exhaustion seemed similarly grey, weighing me down, and creeping through all my limbs, sapping my energy like a parasite. I tried to muster the vigour with which I'd sped up the bridge just a few weeks previously, but couldn't – it was as if I were now a different person.

'Come on!' I urged myself. 'You're a courier – this is what couriers do.'

That became something of a refrain for me during my first few weeks: a constant reminder to myself that couriers were tough and strong and uncomplaining; that they worked five days a week in all weathers; that they kept going when they had a cold; that they stopped and fixed their bikes by the side of the road when they went wrong; that they were as fast on Thursday afternoon as they were on Monday morning; that they never got tired – that, just like when I was strap-hanging and coffee-buying in my first summer in London, pretending to the other commuters that I was really one of them, I had announced myself to be one of these people, and now had to live up to this foolhardy proclamation, and my own exaggerated notions of what a courier was.

It took me quite a while to get to know other couriers, and of course I assumed this was because they would never deign to notice a lowly novice like me. There were actually more subtle reasons than this – a main one being that my shyness presented a far bigger barrier than their superiority; another being that what comes across as aloofness in many couriers is actually their own social awkwardness; a more obvious one being that couriers are constantly on the move, and rarely share space for very long. If you work in an office or a bar, you'll get to know all the lovely and annoying qualities of your colleagues very quickly, but if you only ever see them as they flash past you, riding very fast in the opposite direction, it can take many months, or even years, before you'll reach the same level of familiarity. And if you're particularly shy, or unfriendly, or just uninterested in getting to know other couriers, it would be quite possible to avoid them for your entire career.

One of the first couriers I met was Sid. He joined me on one of my favourite benches, near the junction of Moorgate and London Wall, where I would sit and idly watch the traffic collect and disperse at the lights, and remarked that he hadn't seen me around before. He didn't look like everyone's stereotype of a cycle courier – he was probably in his mid-forties, not especially tall, wearing tracksuit bottoms and a roomy anorak, and riding a battered mountain bike. He had, however, been on the road for fifteen years, and when he found out I was new, started regaling me with tales of the Good Old Days, when there was so much work that no one had time to sit on park benches watching the traffic, and his girlfriend used to phone up his controllers at seven in the evening and beg them to let him come home for dinner. As he talked, his rather stern, weathered face softened and became more animated, and he asked, with big-brotherly concern, how I was getting on. I was doing OK, I told him, but not looking forward to the colder weather, which by now was just around the corner.

'Ah, you're not a real courier till you've done your first winter, that's what they say!' He grinned, little realising how much I'd take these words to heart. Surviving the winter became my first objective benchmark of courierhood – if I could meet this challenge (November, December, January and February, I decided), then I would have earned the title of courier. I would be one of them, rather than an outsider who could do a convincing impression.

One of the only couriers I knew prior to taking up the job was Will, a dour, sarcastic, curiously lovable intellectual from Wigan, who'd been on the road for close to two decades, and whom I'd met a couple of months before I started, when he photographed me and my bike as part of one of his projects. I, of course, asked him all about being a courier, and enthused about how I was planning to become one myself. A couple of years later, over a pint, he cheerfully admitted having thought I was full of shit, and wouldn't last a week. Sometime during my first month, he pulled up next to me on Hampstead Road, and said, 'Hello, Emily,' which was just as well, because I was riding in a haze of grey exhaustion that made me oblivious to all but the traffic, and wouldn't have recognised him otherwise. I dimly remember commenting on how exhausted I was, but also how surprised, because I'd regularly been cycling sixty, seventy and eighty miles over the summer, and couldn't understand how this could be so much more tiring.

'Yeah, courier miles are longer,' he reassured me, and then introduced me to a useful cut-through that led me straight down from the Euston Road into Soho, via Fitzroy Square, Charlotte Street and Rathbone Place, and which I still use several times a day, occasionally remembering our conversation as I pass the spot where it took place. Courier miles might not actually be longer, but they are certainly harder. I was used to riding long distances along intercity A roads, often cycling for fifty miles or more without needing to stop, or modify my speed or direction more than a couple of times per hour. In central London, I was covering relatively small distances, but every other minute I'd have to stop for traffic lights and then sprint away from a standing start, only to stop again at the very next junction. And you don't ride in a straight line in London. A city this ancient has few straight roads, and most are arranged into complex one-way systems. You can't ride fast for very long before you have to slow the bike down and rearrange your weight in order to manoeuvre it round a corner, concentrating furiously not only on this corner, and on remembering which way the next one will take you, but also on dodging through the minefield of pot-holes and slippery manhole covers and – most draining of all – negotiating fast-moving, suddenly braking traffic, and trying to anticipate the movements of dozens of indecisive pedestrians.

So exhaustion is my most pervasive memory of those first few months, but it is closely followed by frustration. I thought I knew London reasonably well after a couple of years cycling around it (unlike many people I know, who still navigate entirely by tube map and smartphone), and could at least tell you in what direction most major landmarks lay from wher-ever I happened to be. But my enjoyment of urban cycling until that point had been based on freestyling – on launch-ing myself in any direction that took my fancy, turning left or right at random until I no longer knew where I was, and then spending the next hour or so trying to navigate myself, via trial and error, back to something I recognised, without stopping, backtracking or referring to the map. Couriering called for a level of precision that this, my cursory revision of bridges and main roads, and my reasonably reliable sense of direction, had not prepared me for.

It was not good enough, I quickly learned, to find a street in the A–Z, ascertain roughly where it was in relation to where I was, and then set off in that direction, assuming I'd bump into it in due course. Sometime during my first week I was sent from Soho to Hertford Street, which lies at the bottom corner of Mayfair, near the junction of Park Lane and Piccadilly – really not very far away. I was still anxious about my speed, convinced that at any moment Derrick was going to phone me up and sack me for being too slow, and so after a cursory glance at the map I raced off down Maddox Street, which seemed to point in the right direction, and a few minutes later found myself in Grosvenor Square, where I hadn't intended to be at all. I circled the square, tried to head south via Carlos Place, and ended up in Berkeley Square instead. It finally dawned on me that I wasn't going to stumble across the right street by accident, so I wearily pulled over, got off the bike, got my A–Z out of my bag, and wasted several precious minutes working out exactly where Hertford Street was from where I was, and memorising the exact turnings I'd have to take to get there. The traffic roared relentlessly past me; everyone else seemed to know exactly where they were going.

'Charles Street, left onto Chesterfield, left onto Curzon Street, right onto Trebeck Street, right onto Shepherd Street, left onto Hertford Street,' I muttered as I got back on the bike, still forgetting which number I was looking for on Hertford Street, which meant I had to pull over yet again when I got there, to check the address on my Xda.

I eventually found a better route than that, and it soon became second nature. If you sent me from Soho to Hertford Street now, I'd probably take no more than two or three minutes. I know the way so well that I've forgotten half the street names (which admittedly can cause its own problems), and I'll pull up at the right address with barely any memory of how I've actually got there. Despite the urge to get on the bike and start moving as soon as possible, I've learned that when I'm sent to a street I don't recognise, it always saves time in the long run if I get out the A–Z, and spend several minutes planning a route before I set off.

Another mistake showed me the value of learning one-way systems. I was given an address on Duke Street, which I quickly noticed joined Manchester Square, which I already knew. So I sped off to Manchester Square, tried to turn south onto Duke Street, and only then discovered it was one-way, running south to north. I could either ride against the traffic, risking the wrath of cabbies and the tickets of policemen, or I could get off the bike and walk, which is what I did – all the way south almost to Grosvenor Square, waiting irritably for the lights to change so that I could cross Wigmore Street and then Oxford Street, fighting my way through the hordes of pre-Christmas shoppers, because of course the address I wanted was right at the other end. A couple of couriers passed me as I went, flowing along with the traffic in the right direction. Lesson 2: always start at the right end of a one-way street, especially if you don't know where the address is that you're looking for.

And one of the most frustrating lessons of all – the lesson of the loading bay. Most large buildings, I quickly learned, have a glamorous reception at the front, for employees and clients and honoured guests, and a dusty loading bay round the back, for couriers, kitchen staff, cleaners and other regrettable necessities. It isn't always easy to find the loading bay, or obvious that there is one, and so you locate the main reception of the building, find somewhere to lock up your bike, negotiate the revolving doors, and queue up among the suits waiting to speak to the receptionist. On very rare occasions, she'll actually sign for your package then and there. On almost equally rare occasions, she'll apologetically explain that packages need to be taken to the loading bay, and politely and patiently explain how to get there. But more often, she'll turn to you from the suit she's been dealing with, her smile will fade slightly, and she'll inform you that 'you need to go round the back', gesturing vaguely in the appropriate direction. Sometimes you won't even make it into the reception – as you lock up your bike, a security guard will get your attention by banging on the window, and make a brushing-away motion with his hand. It's difficult not to take this personally.

So you follow the directions to the rear entrance. It's not always just 'round the back' – sometimes you'll have to find your way round a whole block of buildings, and possibly even cross a few streets before you find the yawning mouth of the loading bay, with its concrete ramp leading down into the bowels of the building, and bored and officious security guards standing around in their oversized hi-vis jackets. And as London develops, more and more of its office buildings are built in clusters on private estates, with pedestrianised plazas in between them, and a massive shared loading bay underneath. Once you've got past the security guards and rolled down the concrete ramp, you'll find yourself on a subterranean road, with speed bumps every few metres, signs warning you to keep to the 5 mph speed limit and a lofty ceiling with a tangle of pipes and ventilation ducts. Alongside the road is a series of caverns – the loading bays for each particular building – with raised platforms at one end, against which the lorries will reverse when they come to unload, and around the side a miscellaneous clutter of anonymous cardboard boxes, wooden packing crates, wheeled metal cages full of kitchen supplies and cleaning products, assorted skips and bins and trolleys, and stern signs warning that nothing is to be left in this area, which are ignored, because there is more available space here than anywhere else in this tightly packed building. Some loading bays will have a wing devoted to employees' bicycle parking, and I always eye this with particular interest, sizing up the ranks of carbon and steel, noticing the jerseys and towels draped across handlebars and top tubes to dry or air in time for the homeward commute, and sometimes envying the owners their on-site showers and comfortable offices.

Often there is a post room adjacent to the loading bay, and it's a pretty simple matter of handing your package to one of the post-room guys (they are almost always guys), asking his name, making some mindless comment about the weather as you type it into your Xda and then getting him to sign the screen. Occasionally, they'll put the package through a scanner to make sure you're not trying to deliver a bomb. In other buildings, you park your bike in the loading bay and follow the security guard's directions to the goods lift: sometimes a noisy, shaky old thing with heavy concertina doors that you have to close yourself; sometimes as smooth and swift as the other lifts in the building, though much busier – if five different people are going to five different floors with five different heavy loads, and then someone stops the lift on its way back down, in order to cram in another load, it can take a good ten or fifteen minutes to do a single journey, during which time those waiting will get more and more vocally impatient, the attendant security guard will get out his two-way radio and start barking at his colleague in the lift, trying to find out what the hold-up is, and I'll make smart-arse comments about how this is like waiting for a night bus. (Someone usually laughs, so I make the same joke every time a lift is delayed.)

The lift will sometimes deliver you back to exactly the same reception you started in, and you'll scowl at the receptionist, wondering what the point was of adding an extra five or ten minutes to your journey when this is an important package, and surely the recipient would like it sooner rather than later. But more often you'll be taken to the company's own post room or reception, on whichever floor they inhabit, the package will be signed for, and you'll retrace your steps, back to the goods lift, back down to the loading bay, back up the ramp, and back to the road, which is where you wanted to be in the first place.

When I dreamed of a being a courier, I hadn't pictured this. I'd imagined the freedom and exhilaration of cycling through the traffic all day while everyone else envied me from their traffic jams and offices – because that is the most visible side of courierhood, and consequently the most well known among non-couriers. They don't see the tedium of the loading bay, or feel the frustration of having to stop the bike, yet again, unclip your bag, swing it round to the front, reach inside for your A–Z, and then spend more precious minutes figuring out where you are, where you need to be, and how on earth you're going to get there. And nor do they imagine the boredom of being asked the same questions again and again and again, by security guards, by post-room guys, by the assorted people you meet in goods lifts:

'So you just ride your bike around all day?'

'You must be very fit!' (This isn't a question as such, but it might as well be, given that I still have to think of something either affirmative or self-deprecating to say in response.)

'Isn't it dangerous?'

'How many miles do you do per day?'

'Do you wear a helmet?'

'Do you have a boyfriend?'

These questions were the first thing I tired of. I would greet them with an insincere smile, and launch into an already well-worn explanation of the job I was still only learning as I went, so that initially the explanation felt more familiar than the job itself.

2

Despite my sense of aspiration and inadequacy, I wasn't really that different from the other couriers – couriers are, in fact, all mostly very different from each other, aside from the superficial stereotypes of muscles and sweat and attitude – but I always focused on the ways in which I failed to measure up, rather than on what we had in common. I was in awe of gnarled old prophets like Sid, who bent my ear with news of the courier's imminent demise. Everyone told me it was better five years ago. Of course, five years ago, they were saying the same thing. But it took me time to learn this. In my first winter I just got to know the faces of the other couriers as they passed me on the road, and wondered how long it would take before they decided I'd been around long enough to be worth talking to. Or maybe there was more to it than simple longevity. Even after I'd started to be on nodding and waving terms with most of my fellow couriers, one man persistently ignored me, although I couldn't help but notice him, since he was tall and pale, had long flowing red hair, and rode a bright yellow Concorde frame. If I nodded at him in passing, he'd carry on exactly as he was, grimly staring down the road ahead. If I raised a hand in greeting, I went similarly unacknowledged. Eventually, I took to waving frantically and mouthing 'Hello!' whenever I saw him. He never gave any indication of having noticed me.

He was probably shy, I thought – but this assumption was dispelled one Friday evening as I stood on the fringes at the Foundry, and saw him a few feet away from me, laughing at something another courier was saying, animated in a way I'd never witnessed in our one-sided encounters on the road. He became a running joke between Ash and me. We hypothesised that it was just women he didn't like, or Condor riders, or people wearing green trousers, and speculated over what absurd things we might do to gain his attention, or even win just a momentary nod of recognition, or a raised eyebrow of acknowledgement. Eventually, he disappeared: I noticed that I hadn't seen him around for a while, and realised that he must have moved on to something else.

It seemed that for my first few months on circuit, the only people who'd design to speak to me were the self-appointed elders, exclusively men, who'd noticed me on the road, observed that I'd lasted for longer than a couple of weeks, and might therefore conceivably be around for a while, and taken it upon themselves to educate me. Not that they weren't friendly, of course, and not that I wasn't grateful.

Not long after my conversation with Sid, I met Von, who approached me on Southwark Street as I unlocked my bike after dropping off someone's visa application at TCLS. I had already seen him several times, always in this same place, and in the course of our conversation I learned that he was actually employed by TCLS, presumably delivering nothing but passports and visa applications for people who were too busy or too lazy to stand in line themselves. Von would be rather imposing if he wasn't also so evidently friendly. He is tall and broad and fearsomely muscular, and rather than the battered fixies and ancient road bikes that most of the couriers ride, he alternates between several futuristic carbon triathlon frames, pairing them with black Lycra and blacked-out sunglasses. In action, he looks like a machine. Close up, there's a tinge of eccentricity. His streamlined bicycle is equipped with two clunky rearview mirrors, and in summer he wears SPD sandals with socks. Years later, I was amazed to learn that he was in his late fifties at the time I met him. I wouldn't have put him at much older than forty.

'How long have you been on circuit?' he asked.

'About six weeks,' I responded, wishing it was a fortnight hence, because 'two months' would have sounded so much more impressive. 'What about you?'

'Pretty much twenty years!' he replied, with a friendly grin that somehow also implied that I was a bit of a fool for asking. He told me his name, and then cast himself off into a sea of reminiscences, with the slightly urgent gregariousness of a talkative person who hasn't found anyone to listen to him for a while. I didn't mind in the slightest. He was fascinating.

First he told me about a book that a photographer had compiled at the turn of the millennium, with portraits of people doing their jobs in London, stretching predictably from the mayor to the people who pick up his litter and clean his office. And he, Von, was featured, he informed me, describing in great detail how the photographer had found and selected him, how he'd posed during the shoot, and how they'd decided that he, above all others, should be on the cover. I came across the book in Clerkenwell Tales a few months later and, sure enough, there he was, a strange and beautiful silhouette with his slick black bike and sleek b|

skin, not looking very much like anyone's idea of a cycle courier, but then, perhaps that was the point.

I can't remember whether I asked about his life outside couriering, or whether he just told me (probably the latter), but it turned out he was also an illustrator and, what's more, the artist behind the Shakespeare comic books I'd devoured as a schoolgirl, ten years previously. He could tell I barely believed him, so he wrote down a website address for me, which I checked that evening, and sure enough, it was him.

But for the most part I watched the other couriers pass me by, getting to know them all by sight rather than by name. There was the courier with the bare arms: a spidery-looking rider with hair somewhere between dreadlocks and an Afro, which added almost a foot to his height. He wore big round glasses and a big toothy smile, and unlike the unfriendly redheaded man, he would greet me with an expression of delight every time he passed me. But what struck me the most was how scantily he dressed. As the winter set in, and I began to add a new layer of clothing every other week, and other couriers started to look like birds do when they puff up their feathers to keep warm, Ephraim, as I later found out his name to be, was still charging around in a singlet and skinny jeans, long, dark, muscled arms gripping the bars of his track bike, dazzling passers-by with his dentistry. I wondered what his secret was.

There was the man without a face, who wore a full balaclava with a long ponytail of dreadlocks comically extruding from the back. We'd nod and wave in passing, and I'd think about how strange it was to recognise someone, yet to have no idea of their facial features. Many months later, spring came, the balaclava went, and it was like seeing a friend with a stranger's face.

There was the man with the crazy socks, who rode a red lo-pro, had a face full of piercings and wild blond hair, and always wore long fluorescent striped socks that didn't match.

There was the fierce-looking girl with a mohawk and a brakeless fixie, whose eye I never quite managed to catch, though, unlike the red-haired man, she seemed more oblivious than unfriendly.

And there was Nhatt, whom I felt I already knew very well, even though we hadn't met and I didn't know what she looked like. A few months before I became a courier, when I was busy procrastinating my master's thesis and going out on long bike rides as an excuse for not doing my research, Radio 4 had aired a documentary about London bike messengers, to which I'd dreamily listened, leaning on an open book at my desk, and which had made me (and probably half the cyclists in London) want to be a courier even more. Nhatt was one of two riders they'd followed, and it was a good choice – she managed to distil her job's irresistible mix of romance, suffering and humour, and her enthusiastic American accent was the perfect foil for Wigan Will's rather more cynical commentary. I was both excited and daunted by the possibility of meeting her one day.

But for now, still hesitant to approach other couriers in the street, worried that they might all turn out to be like the beautiful man with the flowing red hair, I sought them out on the Internet, already knowing that I was much better at getting on with people textually than verbally.

This was the era of the Internet forum, of big baggy monsters like the London Fixed Gear and Single Speed (LFGSS) forum, with endless sub-forums hosting endless discussions, arguments, riffs and repartee, with all their cliques and in-jokes; before we started broadcasting all our wit on Twitter, and pouring all our rhetoric into the discussions below the line on online newspaper articles. I had very successfully found my niches in the London gay scene and the recreational cycling scene via their respective Internet forums, so now I sought out the courier version. It turned out to be an offshoot of *Moving Target*, which was currently a blog, but had started life in the 1980s, as a 'zine, and had been edited by Buffalo Bill throughout. Bill was widely considered to be the godfather of the London courier scene. He had started out as a courier in the hazily recollected days of the early 1980s, when (so it was rumoured) pushbike couriers regularly earned £500 a week, and sometimes even twice that, and, unlike most of his early colleagues, who had melted away into other industries, easily losing touch with a community that had existed only tenuously, he had been one of the first people for whom 'courier' was as much an identity as a job. As well as writing *Moving Target*, he had been one of an international band of brothers (and sisters) who had made contact, somehow, with couriers in other cities across the world, establishing life-long friendships and setting up the Cycle Messenger World Championships, which began in Berlin in 1993, was held in London in 1994, and hasn't missed a year since then (recent events have been held in Tokyo, Warsaw and Mexico City).

As with Nhatt, I knew Bill by reputation long before I met him in person, and had somehow imagined that he'd be a grizzled patriarch with a long beard, tall and still physically powerful, though perhaps with a bit of a paunch. When I eventually met him I discovered that I'd been completely mistaken – he's lean, energetic and somewhere in his mid-forties, though he hasn't a grey hair on his head, and could easily pass for a man ten years younger.

At the time I discovered it, *Moving Target* was undergoing what Bill referred to as 'one of those "my work here is done" interregna', since, after a couple of decades of exposing and explicating the courier experience, and not having been a courier for quite some time, he had run out of things to say, and most of the posts on the blog were now just flyers for Friday-night alleycat races, or the occasional appeal to help find a stolen bike, or donate money to a courier who had broken a bone. Most of *Moving Target*'s traffic in those days was on its forum, which seemed to fulfil much the same purpose as the street corners on which couriers gathered to bitch about their job, save for the fact that these were probably different couriers – the ones who might hover on the fringes at Creative Corner or the Foundry (or avoid them altogether), but still had plenty to say.

It was through this that I made my first real courier friend, a dry-humoured rider called Lukasz, who had been on the road only as long as I had, but who stood out for the fluency of his observations, and who was as happy to meet me as I was him when our paths finally crossed in Covent Garden. He was slightly older than me, swathed in the courier's winter uniform of jumpers and jackets and a dark-blue woollen hat, and had a handsome face made interesting by well-placed lines and what looked like a semi-permanent scowl. His crooked smile, as we shook hands and introduced ourselves, shone out like a reward. I liked him instantly.

'How's work?' I asked, knowing by now that this was one of the standard courier greetings, opening the floor for whatever particular complaint might be weighing on the other party's mind.

'Fucking awful!' He grinned darkly. 'Two jobs all day. I think I might go home if it doesn't pick up. Just gotta make enough to pay for this coffee.' He indicated a Costa cup on the bench next to him.

'That's awful!' I commiserated. 'Who're you working for again?'

It was one of those companies that no one's really heard of, mostly white vans and surly motorbikers on unglamorous assignations between industrial estates in Acton and Croydon, and just one or two pushbikes to save on petrol by mopping up the few jobs that stay within the West End.

'I'm only gonna stay there till I've done it long enough to get a job somewhere else,' he said. I resumed my commiseration and then, feeling like I'd had a brainwave, suggested he go into Pink and ask Derrick if there was any work.

'I mean,' I added conspiratorially, 'I basically blagged my way in with no experience, so if they'll take me, they'll definitely take you.'

'I – hang on a sec.' His radio rumbled at him (the sound quality was markedly lower than Pink's) and he shoved it further up the strap of his bag with his right hand, cocking his head to get his ear as close to the sound as possible, in what I now recognise as one of the universal courier gestures.

'Got a job!' he announced triumphantly, a minute later.

'But yeah, maybe I'll give Pink a go. See you round, anyway.'

He tightened the strap of his bag, giving a little jump to settle it on his shoulders, picked up his coffee cup and, after a quick scan of the vicinity, revealed that there were no bins within reach, put it down again and swung a leg over his grubby blue road bike. I watched him weaving through the crowds of shoppers as he set off towards King Street, his smile fading into a frown of concentration.

It was a few more months before I ran into Nhatt, during which time I built up a rather formidable picture of her, through word of mouth and word of Internet, as the de-facto princess of the courier scene. She had contributed witty articles and drawings to *Moving Target*; she was a capable bike mechanic and a trained vegan chef; she organised alleycats and designed flyers; at any given moment half of London's couriers and fakengers seemed to be in love with her. Her full name (chosen, I assumed, rather than given) was Nhatt Attack, but where most other people might have been reduced to a caricature by such a zany appellation, Nhatt somehow wore it well, her other attributes too substantial to be belied by the eccentricity of her name.

Despite her ubiquity, I still had no idea what she looked like, but nonetheless kept an eye out for female couriers, and every time I saw one whose name I didn't know, I wondered whether she might be the famous Nhatt, and attempted to imbue her with what I knew of Nhatt's reputation and personality. The robust-looking dark-haired girl who wore baggy T-shirts and combat shorts looked as if she might be capable of winning an alleycat. The rangy blonde on the vintage road-bike conversion seemed a likely candidate to have stolen the hearts of half the city. But I usually only ever saw them riding very fast in the opposite direction, and would have been too shy to approach them even if I did catch them off the bike. Eventually, one sunny spring afternoon, an unusually pretty girl on a loaded cargo bike crawled past in the sticky Goodge Street traffic, smiled at me, and said, 'Hello there.' Vivid tattoos of snails and dandelion clocks blossomed up her arms, and a heavy fringe stuck out from under her cycling cap. She told me later that I had looked a bit confused, as though I wasn't sure whether she was talking to me, or whether I was supposed to recognise her. That was Nhatt, and that was that.

The following week I saw her again, pushing her bike along Endell Street, took a deep breath and strolled over to say hello, more frightened of offending her by failing to greet her than by anything stupid I might accidentally say.

'Oh, hi!' she said, with a grin that lit up her face and showed a mouth full of lopsided teeth. 'How're you doing?' She was taller than I'd expected (which often happens, when you've only ever seen someone on a bike or on the Internet), and had a bright, hurried way of talking, the words tumbling so quickly from her mouth that they sometimes seemed to tangle themselves up and get caught on her teeth on the way out.

'Good, yeah. How are you?' was all I could think of to reply.

'Oh, you know. Just turning my machine off and turning it on again.' She waved her Xda at me, with an exasperated rolling of eyes that suggested this wasn't the first time today she'd had to do this, and wouldn't be the last. 'I like your skirt.'

I had recently cut the legs off an old pair of jeans and was experimentally wearing the result over my cycling tights, in an attempt to hide my Lycra-clad rear from lascivious drivers.

'Thanks! I've been having a bit of trouble with it getting caught on the saddle.' (This was an understatement. A few minutes earlier the skirt had unexpectedly stopped me in my tracks as I tried to ease my way off the saddle and put a foot down at the lights, and I had panicked, almost fallen over, and ended up whacking my crotch on the top tube. The momentarily excruciating pain had now faded to a troubling glow that harmonised nicely with my corresponding blush of embarrassment. But she didn't need to know that.)

'Yeah, watch out for that. You remember the girls' alleycat last summer? Oh, no, I guess that was probably before your time. My boyfriend did it in drag, and he nearly crashed getting his skirt stuck on the saddle.'

We laughed, and over her radio Bill's voice said, 'Zero-four, zero-four.'

'I'd better go,' she grimaced, and was on her bike in an instant, accelerating off down Endell Street, one hand on the bars, one on the radio.

'Zero-four?'

She raised her hand in a wave as she swung right into Shelton Street, and then she was gone.

But despite these nascent friendships, during those first few months I felt as though the world were holding itself at an arm's length, leaving me hemmed in by exhaustion and muffled in a haze of concentration that spared scant attention for anything beyond the road and the traffic, the routes between the West End and the City and all the shortcuts I was learning – and devising – as I went along, and the constant need to keep going, and to go faster, and to avoid making mistakes at all costs, for fear of being shouted at over the radio and humiliated in front of the whole fleet, or, worse still, of being fired. The world of the courier is, I realised, mostly a solitary one. For most of the day you're on your own on the bike, your human contact reduced to monosyllabic exchanges with receptionists and over the radio. And as soon as you get in from work, your body insistently and decisively puts itself to sleep. The friends I had seen almost daily while I was a student I now managed to catch up with only every couple of weeks. For those first few months, couriering filled up my life, to the exclusion of almost everything else.

3

By the end of my first Friday, I was counting the hours till the end of the day, trying to calculate how many more jobs I was likely to be given, hoping they wouldn't force me to ride too far, and wondering if I'd get any time to rest in between. At ten to five I rolled past the John Snow pub on Broadwick Street, and was loudly hailed by some cycling friends, who were already standing outside with pints, looking crisp and untouched in their office clothes, as though it were the beginning of the week rather than the end. I shouted that I'd join them in five minutes, and hastened slowly off to Golden Square, for my final drop of the day. But before I'd even got there, I heard my name over the radio.

'One-four, one-four Emily.'

'One-four?'

'Once you've dropped that one, got another one for you.'

And the pixellated voice of my Xda said, ATTENTION! NEW JOBS!

'Roger-rodge,' I replied bleakly, stopped, and checked the Xda to find out where I was being sent this time, hoping oh so fervently that it would be a nice easy job within Soho, or just across Regent Street to Mayfair, preferably between clients that I already knew, so that I wouldn't waste time and leg power trying to find them. It wasn't. It was a multi-drop, picking up from a private equity firm in St James's, and delivering to four different addresses in four different postcodes, right across the city.

Knowing what I do now, I'm surprised that Andy gave this job to a novice courier at the very end of her first week. Like many controllers, he'd started out as a courier himself, and remembered the feeling of being given a job going north at the end of the day, when you live south, and just want to get home; the annoyance of being asked to ride several miles with no package on board, because someone had booked an urgent pick-up and there were no other couriers in the vicinity; even the irrational frustration of being zigzagged continuously between w1 and sw1, or the City and the West End, despite having work going both ways, with the sense of constantly just retracing your steps, rather than a token illusion of progress.

Andy was a master of the long run (at least when enough clients were booking jobs that he could pick and choose which courier to give them to). He'd load you up with work in Soho, asking you to hang around for five minutes or so before setting off, in case anyone booked another job going the same way, and I'd use this time to plan my route between the different addresses. There might be a long job, going all the way from a Soho editing house to a production company in Shoreditch – but to make it worth the courier's while there'd be another one to drop at the old Guardian offices on Farringdon, and one for North One TV at the top of Pentonville Road. Then, on my way along Clerkenwell Road, I'd be sent in to pick something up from Hungry Man (production companies often have silly names like this) on Herbal Hill, going to a studio off Folgate Street, just into e1.

[32]

The Guardian building, although its address was Farringdon Road, actually backed onto Herbal Hill, so I'd lock my bike up in between their door and Hungry Man's, and have one package delivered and one on board within seconds. I sometimes wondered whether Andy had planned my route to be quite so smooth, or whether it was just chance. After a few months of working with him, I learned that it was more of the former; less of the latter. He was a man who prided himself on knowing things, be they the intricacies of current and historical affairs, the specifications of every bicycle he'd owned since he was a teenager, or the precise location of every back street, cul-de-sac and loading bay in London.

From there I'd head up Rosebery Avenue (a much gentler climb than Pentonville, even though it goes up the same hill) for the N1 drop, half of my mind on the road, and the other half constantly rehearsing where I was going next, and where I was going after that, and how I was getting there, whether each address I had in mind was a pick-up or a drop, and whether this corresponded with the number of packages still in my bag. (It's every courier's nightmare to get to the end of a run like this, and find that she still has one package left, that was supposed to be delivered half an hour ago, on the other side of town, or to get to a drop in the City, and realise that she forgot to pick up one of the jobs coming out of the West End.) At this point I ought to have the Shoreditch job, the Folgate Street job, and the one I was about to deliver in N1.

I liked delivering to North One TV. They had a courtyard screened off from the main road, where I could probably have left my bike unlocked if I wanted to, though I never did. The receptionist was a plump, smiley blond girl called Daisy, and although we never had time to say much to each other beyond the usual pleasantries, we both took the trouble to imbue them with as much sincerity as possible, and I'd always make a point of typing her name into my Xda without asking her what it was, to show her that I remembered it.

And from there it would be a lovely straight downhill along City Road, heading for the Shoreditch and Folgate Street deliveries, but stopping to pick up an EC2 from Underwood Street along the way. I'd drop the Shoreditch job (the first one I'd been given coming out of Soho, though the pick-up was by now a distant memory, or forgotten entirely, cast off by my brain as no longer relevant, since it had so many other addresses to hold in mind, while also devoting significant energies to route-planning, traffic-surfing and pedestrian-avoidance), and then head down into the City to deliver the two remaining. By the time I made the last drop, Andy would already have sent me more work coming out of the City, shuttling legal files over to the Temple, almost closing the big circle I'd effectively traced round the capital.

If there was enough work for a run like this to be put together, and if the courier's speed and reliability were such that she could be given multiple jobs, it often worked like a dream. 'Courier and controller in perfect harmony,' Andy would sometimes say, concealing his pride under a veil of sarcasm that fooled no one. But all too often things would go wrong. One client wouldn't have their package ready when the courier arrived, and all the other jobs would be held up. Or a job would be cancelled at the last minute, leaving a gaping hole in an otherwise perfectly linked series of deliveries. Or the courier would forget a pick-up, or deliver a package to the wrong place, or ignore Andy's instructions and deliver the jobs in the wrong order, either mistakenly prioritising standard jobs over urgent ones, or ending up in the wrong part of town to pick up another job that he'd lined up for them, but not yet told them about.

Or sometimes the courier simply doesn't want to do the jobs, because she's exhausted and wants to sit in Soho Square and stare at the pigeons for half an hour, because it's raining, because she's just bought a big cup of coffee, or because she's due to finish her shift in ten minutes' time, and knows that the jobs she's been given will take a lot longer than that. Controllers vary in their sensitivity to this. Of course, from another perspective, a controller is doing a courier a favour by giving her work, since, as I've heard many controllers and a few older couriers say, 'a turning wheel is an earning wheel', and there's no reason to suspect that, on an ordinary Tuesday morning, the courier might be anything other than delighted with the opportunity she's being given to earn another £2.75, or whatever that particular job's paying. But on a Friday afternoon, a good – or, at least, a sympathetic – controller will try to avoid giving out work going in the opposite direction from home, or that's going to keep the courier busy for another hour when she'd rather be in the pub. If it's inevitable, he'll at least apologise, or even go through the charade of offering her the opportunity to turn the job down, while making it very clear that he'd rather she didn't.

My normally healthy work ethic had been completely overpowered by exhaustion that Friday evening, so had

Andy given me even the slightest bit of leeway, I'd have ducked out of the job and been back at the John Snow as the clock struck five. But he didn't, so I found my way to the address on King Street, where I was sent round to the side entrance on Rose and Crown Yard and shown into the lift by a monosyllabic security guard, who was probably as keen for the week to end as I was. The top-floor reception, lined with sleek golden wood and panoramic photographic prints of calm and mostly featureless landscapes, was eerily quiet. Judging by the walls of pinstriped masculinity crowding into the well-heeled Mayfair pubs I'd passed on my way there, it wasn't difficult to guess where everyone had gone. The two receptionists were just on their way out too: one doing up her coat; the other bending over the switchboard, almost certainly turning on the weekend answerphone message. ('Our offices are now closed. Our opening hours are Monday to Friday, 8 a.m. to 5 p.m.') They looked at me with mild irritation, as if I were the only thing stopping them from leaving, and indicated a messy heap of white A4 envelopes, from which I extricated the four whose addresses corresponded to those on my Xda, and scurried apologetically back to the lift. On the way down I double-checked the addresses, repeating them over and over to myself in the hope that I'd imprint them on my memory, and not have to stop the bike every few minutes to recheck the envelope to find out where I was going next, and recheck the A–Z to remind myself how I was getting there.

'Hundred Victoria Embankment; umm, Leadenhall Street' (I couldn't remember the number) 'Fenchurch Street; One London Bridge.'

I couldn't picture any of them, apart from One London Bridge, which squats at the southern end of the bridge in question like a gigantic Rubik's Cube with one chunk missing. I designated that my last drop, since it was closest to home, and tried to work out the most sensible way to get there, via the other three drops. I can't remember by what convoluted route I reached Victoria Embankment, though now, with my much improved street sense and Pall Mall having been made two-way, it would be a very straightforward ride of about two minutes, via Cockspur Street, Trafalgar Square and Northumberland Avenue. What I do remember is how impossible it was to find number 100. Victoria Embankment is a fast urban dual carriageway, with the Thames on one side and on the other a series of looming government buildings, set so far back from the road, behind fences and gardens and armed police guards, that it was impossible to see whether they had numbers; also very unlikely than any of them was the address I was looking for. So I carried on east, past the Embankment Gardens and the blind arches and battlements that embank Somerset House from the road in exactly the same way that the road itself is embanked from the river. I halted briefly to investigate an Australian bar that seemed to be the only obvious address on the Embankment for about half a mile, but it had no visible door number, and very definitely didn't house the company for which the package was intended. Further along the road was once again flanked by gardens, and then disappeared into the labyrinthine junction north of Blackfriars Bridge. I hadn't found number 1, or any other number, let alone 100, and couldn't even tell whether the buildings were numbered west to east or east to west. Grimly, I turned the bike around and pedalled back towards Westminster, trying with no success at all to ignore the homeward-bound commuter cyclists shooting past me, and even more vainly to enjoy the painful heaviness in my legs, which was doubtless leading to improved fitness and strength and muscle tone, but right at that moment required almost more willpower than I could muster to keep the pedals grinding round.

After riding all the way back to Westminster Bridge, and then all the way back to Blackfriars again, without any more luck than I'd had the first time round, I called in on the radio.

'One-four, one-four?'

'One-four, go ahead.' Andy had gone home, and one of the other controllers was on the box – the ones who stepped in for his lunch break and took over in the evenings, and were slightly less experienced, slightly less intuitive, slightly more prone to mistakes, or to sending you all the way across town with a single standard delivery.

'Umm, really sorry about this, but I'm having trouble finding 100 Victoria Embankment. I've been up and down twice. Could you just give me a rough idea of where it is?'

There was a pause, which went on and on until I realised that it wasn't a pause at all; he wasn't going to answer, perhaps out of sheer disgust at my stupidity, though in hindsight it's much more likely that he simply didn't know himself, or was asking the other men in the control room, and finding that none of them knew either. A minute later he called someone else's number and sent them to pick up a job on High Holborn, and I knew I wasn't going to get any help.

After another couple of laps I stopped my bike under Waterloo Bridge and wheeled it along the pavement, scrutinising every park, gateway, unmarked door and unpromising building I saw that might conceivably have an address. I detoured round Temple Place, peered into the Inner Temple Gardens, scanned the hulls of a couple of riverboats, and eventually found number 100 at the Blackfriars end, next to a large ornate doorway on a building that was clearly far more on New Bridge Street than Victoria Embankment. (Another lesson: buildings are often found round the corner from where they claim to be, particularly if the adjacent street is better known than the one they're actually on. Having a Harley Street office, for example, carries such kudos, that the first few doorways along Devonshire, Weymouth and New Cavendish Street are generally labelled as Harley Street as well, to the perpetual confusion of novice cycle couriers.) I was met on the steps by a security guard, who seemed anxious to keep me as far away from the building as possible, and directed me to a delivery entrance around one more corner of the building on Watergate, where I finally got rid of the package, and turned my attention to the other three.

Leadenhall Street posed further problems, as it lay beyond the formidable eight-way junction of Bank, which I had entirely failed to memorise when preparing for my non-existent interview, and which still terrified me. I was distracted by the picturesque nomenclature of the streets (Poultry, Cornhill, Threadneedle Street), but even if I could remember the order in which they led off the main interchange, what they led *to* was still a mystery, and not one I was equipped to penetrate on the hoof, carried through a green light by the swell of rush-hour traffic and diving for whatever exit was at hand and seemed less likely to result in my being swallowed by the maelstrom. I found myself on Threadneedle Street, pulled over once again to inspect the A–Z, and discovered that I was supposed to be on Cornhill. Rather than making a detour, or risking being ticketed by the police for riding against one-way systems, I wheeled the bike down Finch Lane, and then along most of Leadenhall too, preferring to search out the number on foot rather than repeat my experience on the Victoria Embankment.

The building, by the time I found it, was deserted. It was older than many of those surrounding it, and its brass fittings and wood panelling seemed out of place beside the glass and steel of the Lloyds Building and the nearby Gherkin. Whatever receptionist had been on duty during the day had by now been replaced by a security guard, who, by the sounds of things, was watching an action movie on a laptop hidden behind the reception desk. He looked up as I approached, saw that I wasn't anyone important, gave the envelope a cursory glance and muttered 'Third floor,' waving me towards the lift beyond his desk. Up on the third floor, a thickly carpeted corridor led away from the lift, and I crept along it, past a series of closed doors and round a corner to the post room: another closed door with a glass panel next to it through which I could see from the blank computer screens and rows of empty pigeonholes that everyone who worked there had finished their week's work and gone home. I knocked anyway, thinking that the sound might summon someone from one of the other offices. I tried the door, but of course it was locked. I wondered if the security guard downstairs would be willing to sign for the package, but already knew that such a responsibility would be far beyond his remit. The radio had been quiet for a while now. The jobs had dried up, and the clients would all be in their habitual wine bars, or on the train home. My friends at the John Snow were probably on their third pint. Ash was waiting for me in a pub in South London. The men in the control room would be packing up for the day, thinking of the drive home, the wife, the football and the weekend. And who knows where the couriers were. Muffled by wood panels and carpet pile, unable to hear the city around me, I felt a very long way from anyone. But, mercifully, my radio still had a signal, and someone answered it when I called.

'Yep? One-four. What's the problem?'

I explained that there was no one around to sign for the package.

'Can you post it?'

I wondered what he meant by this. In a letterbox? But it didn't have a stamp. And surely a client who'd paid money for a letter to be hand delivered wouldn't be happy when it turned up several days later, and the recipient was obliged to pay the postage? Were couriers supposed to carry a supply of stamps for occasions like this? It seemed unlikely.

'Umm, sorry, I'm not sure what that means,' I replied, feeling wretchedly stupid, and wishing passionately that I'd had the courage to turn down the job, or the foresight to lie about having a puncture.

'Is there a letterbox or anything? Somewhere you can leave it where it'll be safe?'

'Uh, yes, I think I can get it under the door . . .'

'Roger-rodge. Do it.'

I did it, and hurried out of the silence of the building back to the street, where the rush hour was already beginning to subside. The Fenchurch drop was mercifully straightforward – the security guard smiled and signed and wished me a good evening – and finally I was at One London Bridge, my cycling shoes ringing noisily on the lacquered floor as yet another security guard escorted me through the draughty reception to the post room (which was still open), a gloomy twilight falling over the river outside.

By the time I called in on the radio to let them know I was empty and heading home, it was seven o'clock, and the tiredness had spread from my muscles to my mind itself. I have no memory of the journey home, only a brief recollection of sitting in a Herne Hill pub with Ash (who wouldn't find her own courier job till the following week, and was thus still wide awake and fully functional) incoherent with exhaustion and both of us giggling at my inability to focus my eyes or finish a sentence.

The following Monday, someone phoned me from the control room to ask what had gone wrong on my Friday evening job. Nothing had, I protested. It had taken me a while, but I'd delivered all four envelopes, and got signatures for all but the Leadenhall one, which I'd posted under the door with the permission of the evening controller.

There had, it transpired, in fact been two envelopes for each address. In my hurry to get the job on board and get out of the building, it hadn't even occurred to me to keep checking through the pile once I'd found the four addresses I was looking for. To my surprise, whoever it was on the phone didn't seem unduly bothered. He advised me to be more careful in future, I cringingly apologised, and nothing more was ever said of it.

Sometimes a mistake would cause slightly wider ripples. Not long afterwards I was late picking up a job from a design firm on Long Lane in Southwark, having spent twenty fruitless minutes searching for it on Long Lane in Smithfield. Once I'd obtained the package (from a distinctly unflustered receptionist), Andy informed me that it contained important tender documents, with a 12 p.m. deadline up in King's Cross, and asked if I thought I could make it. I assured him I would, but after several unplanned detours, including at least one full circuit of Smithfield Market, it was 12.16 by the time I had presented the package to a similarly serene receptionist and sheepishly called in empty. My tardiness went unremarked for over a year, until a chance conversation with a journalist who listened to the story (which I had barely bothered to embellish) said, 'Oh, yes, I think I know the one!', and proceeded to tell me about a friend of hers who worked for the firm in question and had seen weeks of hard work go to waste when a major tender bid was delivered fifteen minutes the wrong side of the deadline.

'Oh, but it was fine,' she said, seeing my horrified face. 'They were philosophical about it. And I think they'd left it a bit close to the line themselves. No harm done.'

As I gradually got to know the circuit, the addresses of the major clients and the routes between them, I became swifter and surer – and as I made friends with more of my fellow couriers, I found out that my own minor errors were nothing compared to some of their monumental fuck-ups. A few of the more reckless couriers (I already knew them as such from their riding style, the risks they took cycling through traffic and their flexible attitude towards red lights) boasted of having been sacked from more than one company for misplacing an important package, either as punishment for the company's loss of a major client, or as a condition of their keeping one. One or two seemed to have worked for almost every company in town, relying on the fact that the industry has a short memory (and is ultimately fairly forgiving), and hoping that no one would notice when they eventually ended up back where they'd started.

At first it seemed unfair to me, when I started, that there was no training manual, no rules or guidelines, no list of the city's loading bays and how to find them; that no one bothered to tell you what the common pitfalls were; that there wasn't even a canteen or a common room where I could talk to my colleagues, ask my stupid questions and learn the tricks of the trade. You don't get much help as a courier – you have to do it all yourself. Perhaps this is why there's such a high drop-out rate in the first couple of weeks.

I wasn't used to learning on the job, working it out as I went along, and realising what the usual mistakes were only once I'd already made them. I preferred to know the rules in advance – and there are just as many rules in couriering, tacit and official, as there would be in any other industry. It's just that no one tells you what they are, so your first challenge is to find out, and only then do you learn how to follow them. It was quite the opposite of the academic world I'd just come from, with its libraries and workshops and reading lists and style guides. Here you learned by listening, by watching, by trial and error, by fucking up and being yelled at, the embarrassment a firm deterrent against making the same mistake again.

Observing other couriers from a distance I learned that carrying my key on an elasticated hair band round my wrist would save me fumbling for it in my bag or pocket every time I wanted to lock up. I noticed how some couriers were hung all over with their equipment: phone and Xda in holsters on the strap of the bag; A–Z easily accessible in a Velcro-sealed pouch on the hip; D-lock thrust through the belt, or held there with cable ties, old inner tubes and recycled seatbelt straps. Some had similarly complicated arrangements holding their radio to their bag; others simply gaffer-taped it in place, or wrapped a couple of strips of Velcro around it. One courier I saw had a collection of about thirty hair bands threaded onto the strap of his bag, gripping his radio like a multicoloured fist. I admired the ingenuity with which everyone seemed to have developed their own solutions and refined the procedures of their job in a slightly different way. Not all couriers kept their key on an elastic band. Some tied it round their wrist with a shoe-lace, the knot sealed with electrical tape. Nhatt wore hers on a complicated bracelet made out of keyrings and retired bicycle chains by a friend of hers in New York. Others had their key swinging from a lanyard round their neck, or trailing from the strap of their bag, or chained to their belt loop and stuffed into their pocket. Gertie, a small, wiry, irrepressibly cheerful old-timer, showed me how his was fixed to his belt with two ski-pass holders (doubled up for safety). 'It's kind of like a reverse yoyo,' he explained, showing me how his key was looped onto the end of a long wire, which reeled itself back up automatically into its casing when he let it go.

I also began to get the hang of radio protocol, occasionally by being corrected or told off when I got something wrong, but mostly by overhearing Andy's exchanges with the other riders. These were mostly one-sided: Andy wore a headset through which he heard what the riders said to him, but what he said to them was broadcast over the radio so that the entire fleet could hear it, sometimes speculatively piecing together a conversation or argument by filling in the blanks between his retorts. Occasionally, he'd accidentally (or deliberately) keep his foot on the 'transmit' pedal while the courier was speaking so that we could hear both sides of the exchange.

Andy was well known, and variously loathed and loved, for his short fuse. Several times a day he'd take his fleet to task, individually or collectively, for interrupting each other on the radio, or for trying to talk to him when he'd asked them to stand by, so that he could answer the phone, hand over to whoever was covering his lunchbreak, or deal with some other miscellaneous control-room business. I must have heard the same admonitions hundreds, even thousands of times, and can still recall them word for word, tone for tone.

'Everyone – stand by – a moment – please!' (in a tone of escalating irritation).

'If I want to hear from you, I'll say, "'Oo else?" or "'Oo's next?" If you don't hear me say, "'Oo else?" or "'Oo's next?", you wait your turn. Is that clear?'

Somehow it was never quite clear enough. At any rate, I heard him issue the same reprimands and warnings several times a day, always sounding as if he were just about at his wits' end, but never quite getting there.

At first this put me constantly on edge, afraid of the public humiliation of being told off over the airwaves, imagining the rest of the fleet pedalling through the traffic and smirking at their radios. But it soon became apparent that Andy's irritation was usually fleeting, and that beneath it lay a sincere, though often grudging, affection for his riders, some of whom had clearly been with him for a long time. I got to know their names and numbers, gradually, and even more gradually learned the tones and phrases Andy would use to speak to them.

'Double-one JP!' was always said with a flourish, as though trumpeting the return of a prodigal, so JP was clearly a favourite – and so openly so that whoever JP was, he must be a favourite among riders as well, for the favouritism to have gone unchallenged and unresented. I eventually met him on his way out of a loading bay behind High Holborn. He was tall and athletic, and smiled when I greeted him, but he spoke quietly and hesitantly, and wore round glasses that gave him a vaguely bookish appearance. You couldn't have resented him if you'd tried. Shortly thereafter, he moved to Citysprint, and was promptly elevated to Andy's personal pantheon – a small handful of exemplary couriers he'd worked with over the years, and now reminisced fondly over with the inevitable nostalgia that seems to pervade the industry. Another was one-four Sophie, whose number I had inherited, and whose shoes I felt I would never be able to fill. She, I was told, had turned up on a borrowed mountain bike, and no one thought she'd last a week. Within a year she was hooked, within two she was racing professionally, and then she had fallen in love, got married, moved to Australia and was now ferrying her two children around Melbourne in a cargo bike.

There were other radio relationships, harried and hilarious. For a week or so, we all listened to a newish courier who would never be less than half an hour late for work, and would respond with explosive self-righteousness when Andy took him to task. As the days progressed, this became something of a circus, and Andy would keep the pedal down so that we could hear both sides of the exchange. We in turn would roll our eyes, listening to the courier getting angrier and angrier as Andy remained dangerously calm, knowing that there could only ever be one winner. Eventually, Andy lost patience.

'Right, one-eight, I've 'ad enough of this. Can you come into the office, please?'

And that was the last we heard of one-eight.

But most of what came over the radio was a constant buzz of numbers and acronyms, which I very quickly learned to ignore, once I'd got sufficiently used to my number that the words 'one-four' would leap out at me from the background noise. In time, I became so finely attuned that I would jump to attention whenever Andy sent someone to 142 Wardour Street, realising only a second later that he hadn't been talking to me after all. Months later, on summer afternoons where the dazzling heat of direct sunlight would sometimes send me to sleep if I was tired enough, and sat still for too long, I'd lie down on the warm grass of Lincoln's Inn Fields or St James's Square, one hand on the bike, bag under my head, radio chattering away right by my ear, and only when Andy called my number would his voice reach down into the depths of my slumber and yank me back up to consciousness.

Most of the time the exchanges over the radio are terse and laconic, with no more than a handful of acronyms and phrases required to convey the vast majority of what needs to be said. 'POB' means 'package on board'. 'Empty' means the package has been delivered and signed for, and you're ready for the next one. Occasional variations include 'Whitfield, going on', which means you've delivered the package addressed to Whitfield Street (or wherever it happens to be), and are still holding the one that's going to the other end of town, hoping that your controller will find you other work to go with it, to make the journey more worthwhile. Or the controller might ask how full your bag is, wondering if there's room for one more (potentially bulky) package, or request your current location, knowing that the route from your recent pick-up to your imminent delivery is likely to take you past the client who's just this minute booked a new job going in the same direction. All of this can be accomplished in startlingly few words.

'Seven-eight, seven-eight, location, please?'

'Shaftesbury.'

'Roger. Details for you, High Holborn.'

'Roger.'

And that's it. The controller sends the details of the job down to the courier's Xda; she stops momentarily to check the pick-up address, adjusts her route slightly in her head, and pushes off into the traffic once again.

It isn't always quite so slick, of course. There are mishearings and misunderstandings, arguments and ego clashes. Sometimes radio protocol falls apart altogether. Sometimes complications arise that are too complicated to be explained in any sort of brevity. A novice courier might call in with a query like this.

'One-four, one-four.'

'One-four, go ahead.'

'Umm, well, I'm standing outside the building, and I've tried ringing the bell, and I've been here like five minutes, but there's no one answering the door – what should I do?'

'Roger, one-four. Is it postable?'

'Umm . . .?'

'Is there a letterbox you can put it in?'

'Oh, yeah, hang on, I'll have a look . . .'

And there's a pause while one-four looks around for a letterbox and, if he or she possesses any initiative at all, checks to see whether the package will actually fit through it.

'One-four, one-four.'

'One-four, yes?'

'Uh, there's a letterbox, but I don't think I can get the envelope through without folding it, and I think it's photographic prints, so they're not going to be too happy with that.'

'Stand by, one-four. I'll call the client and get back to you.'

'Roger-rodge.'

A slightly more experienced courier would simply say, 'No answer; not postable.' That's all the controller needs to know. Although he'll occasionally have time and inclination for a bit of banter, he doesn't want to be bothered with superfluous information.

The same few words are churned around the airwaves over and over again, too innocuous to really become boring, though everyone found their own subtle ways of personalising them, or of loading them with the sarcasm or chirpiness or indignation or suffering or energy that we had no other immediate means of unburdening.

'Roger' became one of those words you say so often that it loses its meaning, and then finds others. Most controllers I've worked with end up using it as a means of punctuating their speech, sticking in a 'roger' every other word, the way other people do with 'like'. Bill uses it as a space-filler: when you've called in empty and he's going through his list trying to figure out whether there are any more jobs he can give you, he'll stretch several 'rogers' over the hiatus as he searches, keeping the airwaves busy, letting you know he's still talking to you, stopping anyone else from calling in until he's decided what to do with you.

'Roger, seven-eight. Roger-rodge. Ro-o-o-o-o-o-o-o-o-oger.' And seconds tick by as I imagine him scanning down the list of jobs on his screen, flicking a pencil between his fingers before finally coming to a decision. 'Roger-rodge, seven-eight, head back in, head back in.'

Andy tended to use 'roger' as an all-purpose term of address, or a substitute for 'mate' (a term he disliked: 'Don't call me mate – I'm not your friend'), meaning that for my first few days on the road I assumed there was actually a courier on the fleet called Roger, and thought that the poor man must never get a second's peace. Then I overheard an exchange between Andy and Aga, the only other woman on the fleet, and understood it was something he said to everyone, a reassuring little quirk of personalisation.

'Zero-nine, Aga? You POB, rodge?'

'Roger-rodge.'

'Carry on, rodge, carry on.'

For a few years, 'roger' was probably one of the most frequent words to pass my lips, and I developed a thousand variations, though I disliked one controller's habit of issuing jokey neologisms like 'roger-todger' and 'roger-dodge', which to my mind interfered with the simplicity and elegance of the restricted radio vocabulary with which we nonetheless managed to say almost all we ever needed to. The beauty of it, I felt, was that the words we used were completely impersonal, that each word meant the same thing no matter who said it, that, by and large, several different controllers were able to communicate with a multilingual bunch of couriers, and to move hundreds of packages thousands of miles a week, with only a few words.

I got to know 'roger' as intimately as I did my bicycle – I savoured the way it would flow through my mouth, the way my tongue would initially retreat and then flick forwards as I pronounced the first syllable, the juicy feel of the fricative. Sometimes, especially when the circuit was busy and I could tell that Andy wanted to finish with me and move on to one of the other riders waiting patiently to talk to him (or calling in over the top of me, which he hated), I'd rattle it out in two tight syllables, as if responding to a sergeant major.

'Roger!' ('Sir, yes sir! Leave it with me.')

On easier days, when everything was rolling along nicely and work was steady enough to keep the radio talking, but slow enough that Andy might tolerate (or instigate) the occasional bit of badinage, I'd revert to a more expansive 'roger', taking my time over the word, adding in a couple of extra syllables, drawing out the vowels, polishing the consonants, savouring the opportunity of having something to say.

'Uh-ro-o-o-orger-rodge.'

And then sometimes there's only the ghost of a 'roger' – when it's the tail end of a conversation, a mere acknowledgement of what's already been made crystal clear, a verbal nod, a lick of sealing wax. Here I top and tail the word as much as I can, amputating consonants, abbreviating it so far that all you'd catch is the briefest susurration, unintelligible except to those who have already had this conversation several times an hour for the last ten years of their career, and know exactly what comes next:

'–dge.'

'–juh.'

'–ch.'

'–sh.'

You spend a lot of time alone as a courier, though the constant sound of your controller's voice on the radio can sometimes make you forget this. Andy's perpetual monologue, crackling out of the radio and into my left ear, quickly became such an essential part of cycling that if I ever rode my bike through Central London at the weekend, without my radio, I'd have the sensation of having gone slightly deaf; of something missing, of the world being quieter and at more of a distance than usual, since the noise around me came from the pavements and the traffic, rather than a small black box strapped to my chest.

I found that Andy's voice, accent and figures of speech were more immediately familiar to me than anyone else's, even people I consider myself very close to. The voice on the radio is the courier's only means of sustained human contact, and after a few months she'll become attuned to it as one does to the voice of a spouse or a childhood friend – able to pick up on the tiny tics and changes of cadence that show when the person is annoyed, or upset, or distracted, or hasn't understood you. Sometimes it'll work the other way too – if you become friends with your controller, or are good enough or bad enough to stand out from the rest of the fleet, he might start to recognise your moods as well – but this is much less likely to happen. He has other voices to listen to, and is sitting in a busy control room with phones ringing and people coming and going, his colleagues discussing the football and his wife texting him about their dinner plans.

The sense of intimacy the courier feels is mostly illusory, or at least one-sided, but it's not always easy to remember this. When something's gone wrong, or when you're exhausted, frustrated, angry or in pain, often the most obvious person to vent this at is the one with whom you spend most of your time, whose voice is constantly in your ear. Occasionally, being former couriers themselves, controllers might sympathise when you tell them about the violence of a driver or the inhumanity of a security guard, but most of the time they're just interested in getting the necessary information across as quickly as possible, because the phone's ringing, and there are half-a-dozen riders waiting to call in with queries.

Nor does he really need to know when your knees are hurting, when your brake pads are about to wear out, or when you're so hungry, cold or exhausted that having stayed on the road for nine hours feels more like a heroic achievement than a day's work. You're often tempted to inform him though – partly to pre-empt and justify any errors or delays, partly to remind him that in between your clean and curt radio responses are miles and miles of pushing and panting and sweating, of dirt and noise, of shrieking ambulances and snarling taxis, of blazing sun or pouring rain or driving snow, while he sits there in his unchanging office, watching the jobs come and go on his computer screen.

There is respect and solidarity in this job, of course there is. But it occurs against a backdrop of almost constant solitude, of private pain and private pleasures, of knowing that the world can afford you little sympathy when things go badly. This, in fact, is probably the very reason for our solidarity.

I stopped at the lights next to another courier once, during a sudden torrential rainstorm that had sent all other cyclists and pedestrians running for cover, so that the streets were curiously deserted, save for us, a few cars, and a million raindrops. I remember the squelch of my sodden gloves on the bars, and seeing the drops of water from his hood dripping past his smiling face. Until the lights changed we simply sat and grinned at each other, and it would take me more than a thousand words to explain exactly what was behind that grin. It acknowledged suffering and discomfort that was so obvious there really wasn't any need to say anything about it. It said, 'We're crazy to be here, aren't we? But we chose this.' And it laughed at the absurdity of two couriers, sitting at the lights, soaked to the skin while everyone else waited inside. Most of all, it spoke of the relief of company and sympathy, because no one but another courier could know exactly what we were going through at that moment – no one, in fact, could have understood that grin without the need to resort to language. The lights changed and we pushed on into the rain, both of us feeling, I suspect, momentarily less alone.

4

Ash started couriering a couple of weeks after me. I hadn't known for sure that she would – it was one of several options she was mulling over, along with going back to Dublin, or picking up another web-developer job through her contacts in London. Secretly, we both knew that whether she stayed in London depended predominantly on whether she wanted to stay with me. Then one afternoon I had an excited text from her, announcing that she'd found a job with One-To-One, and was starting the following day.

It was only then that I realised how lucky I'd got with Pink. Like Lukasz's former company, One-To-One was primarily a passenger car firm, who kept a bike or two on the books in order to save money on the sly when clients asked to send packages by car. In practice, this meant that, save for the odd flurry of last-minute theatre tickets or forgotten mobiles, Ash spent most of her days waiting around for work, and her number of drops rarely stretched into double figures. This, apparently, was how many couriers started out – working for companies who were known for their low workloads, or for treating their riders badly; building up a few months of experience, with which they would then attempt to blag a job at a better company.

Through eavesdropped conversations, and brief exchanges with other couriers in loading bays and post rooms, I began to get an idea of all the different companies. Top of the pile were CitySprint (who didn't pay well, but had enough clients for there never to be any shortage of work, so a fast and reliable courier could still make good money) and Creative (where Nhatt worked and Bill controlled), which had started off ferrying tapes between production houses in Soho, and was still considered one of the cooler companies to work for. Its fleet, unlike many, had a low turnover, and a high incidence of courier personalities and legends. People tended to make it to Creative, and then stay there until they retired, knowing that the company, although far from perfect, was run by ex-couriers who would look out for you – or, at worst, screw you over slightly less frequently and slightly more apologetically than anyone else.

Further down the scale were eCourier, unique in that they worked without a controller, the jobs being allocated automatically, based on the riders' GPS location, and Courier Systems, whose website informed me that it would take on only riders with at least three years' experience, and whose riders informed me that this was bollocks, and anyone could get in. Then there were the smaller boutique companies like Cyclone, whose riders I'd often see lounging like a pride of lions in the park opposite their offices at the bottom of Whitfield Street, and Metro, a printing company in Clerkenwell whose small fleet was recognisable by the fact that they habitually rode around carrying poster tubes longer than they were tall, carefully strapped onto their bags, protruding fore and aft like a lance.

Pink, I would have guessed (it's hard to be objective about your own family) was somewhere towards the top of the second tier of companies – not quite as impressive as CitySprint or Creative, but somewhere you could make a halfway decent living and not have to feel embarrassed when another courier asked where you worked. No one even seems to have heard of One-To-One, so I'm not quite sure how Ash found them. Probably, she followed a similar strategy to mine – calling every listed company in London until one of them had an opening. Her introduction to the circuit was therefore different from my own. Rather than riding and riding and riding until her legs were heavy and stiff, her stomach growling and her eyes threatening to close every time she stopped for more than a few minutes, she became accustomed to waiting on street corners and, as the weather got steadily colder, sitting in cafes, judiciously eking out a cup of coffee for anything up to three hours, and trying not to think about how the £2 she had paid for it compared to the amount of money she'd earn that day.

After a couple of weeks, she discovered a busy little cafe at the bottom of Wimpole Street, incongruously serving cups of tea for 65p and coffee for 75p in the midst of Marylebone's plenty, and I got used to spotting her there, bundled up in her bright orange jacket and deerstalker hat at one of the outside tables, flanked by leathered motorcycle couriers and morose gentlemen who might not quite have qualified as tramps but certainly weren't too far off, scanning the street or browsing one of the free newspapers, radio turned up just loud enough to hear when her number was called. I'd usually stop, for a chat or a kiss, full of delight at the dubious coincidence of our meeting. She was a beacon for me in those first few months – one of my only points of familiarity before I got to know any of the other couriers. My favourite encounters were when she shot obliviously past me in the opposite direction, concentrating so fiercely on the road that her tongue appeared at the edge of her mouth, or when I caught sight of her auburn hair and jaunty red Raleigh frame disappearing round a corner, made a split-second U-turn and gave chase, nonchalantly pulling up alongside her at the next lights and remarking 'nice bike', just as she had when we first met, quite by chance, on our way through Epping Forest one summer evening.

She moved from her temporary room in Thornton Heath into a cheap house share in Walthamstow, and we took to spending alternate weekends there, and in my tiny flat in West Norwood, ruefully amused that we had ended up living almost as far apart as was possible within the same city. Some Friday evenings, in a half-hearted attempt to celebrate the end of a hard week, and to gird our loins for the final eight miles up the A10 to E17, we'd stop for a drink at the Foundry, which was at that point the favoured courier watering hole. It wasn't difficult to see why. The Foundry was a roomy, rambling, wrecked-looking venue, squatting on the wide junction where Old Street met Great Eastern Street, with several metres of open pavement out the front, which meant that the couriers had plenty of space to lock up their bikes, and also to stand around with the cans of lager they'd bought at the off-licence across the road. I suppose if anyone had made a fuss they could have claimed that they were standing several metres away from the entrance to the bar, and it was, as far as anyone knew, not illegal to drink in the street in that part of London, so what are you going to do?

But no one ever made a fuss. The couriers were, in all likelihood, a big part of what gave the place its cachet, and when you peered through the cracks in the crowd, you'd make out the skinny jeans and witty T-shirts of all the graphic designers and web developers whose start-ups had begun to populate the area, and even a few young suits, stopping off for a drink with their flatmates or uni friends on their way between Bishopsgate and their canalside residence off Broadway Market. We're not all that different, you and I. A couple I know – both corporate lawyers – had their first date at the Foundry, long before I ever went there myself. The couriers gave the place its visual energy, its air of slightly maverick rebellion; everyone else put in the money.

Ash and I would hover on the fringes, talking mostly to each other; occasionally saying hello to another courier one of us knew, or a cycling friend who'd stopped by on their way home, still not feeling as if we really belonged to this fabulous crowd of tall handsome men – and the occasional handsome woman – their skin still dark from months of suntanning, but now mostly encased in expensive-looking waterproofs, gloves, overshoes and hats. All summer they had ridden around in singlets and cut-off jeans, looking like they were having the time of their lives – now things had got serious.

The evenings were dark by now, and colder every week. We would have had our lights on for over an hour by the time we reached the Foundry, and after standing around for the time it took to drink a can of lager we'd be shivering miserably, dreading the forty-five-minute crawl home with our stiffening muscles, almost too tired to be hungry, although we'd bring ourselves to cook a pot of pasta or pota-toes as we took turns in the shower, and force it down before we fell into bed. It makes sense to me now, that the rest of the couriers seemed so hyperactive, laughing and shouting and jostling each other, practising skids and trackstands and playfighting like a litter of puppies – it was a way of cling-ing onto the energy of the day, maintaining its momentum, because once it was allowed to ebb, there was only exhaus-tion to take its place.

Everything is harder in winter. The weather exerts its own tax on your finite energy resources, tiring you out even more just in the effort of keeping warm. I began to notice, when the temperature dipped below zero, that I'd fall asleep an hour earlier than usual, no matter how slow work had been. In fact, when work was slow it got harder, because I wasn't able to keep myself warm by cycling. And where in the sum-mer you'd simply prop your bike up outside a building, close your lock around the front wheel in one swift movement and jog into the reception, at half-past four in late December, you first have to take your gloves off, plucking awkwardly at the Velcro around the wrist with fingers that are still numb from the cold, despite the layers of fleece and Gore-Tex they're wrapped in, and biting the tips of your fingers in an effort to get them out of the gloves without turning the lining inside out, which will make them even more difficult, fiddly and time-consuming to put back on. Then you lock your bike up, then you start to put your gloves back on, then you remember about your lights, and remind yourself that it's not worth risking it, because you've already had two sets stolen when you left them on the bike as you ran into a shop to buy pasta or milk, and you never know when a usually straightforward pick-up might take much longer than usual (maybe the receptionist will be away from her desk, or the files will still be downloading, or the person who booked the job will have got the address wrong, and after twenty minutes of confusion you'll figure out that you were actually meant to be four doors down). So you unhook and unscrew and unwrap your lights from seatpost and handlebars, these now-familiar motions prompting the now familiar resolution to find a way of attaching lights to your bag and radio, as you've seen other couriers do – a resolution that grows fainter with every reiteration, and that you won't actually get round to fulfilling until your third winter on the road.

Most large buildings have heaters that blow a warm wave of air over you as you walk through the doors, and within an instant the world feels like itself again, the cold recedes in memory as much as sensation, and you grin reassuringly at the kind receptionist, who asks, 'Gosh, aren't you cold in this weather?', and say something brave and dismissive about how you just get used to it, or get on with it. Then you look for excuses to delay your departure, even if only by a matter of seconds. You initiate a conversation – about the weather, or how close the weekend is, or anything else anyone wants to talk about, including flirtatious overtures you'd normally ignore. Or you find a bathroom and spend a minute or two holding your hands under the driers to try to send the heat a little further than skin deep, and thaw out the crooked icicles that you imagine have now taken the place of your veins. Or you might just stroll to the door at roughly half your usual pace, and then linger on the threshold for another minute or so, finishing off the job on your Xda, fastening your bag, tightening the straps, checking everything's in place, and getting your lights out of your pockets ready to put them back on the bike once you're out in the cold again.

On the very worst days, stepping out from under the heaters takes the same sort of resolve as does jumping into an unheated swimming pool. The first shock of cold is the hardest, and then, as long as you keep moving, you're OK for a while. Then you start to notice how the chill has crept into your bones and muscles, slowing you down, blurring your coordination and your judgement, making you clumsy and stupid. I often embarrass myself on cold days, by slightly misjudging a gap in the traffic, so that I have to put my foot down, or anger a driver by leaning on their bumper for a moment – or by mishandling the bike as I bring it to a halt, so that my usual graceful dismount becomes more of a crash landing, or simply by dropping my lock as I try to juggle it with my key, my front wheel and whatever railing or signpost I'm trying to lock it to. My toes reach a complicated zenith of sensation where they manage to be simultaneously numb and sore, so that, between bike and reception, I tread cautiously, afraid of both pain and of stumbling. On particularly cold days, my lips end up numb too, so that I slur my words when I speak, and worry that people will think I'm drunk.

Throughout that first winter I found myself nurturing a pointless and irrational sense of resentment towards everyone around me – my controllers, the receptionists, the bus drivers – and their constant failure to acknowledge or even notice my suffering. I hated the controller's voice as he told me to head up to Clerkenwell for another pick-up as soon as I'd dropped the Holborn, because I'd been planning to go and stand under the warm air vent at the top of Fetter Lane for a few minutes, savouring the smell of bread and croissants rolling out from the Sainsbury's bakery, and holding the snapping snarling winter air at bay for just a few minutes. I hated the breezy receptionist with her impersonal smile, who didn't bother to ask how I was, to notice the sleet melting off my clothing and soaking into her carpet, to recognise how slowly I typed her name into the Xda (because my frozen fingers were so stiff that I could barely grasp the stylus), to marvel at how I'd just carried on working, no matter what the weather, and to remark (in tones of awe and admiration) on how difficult that must be. Mind you, even if she had (and to be fair, some of them did), it wouldn't make very much difference. My dull, mumbling resentment wasn't really directed at her, or the voice on the radio, or anyone but myself, and the weather, which doesn't care what I think of it, and will carry on regardless, and for as long as it pleases.

At some point during that first torturous winter, I developed a detailed fantasy as I rode along, at least in those moments where the intensity of the cold had receded enough to leave me some thinking space around the edges of the pain. One day – and perhaps this might even turn out to be true – I would be a well-dressed, well-paid, well-respected professional in a suit, like the ones I saw walking through the receptions to their offices and meeting rooms as I handed over their contracts and legal files to the receptionist. (In fact, like the ones who five years earlier had been my fellow students, and who, when I glimpsed them walking down Bishopsgate or Gresham Street, reminded me that, with my qualifications, there was really very little reason why I couldn't have followed a similar career path, if I'd really wanted to, or believed I could.) It would be a freezing cold winter day, identical to the one I was currently enduring, and I'd take pity on a shivering cycle courier who'd come to pick up some paperwork from me.

'Do you want to warm up for a bit?' I'd ask, hesitating as I handed over the package, watching the mixture of relief and resignation flicker across her face, knowing that she wanted nothing more than to stay in this warm, bright building, rather than go back out into the cold grey streets, but also that sitting around inside wouldn't pay her rent, or ingratiate her with her controllers.

She'd start to refuse, gruffly, nobly, regretfully, and I'd interrupt her, my plan falling into place only as I issued the invitation.

'I'll sign for an hour's waiting time,' I'd say. 'We've got a hot shower through there if you'd like, and there's a meeting room no one's using today. You can put your gloves on the radiator, have a cup of coffee . . .'

She wouldn't believe it, of course. Why would this immaculate young executive, with her crisp white shirt and blow-dried hair, even notice the winter plight of a cycle courier, much less care about it?

'I was a courier myself,' I'd explain, conspiratorially. 'I still cycle in every day. I know what it's like.' And I'd show her my glove tan, or, if we were far enough into winter that it had faded back into the milkiness of my flesh, hitch up my skirt an inch or so to demonstrate that I still had a cyclist's legs. 'Look, call your controller – what company do you work for? – tell him that the package isn't ready yet. It's not that urgent anyway, as long as it's there by five. Tell him they've asked you to wait.'

And I'd show her through to the showers, point out the dryers and radiators for her soaking clothes, open a packet of biscuits and instruct the receptionist to give her as much tea and coffee as she wanted. An hour later, her gloves would still be slightly damp, so I'd swap them for my newer, more waterproof ones. And she'd be grateful, but not awkwardly, pathetically so – because she'd know that my generosity came from a genuine recognition of her suffering; from having been there myself, and knowing how wretched it can feel; from wanting to make things better, now that I actually could.

Rescue fantasies are almost always founded on arrogance, but I'm not so sure about this one. Is it arrogant to fantasise about rescuing oneself? And if, one day, the tables really do turn, and I find myself at the apex of winter's wheel of fortune, offering warm coffee and dry socks to a freezing cycle courier when she turns up on a January afternoon to collect a manuscript or drop off a contract, I'd rather think of my benevolence as just an extension of my erstwhile longing; a gesture of gratitude to fate for having shown me this suffering, then taken it away, bestowed it on someone else, and given me the means to alleviate it.

Of course, my longing for recognition, however instinctual, was itself fairly arrogant. There are, after all, countless people who suffer, visibly or invisibly, noticed or unnoticed, all over London, all of the time. My own hardship was arguably no worse than that regularly endured by cleaners and night nurses, on their feet for twelve hours or more while the rest of the city goes home, relaxes, sleeps and wakes again – or by the security guards, fighting off boredom, cold and argumentative cycle couriers as they stand at the mouths of London's loading bays. And of course there are the people who spend all their time out in the streets, night and day, summer and winter, because they have nowhere else to go. I had always pitied the homeless, but it wasn't until my first winter on the road that I really sympathised with them, and got close to understanding how the cold will make you desperate, how it will cloud your judgement and realign your priorities. One icy, windy day during that first winter, half crazed with the pain of frozen fingers, I staggered into Condor Cycles and spent £30 on the warmest gloves I could find, without a moment of doubt that this was the right thing to do. On any other day I'd have talked myself out of it, persuaded myself that I could withstand the pain for at least a few more hours, reminded myself that £30 amounted to half of my entire day's earnings, convinced myself that I could probably find the same gloves for half the price online, and could probably make do with the ones I already had anyway. But the cold swept this all aside. As long as my fingers hurt so much, nothing was more important than stopping the pain.

And I had a cosy flat to go back to in the evenings, with a hot shower, and clean dry clothes to change into. The thought of staying out all night in this, with no relief, in a damp sleeping bag on a stone-cold pavement, was terrifying. The firmest resolutions go through a chemical change below a certain temperature. Principles grow sluggish and counter-arguments congeal. Even if the £30 I'd spent on those gloves had taken me down into my overdraft and incurred an extra £30 fine, I'd still have bought them. Even if I knew that I'd struggle to pay my rent as a consequence, I'd still have bought them. If I had spent all day sitting on the pavement, nowhere to go, wild with cold, knowing that I'd be spending the next twelve hours in similar fashion, I would spend my last fiver on cheap alcohol, rather than hoping that I might somehow work it up to a tenner and be able to buy myself a night in a hostel. Numbing the immediate pain becomes more important than anything else. Long-term plans seem laughably irrelevant, because you can't imagine how you'll survive the next few minutes if someone doesn't do something. You'll grasp at any lifeline, clamber into any lifeboat, no matter how leaky.

A tramp once offered to buy me a cup of tea, one chilly January afternoon, as I sat huddled up outside a cafe in my many layers, principles sufficiently frozen that I hadn't bothered to make my usual courtesy purchase of the cheapest thing on the menu, to signify my right to the table – or even to choose a table where I could pretend someone else's dirty cup was actually my own. I turned him down politely, and wondered if this meant I had really hit rock bottom. But at the same time, to be noticed, and to be offered sympathy by someone who might have the slightest inkling of what I was going through, was a rare occurrence in those days. I looked at his retreating back with a rush of affection.

Laboriously, since my thoughts were still clouded with cold and exhaustion, I tried to tell myself that this was no smiling matter. That despite the perceived glamour and excitement of being a cycle courier, I must have taken a very wrong turn to have found myself shivering on street corners, muffled in several layers of stinking clothes, not earning any money, and being pitied by people I usually considered far worse off than myself. Somehow though, I couldn't bring myself to feel any sense of regret – or even, really, any urge to be somewhere else, unless it were somewhere just slightly warmer.

I chewed over this puzzling sense of contentment as I went about the rest of my day's deliveries. What was absent, I noticed, was the tiny nagging doubt that had surfaced again and again during my years in academia – a doubt that what I was doing held any point or relevance for the world beyond me; a concern that I wasn't living out my full potential; a fear that, if anyone ever called on me to justify my career choice, I simply couldn't. What use was it to anyone if I came up with an original way of understanding modern Urdu feminist poetry? Of course, I might just as well argue that it was still of microscopically little use to the world that London's packages were delivered on time; that I really wasn't making the most of my talents and qualifications by loitering outside cheap cafes in the cold; that in fact, I might be wasting my life even more than I was before.

But the doubt had gone. I no longer felt I ought to be elsewhere. At least, no more than the courier always feels she ought to be elsewhere, when there's a job on her Xda and a package in her bag. And this must be part of the strange and seductive satisfaction of couriering. It's not just that the job consists of continual minor achievements ('Yes! Got the package there on time!'; 'Yes! Avoided that speeding cab!';

'Yes! Made it through the green light!'), it's more that it offers a sense of constant movement. There is always somewhere else to be; you're always on your way. For someone who otherwise had no idea where her life was going, this was a pleasantly literal solution.

5

At the tail end of this first winter on the road, it occurred to me that I could carry a book in my bag, and read it in between jobs. This quickly became one of the things I looked forward to most – it made up for the daily hour of almost uninterrupted reading I'd lost when I stopped commuting by tube, and was partial compensation for the otherwise wasted hours spent standing by when work was slow. The lens through which I scrutinised the city adjusted slightly, and began to take in promising reading spots – benches tucked away in corners where I wouldn't be discovered or interrupted, like the one at the bottom of Bedford Row on which I once spent half an hour trying to ignore the unwashed stench of the tramp sharing it, which wafted towards me every time he lifted his bottle to his mouth, until he struggled to his feet and I realised he was a barrister, long dark gown slightly askew, sockless ankles protruding from incongruously polished brogues. He tottered off towards Jockey's Fields, and I wondered whether he was a tramp pretending to be a barrister or, far more likely, a barrister who had fallen on hard times, whose work had dried up, and who now stumbled drunkenly around the Inns of Court, variously tolerated, indulged and ignored by his former colleagues. I never saw him again.

The Inns of Court, particularly Lincoln's Inn Fields and the rabbit warren of tiny secluded courtyards that make up the Inner Temple, afforded me plenty more reading spots. They were one of the first major discoveries I made as a courier. I hadn't even known they existed, or that behind the mundane façades of Fleet Street and Kingsway was a cloistered world where the roar of traffic from the Embankment was held at bay by stone walls and gardens full of roses and magnolia trees, and the constant calming music of the fountain in Fountain Court, tinkling away under a mulberry tree that stains the flagstones (and my fingers) with blood-red juice every August. The first time I had a delivery to Middle Temple Lane, I spent a long time prowling up and down Fleet Street opposite the Royal Courts of Justice, looking for a southbound junction that my A–Z insisted was there, convinced I must somehow have made a mistake and be looking in the wrong place. And then I found the door. It seemed like the kind of door designed not to be noticed, tucked away as it was between a bank and a shop, overshadowed by the jetties and bay windows of the tall half-timbered building that rose above it, bearing no number or any other indication of what lay beyond it. We pass doors like this every day without noticing them, our attention diverted by the bright and busy shopfronts on either side, our eyes passing heedlessly over any portal that doesn't draw attention to itself: the narrow doorways that lead to the flats above shops, the tall padlocked gates hiding the passages between the buildings, the unmarked fire escapes, and the entrance to Middle Temple Lane. The door itself was of heavy dark wood, riveted together with huge iron nails, broad and low, so that with its curved top it seemed almost circular, like a hobbit hole or the entrance to a dragon's lair. It was stout and strong – a door built to keep hordes at bay, rather than as a token demonstration of boundaries like the glass and plywood we all politely observe, knowing that we could put a fist through them if we ever needed to. It was a door that called for a ceremonial knock, a secret password, an ornate key the length of my forearm.

I gave it a cautious push, and it swung open easily, with a satisfying fairy-tale creak. As it thudded behind me, I remembered Mary in *The Secret Garden*, stepping through the hidden door into a garden that no one has set foot in for ten years.

She slipped through it, and shut it behind her, and stood with her back against it, looking about her and breathing quite fast with excitement, and wonder, and delight.

She was standing inside the secret garden.

A narrow cobbled lane stretched down the hill ahead of me, in between tall brick buildings with ranks of white window frames. At the far end, barely visible, was another arch-way, through which a burst of leaves and light gave me the impression that the lane opened out onto the Embankment and the river. It was a scene that might not have changed for several centuries. The lane was deserted, except for two men in rippling black gowns, wads of paperwork hugged to their chests, who disappeared into one of the buildings as I watched them, and the noise of Fleet Street seemed to have been muffled by the thick wooden door; repulsed by the tall brick and stone ramparts; kept out by the air of the

Middle Temple, which seemed fresher, stiller, sweeter than that outside the door. I could hear birdsong, and the play of a fountain – and the intruding echoes of my cycling shoes, ringing out down the lane as they slipped and stumbled across the shining cobbles.

Just inside each doorway, a long list of names was painted on a board in a neat roman font, usually with one or two 'Judges' and 'Right Honourables' at the top, followed by what appeared to be the roll-call of the ruling class, a roaring cascade of double barrels, with here and there a lone Khan or Singh. Stone steps gave way to plush carpets, and I followed hand-painted signs and brass stair rods up to the first-floor clerks' room, where four or five immaculate young men faced each other across a bank of telephones and PC monitors. The vast majority of legal clerks seem to be cufflinked and hairgelled men in their twenties, with an air of ambition and self-confidence seemingly at odds with the mainly administrative nature of their role. I have long wondered why this is. Other administrators are generally much more down at heel, and delightfully variegated. Delivering to Companies House on Bloomsbury Street, before it moved down to Victoria, I'd always enjoy watching the miscellany of employees working behind the counter – the motherly woman in her fifties who wore spaghetti straps over her large mottled shoulders in summer; the tall, slightly stooped man with his cardigans and belted jeans; the shy, scrawny, bespectacled younger woman, with her hand-knitted jumpers and long flowing skirts; the deft, sprightly gentleman in tweeds and bow ties, who had a manicured beard and an energetically friendly way of asking you to wait *just* one moment, please, sign right there in the column at the end, spell out your name, please, *do* have an enjoyable day.

These clerks, however, looked as if they'd be spending several evenings a week rubbing suited shoulders with the rest of the legal profession in the glistening taverns of Fleet Street and Chancery Lane. They were all on the phone when I walked in, some hunched forward and scanning their screens, others leaning back expansively in their chairs, gesticulating lazily with one manicured hand, a performance as much for the benefit of their oblivious colleagues as the unseeing person on the other end of the line. One of them eventually caught my eye, and flexed his eyebrows in a way that very clearly said, 'Yes, I've seen you, now please just wait patiently until I'm ready to deal with you.' I extracted the package from my bag (it was two large ringbinders, sealed in a thick plastic envelope), fished out my Xda and clicked my way through to the POD (proof of delivery) screen, so that it would be all ready for him to sign the moment he came off the phone. The window behind him was open, and a leafy breeze curled intermittently round the room.

'Yep. Yep. Yep. Yep,' said the clerk curtly, bringing his phonecall to a masterful close. Just as he replaced the receiver in its cradle and turned to me, Andy's voice boomed out over the radio, loudly instructing someone to head over to Lower Thames for a pick-up. The airwaves had been quiet for so long that I'd forgotten to turn my radio off as I walked into the building. Four heads jerked up to glare at me, and the clerk frowned with distaste, as I would myself at a teen-ager playing her music out loud on the tube.

'Turn that down please,' he said, with a contempt I more or less shared, despising myself for shattering the peace of his office, and by extension despoiling the newly discovered beauty of Middle Temple Lane. Hurriedly and apologetically, I twisted the knob beneath my chin to shut out this unwelcome intrusion of modernity, held out my Xda for him to sign, and fled back down the carpeted staircase. On my way back up Middle Temple Lane, I noticed a stone archway to my right, between buildings, and followed it through to a tiny flagged courtyard, shaded by two large trees and overlooked by flowering window boxes. Through another and I was faced with the huge golden rotunda of the Temple Church, regarded by a group of well-heeled tourists whose guide was explaining its history in a stage whisper. I walked past them and sat on a stone bench, the church at my back, and watched the bright flagstones as they gradually began to swim before my eyes. It was a sunny morning, but I was still almost constantly tired, and grateful to have found somewhere to hide and rest for a few minutes.

After that, whenever I called in empty in EC4 and Andy replied, 'Got you down, one-four, got you on the plot' (meaning that there was no immediate work, and he'd put my name at the bottom of his list of available couriers), I'd hasten over to the Inns of Court, radio turned down from a shout to a mumble, and find myself a quiet courtyard or garden where I could sit, reading my book or eating my sandwiches, until I was called again. No one ever kicked me out, or even seemed to care that I was there.

As time went on, I found other boltholes. There was Gough Square, a tiny cobbled yard just north of Fleet Street, which would have been unremarkable were it not for Samuel Johnson's old house at one end and a bronze statue of his cat – Hodge – on a small pedestal at the other. Hodge was a stout and surly-looking fellow (he and Johnson probably found they had a lot in common), perched proprietorially on a bronze copy of the Dictionary the way modern cats sit on laptops, two empty oyster shells by his side, to commemorate Johnson's indulgent habit of going out himself to buy treats for Hodge, not wishing to inconvenience his servants and risk them taking a dislike to the cat. Quite predictably, the statue had become a totem of affection and amusement for those who worked in the area. There was quite often a shining twenty-pence piece in one of the oystershells, and most Decembers someone would tie a tartan ribbon around Hodge's oblivious neck. There were benches on either side of the statue, usually populated by smoking lawyers, builders in hi-vis jackets, working their way through their lunchboxes, and myself, bicycle leaned against the back of the bench with one handlebar peering over my shoulder, looking up from my book to smile in amusement as lost tourists discovered and exclaimed over Hodge, read out the inscription from his pedestal, and took it in turns posing for photos beside him.

Other hiding places included the leafily shaded Mount Street Gardens, secreted between houses and a tall Victorian school in Mayfair, not a single side of it facing a road, so that its presence was almost entirely unannounced, and therefore mostly undetected, and I never had any trouble finding a free bench, even at the height of summer. And Postman's Park, a former churchyard now stranded in the middle of the one-way system at the western end of London Wall, and therefore much less frequented than you'd expect, given that one wall of the park is covered in china tiles, each commemorating a Londoner who lost his or her life saving the life of someone else, such as eleven-year-old Solomon Galaman, who 'died of injuries . . . after saving his little brother from being run over in Commercial Street' in 1901, or Frederick Alfred Croft, who in 1878 'saved a lunatic woman from suicide at Woolwich Arsenal Station, but was himself run over by the train', or Sarah Smith, a pantomime artist who died in 1863 'of terrible injuries received after attempting in her inflammable dress to extinguish the flames which had enveloped her companion'. I couldn't say whether I find these plaques more macabre or inspiring, but I think that for me their primary attraction is the curiously vivid and detailed glimpses they give of a London long lost – or perhaps not lost at all, since, after all, plenty of people are still mown down in road accidents, and fling themselves in front of trains. I regularly ride down Commercial Street on my way to a pickup in Tower Hamlets, or a drop in Bermondsey, and think about how it must have looked a century and a half ago, back when Whitechapel was still populated by prostitutes, Irish immigrants and Jewish refugees. Solomon Galaman was no doubt one of the latter, and I wonder if his death finally extinguished the hope and optimism with which his family had reached their new country, or whether years of squalor and penury in the slums of Spitalfields had already done that. Or perhaps, in those days, losing a child or two in disastrous circumstances was almost to be expected.

Reading books in the city that was the natural habitat of their characters turned out to enrich both city and character.

The match isn't always exact, of course. Sometime during the long tail end of my first winter on the road, I kept a dog-eared copy of Iris Murdoch's *Under the Net* in my bag, and read it in between jobs, when it wasn't raining, and when my fingers weren't too cold to turn the pages. A lot of the book was set far out in West London, where I almost never go, so it might as well have been describing Birmingham for all the impression it made on me, but eventually the eccentric ramblings of its characters took them to Holborn Viaduct.

The taxi drove off and left us standing alone on the Viaduct. If you have ever visited the City of London in the evening you will know what an uncanny loneliness possesses these streets which during the day are so busy and noisy. The Viaduct is a dramatic viewpoint. But although we could see for a long way, not only towards Holborn and Newgate Street, but also along Farringdon Street, which swept below us like a dried-up river, we could see no living being. Not a cat, not a copper. It was a warm evening, cloudlessly and brilliantly blue, and the place was mute around us, walled in by a distant murmur which may have been the sound of traffic or else the summery sigh of the declining sun.

They then head towards the Viaduct Tavern, which is still there, and where I sometimes stop to get my water bottle filled as I pass by.

I haven't looked at Holborn Viaduct the same way since I read *Under the Net*. Until then, it was merely one of those arbitrary dividing lines between the City and the Middle; the moment you emerge from the City as you head west, and the moment you finally shake off the tangle of Holborn as you head east. And Farringdon Street, which runs beneath the viaduct, was at first just a nuisance – a steady uphill climb from Blackfriars, with potholes, fast traffic, and a difficult right-hand turn if you want to go east into Smithfield after the viaduct. But now Farringdon's a riverbed, even though the River Fleet, once one of London's busiest waterways, has sunk several metres underground in the last century or so, and is now audible only through a couple of gratings dotted through Clerkenwell, and visible where it trickles into the Thames under Blackfriars Bridge. I had never really paid attention to how the city folds in half at that point, like the pages meeting the spine of a book. A couple of hours after discovering this passage, I stopped on Holborn Viaduct, and looked around me for the first time. In some ways the scene could not have been more unlike Murdoch's description. The sun had already set, whatever summery or wintery sighs it emitted quite drowned out by the traffic roaring up and down Farringdon as the rush hour took hold. Windows and streetlights and headlights beamed a pale yellow light, feebly reflected by the puddles and in the dampness of the pavements, and the sky behind them was an insipid greyish lilac, darkening rapidly as daylight and lamplight concluded their clumsy exchange of powers. The air was too damp to be properly cold, but there was nothing warm about the closed windows, the speeding cars, and the commuters hurrying to and fro in their overcoats. It was not an evening for lingering outside, and yet linger I did, leaning my elbows on the painted parapet, and admiring the way in which the delicate fingers of the statue of Commerce (personified as a coroneted woman in long flowing robes) reached out into the void above Farringdon, as if she had just cast a handful of coins down into the river of traffic below. I looked forward to coming back six months hence, on some warm, cloudless and brilliant evening, in an attempt to recapture more closely what Iris Murdoch must have seen in 1953 or 1954, and which now, through the entanglement of her prose and my own exploration of the viaduct, felt almost as if it might already be part of my own memory.

I went on a similar pilgrimage, in between jobs, when I read Alan Hollinghurst's *The Swimming Pool Library*, to see if I could find the imaginary site of Lord Nantwich's house, which was meant to be somewhere in the vicinity of Huggin Hill, on a street 'so narrow that it had been closed to traffic and was no longer marked in the London A–Z', and boasted an improbable Roman mosaic in the depths of its cellars. And of course, there's nothing to be seen – the area's now just tiny back alleys, sloping down towards the river, featureless except for the loading bays and fire escapes of all the massive office buildings that the city has turned into in the last few decades.

In *Under the Net*, several hours after leaving the Viaduct Tavern, and rather the worse for wear, the protagonist and his cohorts decide to go for a swim in the Thames from pretty much this exact spot. As they cross Upper Thames Street, now a busy dual carriageway spanned by foot bridges, there is 'no sound; not a bell, not a footstep', and Jake muses on 'what used to be Fyefoot Lane, where many a melancholy noticeboard tells in the ruins of the City where churches and public houses once stood'. Even then much had come and gone. The swimmers move 'out of the moonlight into a dark labyrinth of alleys and gutted warehouses' beside the river, all of which has now also gone, giving way to more office buildings, and loading bays, and a brickwork footpath with a view across the river to the Tate Modern, a newly sanitised relic from times when the river was a resource, and the buildings that surrounded it purposed for function rather than display. Hollinghurst, writing in and of 1983, remarks on the unexpected quietness of the streets, that are now occupied by 'somnolent trades – a bespoke tailor, a watch repairer', and one or two remaining warehouses: 'some had battened-up windows [and] bleached and cracked signs for businesses long defunct'.

I often catch myself looking back to the days when the riverside was a maze of decaying warehouses and crumbling wharves – or further, to when it must have been a busy dockside heaving with sailors and stevedores and prostitutes and pickpockets – with a kneejerk nostalgia that's easily dismissed because, after all, all of that was long gone before I even arrived in the world, and even if I could somehow take myself back there, nostalgia would soon be displaced by reality, and the stench and misery of London's earlier incarnations would have me fleeing for the time machine or portal through which I'd managed to shift myself.

Turning the problem round, I realise that at least some small part of my nostalgia is prompted by my lingering dissatisfaction with the present – with how the banks of the Thames are now almost solely the property of the law firms and multinationals whose offices have supplanted the winding alleyways and ramshackle buildings that came before, and whose roof terraces now command the best views of the oozing river – or of the tourists, who are different every day, and yet also always the same, dragging their feet along the South Bank from Borough Market down to the Globe, milling and marvelling across the river to St Paul's, presenting a constant obstacle to anyone who actually knows where they're going. But then I doubt that the honest filth of the old riverbanks would have given me any more of a sense of belonging than the sheer walls and complicated security arrangements of the multinationals. And nor was the older London, just because of its obvious dirt, and the impression of having been thrown and held together by human beings who were just about making do, any more alive or real than what has replaced it. I should know better, I tell myself, since I'm the one who sees round the corners and into the crevices of these buildings, who has an ongoing flirtation with one of their receptionists who always grins when he sees me, bounding over to help me with the lift doors when I deliver to the travel company on the fourth floor, and whose innocent enthusiasm is so endearing that I can't frown at him the way I usually do to nip these things in the bud. I see into the kiosks where tired security guards eat their ham sandwiches over copies of the *Sun* and the *Mail*, radio buzzing with news of minor incidents in the goods lift. I've spotted the tiny dent in the brick wall alongside the river that overflows with cigarette butts, and wondered idly why the smokers from the surrounding offices congregate here, rather than at any other point along the walkway. Humanity will always find a foothold, I remind myself, no matter how apparently inhospitable the conditions.

London's skyline has changed considerably, even in the

short time I've known it. During 2011, I watched the Shard slowly climbing towards the heavens, having known it was coming long before the rest of the city. There used to be an unremarkable office block on that site, and I delivered there quite regularly. Then one day I turned up with a package and it seemed very clear that the building was no longer in use. The doors were locked, the lights were off, and there wasn't even a security guard at the front desk. After a long-winded series of phonecalls and radio conversations, I managed to convey this to Andy and he managed to contact the client, and eventually sent me round the corner to their new office on Tooley Street. A couple of weeks later, the building was taken down (a friend who worked as a nurse at nearby Guy's Hospital told me how the cranes had lifted JCBs all the way up to the top of the building, and they had demolished it from the roof down) and I saw from the illustrations on the safety fences that it would eventually be replaced by an enormous glass building that looked like an elongated pyramid, and dwarfed the rest of the city – though that could of course have been artist's licence on the part of the planners.

All tall buildings, I've learned, are built from the inside out. First the foundations are dug, and all we'll see if we peer through the cracks in the security fence is an unremarkable mess of mud and rubble and earth-moving equipment – if we're lucky a crane or a drill. And then the lift shaft appears: a concrete spinal cord, stencilled at regular intervals with the numbers of the levels that it will serve once the rest of the tower is built around it. Finally, the vertebrae of floors and ceilings and the shimmering reptilian skin of steel and glass are tacked on and another small patch of the sky is colonised by the city.

Not so long ago I was riding south over Blackfriars Bridge (a less frequent occurrence than you might expect, since I have a slightly irrational dislike of Blackfriars, so will always make a detour to use Southwark or Waterloo, unless it's obviously on my way) and noticed that Sea Containers House, one of the largest buildings on the South Bank, had an enormous half-built tower sticking up behind it, which most definitely hadn't been there before. I spent only a few minutes mourning the lost skyline of my earlier days in London before I decided that I was being needlessly emotional. True, my children's children – or indeed, anyone moving to London this summer – will only ever know the city as a forest of skyscrapers, more and more like any other of the world's capitals. But even when I moved here, there was the Gherkin on St Mary Axe, and there was Tower 42 on Old Broad Street, and there was Canary Wharf, and no doubt people a couple of generations older than me were reminiscing over the days when the biggest bumps on the skyline were St Paul's and Battersea Power Station.

What difference does the skyline make to me, anyway? The loading bays under the buildings all look the same, and down in the streets all that really matters is how long the roads will be closed for while the towers are being built.

6

To my surprise, Lukasz followed my advice and asked for work at Pink – and to my even greater surprise, he was taken on. Working for the same company, and picking up from the same clients, we started seeing a lot more of each other. I told him about Ash's cheap cafe on Wimpole Street, and we compared notes on which reception had the best sweets (Blackstone Chambers, but the receptionist wasn't the friendly type, so you had to wait until she was signing the docket before plunging your hand into the jar), and commiserated over the White Cube post run – a monster multidrop that cropped up every afternoon at three, and involved carrying very heavy magazines and art catalogues from the gallery on Hoxton Square up to their warehouse on Wharf Road, then picking up another pile to go down to their other gallery, all the way over in St James's, then back to Hoxton with more, and then finally back to Wharf Road. The White Cube post run was known and feared among the fleet. Its only advantages (for me) were that if I was given a couple of other jobs along the way, I could normally contrive to finish the job at five on the dot, and then go home – and, of course, if the receptionists were still collecting the post when you turned up, I could wander in and have a look at the art. For a few weeks in 2009, an enormous monochrome portrait of Margaret Thatcher took up the entire back wall of the Hoxton gallery, glaring at me as I stood cramming mail and piles of books into my bag. One day I walked up to have a look at her and found that her face was made up of thousands of plastic objects – toys, trinkets, combs, masks, body parts and a whole forest of dildos, which from the side bore a passing resemblance to the London skyline. That summer, White Cube showed a collection of Tracey Emin's etchings, and I became used to the small sketch that hung beside the reception desk; a grainy and indistinct pen-and-ink drawing of a woman lying on her back, legs splayed, hands cradling her genitals. I never got to see the rest of the exhibition.

If I was standing by in Cavendish Square or the Paddington Street Gardens, and heard Andy say, 'Roger-rodge, zero-seven, got you down,' I knew that Lukasz had just called in empty, that Andy had put him on the plot behind me (and possibly several others), that he wouldn't be going anywhere for a while, and that he was too close to the cheap cafe to resist the siren call of a 65p cup of tea. A couple of minutes later, I'd park my bike next to his and stand there waiting for him as he emerged from the cafe, one hand holding a paper cup, the other turning his radio back up. (Turning your radio up and down as you enter and exit buildings becomes so instinctive that I often find myself reaching for the dial as I walk into cinemas and supermarkets at weekends, even though I'm not wearing a bag or a radio.)

He was always pleased to see me too. We'd sit and while away the time until one of us got a job, discussing the idiosyncrasies of the traffic, bemoaning the various ills of our bicycles and comparing notes on the controllers. To my surprise, Lukasz turned out to be a fan of Paul, the lunchtime controller.

'Yeah, I like him, I just think he's a dude. He's so chilled. You can tell he smokes dope at home.'

I couldn't but, as Lukasz pointed out, it takes one to know one. I didn't tell him that for my first few weeks on circuit I had been completely unable to tell Paul's voice from Andy's over the radio, even though I knew from my trips into the control room that they were entirely different people – Paul morose and laddish; Andy bright and sarcastic. I had only gradually learned who was who as I spotted the difference in their controlling styles – Andy would, given sufficient work, keep his couriers moving all the time, and always have a new batch of jobs lined up for them the moment their bags were empty. Paul, slower and less experienced, tended to let the circuit grind to a halt. I always knew, when he took over from Andy at lunchtime, that if I didn't already have a run of jobs in my bag, when I called in empty, he wouldn't have anything else for me. Sometimes I'd wait twenty minutes and then be given a job that had been booked an hour earlier. I didn't blame Paul. I was beginning to understand how complicated controlling must be – keeping track of the direction and whereabouts of up to twenty couriers, and trying to allocate an ever-growing list of jobs, remembering that the specials always had to go first, trying to anticipate when a courier might finish his current run and whether he'd be available to pick up a new job that had just been booked, and if he wouldn't, figuring out the trajectories of the rest of the fleet to see who would.

I told Lukasz about boltholes like the Paddington Street Gardens, which had free public toilets and so many benches that there was always enough space for a resting cycle courier in among the nannies and language students and tramps. He told me about the graveyard at Bunhill Fields, where he liked to hide himself away, revelling in the unexpected peace and quiet a stone's throw from the Old Street roundabout and, he told me, communing with the spirits of Bunyan and Blake, who were buried there. And I introduced him to my friend Lawrence, who was rapidly becoming a benevolent uncle to the city's couriers.

I'd met Lawrence at the height of 2008's summer, on the same ride where I met Ash. Legend has it the Dunwich Dynamo was started by a gang of couriers, who finished work one Friday evening, drank some beers, started riding east, and kept going until they reached the Suffolk coast the following morning. This legend probably isn't true, but neither are half the things you hear about couriers, and since it paints us in a favourable light, and makes a good story, little has been done to dispel it. Two decades later, the ride is bigger and better known and gets more so every year – partly, I'm convinced, because of its openness. There's no entry fee and no support services beyond other riders' tool kits and a few enterprising locals selling bacon sandwiches from their front gardens.

And you can ride it however you want. There are always a few Lycra louts who treat it as a race, competing to be first to the beach and then riding back to London afterwards – and then, at the other end of a very long peloton, the slow-coaches on hybrids and recumbents, taking it easy and rocking up just in time for lunch. People treat the ride as a party, stopping in pubs throughout the evening, exchanging homemade flapjacks and chocolate-covered coffee beans in the early hours of the morning, and tailing off into a well-deserved orgy of pints and fry-ups at the finish.

Unless I'm out of the country, I do the Dynamo every year. For me it's a metronome – a steadily beating annual rhythm that marks out how far I've come, and what's changed since the last one. I can still remember which bike I rode every year, who I rode with, what I ate, and whether I cycled back to London afterwards, or to the station in Ipswich, or subjected myself to the excruciating discomfort of the coaches. In 2008, I was riding alone for the first time, enjoying the freedom of not needing to wait for or keep up with anyone else, and the serendipity of bumping into cycling friends from all corners of my life – because everyone comes together for the Dynamo, fixies riding alongside tourers, roadies racing couriers, middle-aged ladies in yellow jackets on brand new hybrids and packs of students riding old Peugeot racers they've salvaged from skips.

I met Ash early on, as we exited London via Epping Forest, hundreds of other cyclists trailing out ahead of and behind us, their red lights beginning to twinkle as the sky turned orange and the evening tipped over from daylight into darkness. She was riding alone too, pulled alongside me and pointed out that we were both riding Surly bikes – mine a Steamroller I'd had resprayed in an ostentatious shade of pink; hers a more subdued blue tourer. Months later, we admitted with some hilarity that she (noticing I was riding fixed) was desperately trying to shoehorn a reference to her other bike into the conversation, to identify herself as a fellow fixie rider, while I (having clocked her lesbian haircut) was searching around for some subtle means of revealing that I was gay too. We didn't manage to exchange numbers, but rediscovered each other quite by chance on an Internet forum a few days later, after I'd reluctantly gone back to writing my thesis and she'd returned to her web-developer job in Dublin, and we spent the rest of the summer carrying out a remote courtship via email.

I encountered Lawrence at the other end of the ride, somewhere between the beach and the signpost that reads 'Dunwich 7 miles'. Everyone picks up the pace when they pass that signpost, imagining that they can smell the sea and rejoicing that the end is in sight, when in fact seven miles is quite a long way to ride at race pace when you haven't slept and already have a century in your legs. By now the crowds had thinned out considerably – most of the people I'd passed over the last hour or so were young men also riding solo, which led me to suspect that I was closer to the front of the pack than the middle (big groups tend to be slower and more sociable), and quite often I would find one or two of them scratching their heads at a junction, peering down two anonymous green lanes in the grey early-morning light, waiting for someone to come along who had a route sheet and could tell them which one led to Dunwich. For the last seven miles, we were all racing, poker-faced, pretending we weren't, trying to disguise our heavy breathing as we overtook each other. A sturdy man in club kit shot past me as if turbocharged, and I watched his hairy calves disappear round the bend, knowing that I stood no chance of catching him with only one gear at my disposal. I settled for picking off the other fixie riders, one by one, until eventually, I was almost on my own, drunk on speed, rashly burning off the energy I had planned to save for the ride home, enjoying the vertiginous sensation of riding as fast as my legs could turn, right at the limits of control, flying, or falling, along lanes I'd seen only twice before. Even at this heady pace, I could sense that another rider was near me: sometimes directly behind; sometimes moving tentatively so that he was almost along-side me, his front wheel just visible out of the corner of my right eye. Eventually, a right-hand bend gave him a small advantage and we were neck and neck. I gave him a nod, eyes still mostly on the road, and took in the rough outline of a tousled dark-haired man, around half a generation older than me, with an Italian road bike beneath him.

'Nice ride!' he said, returning the nod.

'Isn't it!' I replied, only then realising that he might not have been referring to the last 110 miles, but to my bike – or perhaps even my prowess on it. We were too breathless for much more communication though, and now we had acknowledged each other's presence, it somehow seemed absurd to pretend that we weren't racing each other to the beach as sincerely as a couple of pros slugging it out on Alpe d'Huez. We put our heads down and we battled, eyes drill-ing into the distance, anxiously scanning the road for the potholes and dead leaves and patches of gravel that we half knew were there, but which were sucked into the dizzy blur of tarmac and hedgerows created by our speed.

The Dunwich Dynamo is probably safer than most other mass-participation rides, since the bulk of it takes place at night and on country lanes, meaning that there are no motorised vehicles around and the cyclists have the road to themselves. But by the time the sun comes up, participants are silly with sleep deprivation, and have an increased tendency to ride into each other, accidentally undertake, or swerve without warning. A man I was riding with the previous year had crashed and broken his nose as a result of trying to adjust his brake calliper while riding – something he'd never have attempted when fully awake. And this year, as the road wound downhill towards the narrow opening that funnels riders onto the wide windy expanse of Dunwich beach, a few bedraggled figures in Lycra were stumbling uphill, wavering slightly, on their way to the pub, or wherever their partners had parked the car. I wasn't a courier at that point, but I'd spent enough time cycling around Central London to be used to sudden unexpected inflows of pedestrians, and managed to dodge my way between them. A sharp moan of outrage told me that my competitor hadn't been so lucky and, sure enough, he rolled to a halt at the edge of the sand, a clear second after me, unscathed, amused, and seething with rueful indignation.

We exchanged grins, and a firm nod that was as good as a handshake. And then we joined several dozen more tired cyclists in the long queue for breakfast, snaking out of the door of Dunwich's small beach cafe, which probably serves fewer than ten fry-ups most days of the year, but is always ready to turn out a thousand on the day the Dynamo rolls in. Since we were both apparently riding alone, it made sense to eat together, exchanging our post-mortems of the ride and watching the crowds of haggard men (and one or two women) around us gradually falling asleep into their cups of tea and plates of grease as the post-ride high subsided.

As cyclists will, we ended up discussing our respective stables, and within minutes he had offered to sell me a Condor Pista for £200, suspiciously little to my mind, but he insisted loudly and gregariously that he never used it, and had no other way of offloading it, and I'd almost be doing him a favour. Shortly before a shy, softly spoken woman arrived to pick him up (I was introduced, but not told whether she was his wife, his sister or his chauffeuse), we exchanged numbers, and over the next few weeks he invited me out on various group rides with various smart men on carbon bikes. Everyone assumed we were a couple, of course, and thought that meeting on the road to Dunwich made a wonderful love story. I would patiently correct them, thinking wistfully of the small red-headed Dublin girl from whom an email might be waiting when I got in, and wondering if Lawrence was having the same conversation elsewhere in the pack – or whether he, in fact, thought we were a couple as well.

He was at once enigmatic and wide open. I'd met him several times (and on several bikes) before I discovered that he lived out in Kent, and when I once asked what he'd been up to lately, wondering what it was he did for a job, he mentioned that he'd been helping a friend to build a road. I wasn't sure whether to picture Lawrence operating a pneumatic drill in a fluorescent jacket and steel-toe-capped boots, or to imagine two or three gentlemen in some combination of boiler suits and tweed jackets, resurfacing a track on one of their estates and punctuating their work with nips from a hip flask. Every now and then a scrap of history would float to the surface – I learned that at one point he had been a social worker, though he didn't seem to be any more. His designer cycling kit and Italian road bikes gave an impression of affluence; his accent was downwardly mobile, erudite but with a hint of blokeishness that grew more pronounced whenever we were in the company of other men.

His relationship status remained a mystery (I had an interest in finding out, wanting to reassure myself that I was being befriended rather than seduced), and for a while I even thought he might be gay. Road cycling, despite what many might perceive as its increasing dandyism, is overwhelmingly a straight man's sport, but Lawrence, with his slightly cartoonish flamboyance, and tendency to overact whatever emotion he was bringing to the conversation, did have a certain campy edge. When I wrote off my Surly by crashing it into a lamp post towards the end of that summer, he took me out on my first ride on the new Condor, sat me down in a cafe, and practically wept along with me as I gave him a blow-by-blow account of the disaster.

And he never stopped talking. Loud and enthusiastic accounts of races he had done (and planned to do) in France and Belgium. Colourful recollections of crashes he had survived. Second-hand reminiscences of Merckx and Coppi. Chronicles of bikes he had known, and bikes he planned to build. A plan to become a cycle courier for a few months. A tale of how he had worked in coffee roasting for a while. A plan to set up a cafe in central London that would serve superlative coffee and become a meeting place for bike people, and somewhere cycle couriers could hang out in between jobs.

This particular idea didn't go away, and over the following year, as I became a courier (and Lawrence did not), and we met up periodically in coffee shops in Soho and Covent Garden, it drifted in and out of the conversation like a recurring theme in a piece of music. Sometimes he'd enthuse about how fertile the overlap between the coffee and bike industries was, how many cyclists also seemed to be coffee snobs, and how no one yet seemed to be catering to this market. ('He's right!' I thought. And, as it happened, he wasn't the only person to have made this connection. In the summer of 2009, the zeitgeist took hold and within a few months a generous handful of cycling cafes opened across London, most of which are still there today.)

Fuelled by our Bar Italia lattes, we'd imagine roadies gathering in the early mornings, necking their double espressos before setting off like a flock of starlings for Regent's Park; commuters stamping in with their rain jackets and waterproof trousers, buying a cappuccino to take to their desks; couriers lounging at the tables outside, clad in their intricate uniform of function and filth, bikes propped up at the kerb and radios cackling quietly as they sipped filter coffee and stared into the passing traffic. A friend of his ran a bike workshop near Putney Bridge, and Lawrence thought it would be a wonderful idea to display one of their nicest bikes in the window, replacing it with another whenever it sold. Periodically, he said he was looking for premises, in Soho or Clerkenwell, and I started to think it might actually happen, but then he'd go quiet, and the longer we talked about it, the more cynical I grew, and the less likely it seemed that this idea would actually come to anything.

And then, suddenly, more than a year after I'd met him, he put his money where his mouth was, and opened up a tiny shop on Leather Lane, an incongruous little market tucked in between Holborn and Clerkenwell Road, still full of hollering stallholders flogging piles of fruit and handbags and cheap clothes from among their planks and tarpaulins; lined with hardware stores and greasy spoons and the odd jeweller or wholesaler who had spilled over from nearby Hatton Garden – the kind of place I still hadn't discovered, because there was never anything to deliver there, nor any point in using it as a shortcut, since the ranks of market stalls and their meandering clientele made it all but impassable during working hours.

Except now I had a reason to go there, and found it a remarkably convenient pitstop when I was hanging around waiting for work in Clerkenwell, or stopping for my morning coffee on the way in from Stoke Newington, where I now lived, having reluctantly moved north of the river to be closer to Ash's place in Walthamstow. Lawrence's shop, unlike the spacious cafe I (and perhaps he) had imagined, was a tiny hole-in-the-wall sort of place, barely big enough for the coffee cart he had dragged in from somewhere, a work stand, and a heap of second-hand bikes that seemed to grow every day. As I watched, it evolved into a cavern of picturesque clutter, bikes hanging from the ceiling and piling up in the corners, racks of tools, and all manner of miscellaneous nuts and bolts and screws and skewers and cables and spacers spilling out of the fiddly plastic drawers they were supposed to live in and rolling around on the floor.

Any illusion of this being a cafe quickly evaporated. The

coffee machine remained, and continued to produce excellent espressos and flat whites, but most people who came in seemed to be under the impression that this was a bike shop, and ordered a coffee only when it became apparent that their squeaky wheel would take longer than five minutes to fix.

The walls quickly turned from white to grey, smeared with the fingerprints of the mechanics who had mysteriously turned up and started working there – most of them couriers who didn't want to ride their bikes that much any more, and seemed to have adequate means of supporting themselves over and above the pittance I presumed that Lawrence would be able to pay. Or he wasn't really paying – perhaps they just spent their days fixing punctures and rewrapping bar tape because Fullcity ('It's named after a stage of the coffee-roasting process,' said Lawrence) was a fun place to be, with its clutter and chaos and caffeine, couriers and commuters bustling in and out, all held together by Lawrence's effervescent and improbable cheerfulness.

The mechanics were a colourful bunch. Jim was a friend of Lawrence: a tall, blond, clever American, who had overstayed his student visa and seemed to be verging on destitution. He wore a long overcoat, and a flat cap, and a woollen scarf, and occasionally smelt as though he hadn't had the chance to wash for a while. After a few months (and probably on my recommendation, since I tend to be fairly evangelical about my job) he started riding for Pink, on a handsome Mercian single-speed he'd borrowed from Lawrence, and I got used to hearing his good-natured confusion over the radio, as he made mistake after mistake, but never seemed to be that perturbed, or to register Andy's growing exasperation.

Jack was a window cleaner, which meant he spent several hours of every day abseiling down some of London's tallest buildings, and also that he usually finished work by lunchtime, leaving him free to zoom around the city on his enormous Fort track bike (Jack was about six foot six), and to hang around Fullcity for much of the afternoon, fixing the odd bike and offering to do the lunch run, because he was that sort of guy. Although Jack had a laddish air that might otherwise have put me on the defensive, he was so genuinely and reliably pleasant that I couldn't help but warm to him. More than once, he turned up with his window-cleaning equipment and gave Lawrence's window a quick going over before moving on to the nail bar next door, and he seemed to have gravitated to Fullcity simply because it offered regular opportunities to help people out.

Shortly after the place opened, Arsen walked in and started fixing bikes, and proved to be so good at it that Lawrence let him stay. Arsen was somewhere in his late forties or early fifties, with a grey ponytail, a chain ring full of immaculately gleaming teeth and a mouthful of rotten ones, and he had worked as a courier for years before poaching a few clients and setting up on his own. Most of his work was daily post runs for the same one or two companies, going out to places in north-west London that I'd barely heard of, and which were far beyond the normal reach of the circuit, and he claimed to be able to accomplish this workload in a couple of hours late in the afternoon, leaving the rest of the day free to socialise, drink coffee and fix bikes. It would be easy to be sceptical of this story – I never saw him anywhere near a loading bay or a post room – but there was nothing to be gained from disbelieving him, and it might, anyway, be entirely true. Stranger things have happened. I often wondered whether people believed I myself was really a courier or, given my incongruous accent and naivety, assumed that I was a *Guardian* journalist doing research for a feature, or an anthropologist working on an ethnography of urban tribes, or a trustafarian who thought it would be awfully good fun to try out being a courier, before using Daddy's contacts to break into the art world.

I once witnessed such nepotism first-hand, while waiting for a package at Tracey Emin's studio near Brick Lane. (It might have contained one of her grainy pornographic etchings.) A smartly besuited gentleman was coming out of a meeting with one of her assistants and, while saying his farewells, mentioned that he had a sixteen-year-old daughter who was looking for work experience, and did they think . . .? 'Oh, of course,' replied the assistant, who sounded rather as if she too might not have got her job on merit alone. 'And why don't I get in touch with the people up at White Cube as well – I'm sure they'd be able to find something for her.' I simultaneously felt happy for the daughter – what a wonderful time she was going to have! – and dismayed for all the other teenagers who might want to work in the art world, but have no idea even of where to begin, much less a father to make the introductions for them.

Arsen and I pretended to hate each other, but actually got on very well. He quickly wised up to my perplexing habit of breaking some part of my bike almost every week, and whenever I pushed open Fullcity's heavy, clanking door, he'd look up from whatever he was doing with a theatrical scowl, raise his eyebrows in a display of mock disappointment, say, 'Oh no, not you again!' or 'What is it this time?', and then go through a pantomime of tutting and eye-rolling as he hoisted my bike up onto his work stand and applied his spanners to it.

'You know, Emily,' he once mused, 'you and bikes are really not a good mix.'

We both laughed. It was unfortunate, but true. Just before I started couriering, that lamp post encounter had written off my beloved Surly Steamroller (and left me with a few scars that, six years on, seem to be here to stay) and I was now exclusively riding the evil black Condor Pista that Lawrence had sold me that day on the beach. We were not well suited. I disliked the stiffness of the aluminium frame and carbon forks, and the Condor, for its part, seemed to be doing everything it could to sabotage my career. Within a year of buying it, I had had to replace almost every single part (by the time I finally got rid of it, passing the frame on to a gullible friend in exchange for a bottle of wine and a head torch, I worked out that I had replaced everything but the frame and the stem), and spent many times the original price of the bike on maintenance. Fullcity immediately became a godsend. If ever something went wrong (or threatened to) during the working day, it was never long before an east-to-west run would take me along Clerkenwell, or a south-to-north one up Gray's Inn Road, and I could borrow tools, rummage through Lawrence's drawers for a new brake cable or seatpost bolt, fix the bike myself, or sweet-talk Arsen into doing it while simultaneously sweet-talking Lawrence into making me a coffee, if he hadn't already started grinding the beans the moment I walked in.

Since I had known Lawrence right from the beginning – and in fact, been the one to broadcast the advent of Fullcity via *Moving Target* – I had a much surer sense of belonging here than I did in the rest of the courier world, and when couriers I didn't know walked in, I'd introduce myself to them, feeling that for once they were on my territory.

And the place was becoming the nerve centre for more and more of London's couriers. Many of the people I had long known by sight were now becoming friends and acquaintances as we bought our coffee (or were given it, since Lawrence charged couriers only 75p, and sometimes when he was particularly busy even that seemed like too much effort) took turns with the track pump and, on dry days, sat outside the shop on Lawrence's rickety aluminium chairs. I rapidly learned that many of the riders who'd seemed aloof were actually painfully shy, that some of the ones I'd thought were too cool ever to pay any attention to me were in fact the nicest people in the world and talked to me as if I were too, and that those I'd assumed were old hands had often been on the road only as long as I had. And I had been at Fullcity longer than anyone – since, in fact, the first morning that Lawrence had opened. People treated me as if I was part of the furniture.

Not that there wasn't a lot of other furniture. Although no one seemed quite sure how it had happened, Fullcity was groaning with bikes. The hooks Lawrence had mounted high up on each wall, in order to display a few of his beauties, were now loaded with two or three bikes apiece, and beneath them bikes were stacked against each wall, three, four and five deep. There was barely room to wrestle the bikes customers brought in up onto the work stands, and once they were there, the assorted mechanics danced around each other like capoeira artists, deftly reaching through frames and over workbenches to grab spanners and rifle through drawers for spare parts, occasionally ducking as one of them heaved a bike off the wall and spun round, lifting it high over the heads of his colleagues and placing it precisely down at the feet of the customer who had come in to collect it. At least half of them seemed also to be skilled in making coffee (I later learned that Lawrence was sending them to be trained at Monmouth Coffee, down in Bermondsey), and a few of the people who came in to buy it had the slightly smug air of experts who have discovered buried treasure, hidden in among the bikes and handed to you in a paper cup with greasy fingerprints on it.

'Free bike oil shot with every coffee!' I had once joked to Ash.

'I ingest quite enough bike grease as it is, thank you very much,' she retorted, and carried on buying her coffee on Wimpole Street.

She had recently started a Saturday job as a mechanic in the tiny workshop someone had set up in the gatehouse of the Castle Climbing Centre in Stoke Newington, and claimed she already spent enough time tripping over bicycles in confined spaces, being bitten by chain rings and bruising her shins on pedals. It was only years later that it occurred to me that she could have been as intimidated by the couriers as I initially was. She'd never have let on.

7

Spring came, and with it a storm of plane-tree pollen. I had never suffered from hay fever in my life, but that May I found myself riding along with streaming eyes, sneezing so violently that I sometimes feared I'd lose control of the bike. After exchanging complaints with a couple of similarly afflicted colleagues at Fullcity, I discovered that this wasn't any ordinary pollen – in fact, it wasn't pollen at all. This was the fruit of the London plane tree: tiny unassuming little pods, that were so vicious only because each was accessorised with a little tuft of bristles, much like a dandelion clock, which enabled them to fly about on the breeze, into the city's parks and squares and gardens, and also into the eyes and mouths and noses of its inhabitants. For couriers, out in the streets all day long, there was no escape.

On a particularly breezy day – of which there were many that May – you could see the bristles drifting about on the air like snow. From a distance, or from inside an air-conditioned office building, they were almost beautiful: soft and fluffy-looking, shimmering as they danced about in the sunlight, whirling through the streets and drifting in the gutters. But what looked like fluff was actually a storm of vicious little spikes. If one blew into your eye, it wasn't just uncomfortable – it was intolerable, as I discovered when filtering through six lanes of cars and buses on Hyde Park Corner, on my way south to Belgrave Square, and suddenly finding myself blinking and blinking and blinking, unable to keep my eyes open for more than a fraction of a second. The traffic around me became a blur, and I struggled and strained to keep my eyes open before realising that the only possible solution was to take a hand off the bars and hold my left eye shut, pressing the spike into my eyeball, hoping that the right eye would remain clear of fluff long enough to get me out of harm's way. I pulled over as soon as I'd turned onto Grosvenor Crescent, dug my finger into my eye, and pulled out a string of greyish jelly, full of tiny specks of grime and one long needly fibre. For the rest of the day, I rode around with a face like a fortress, mouth closed, brow creased into a heavy frown, eyebrows drawn down low over my eyes, which themselves were narrowed to slits.

But there was no way of avoiding the fluff. Sometimes I'd feel a spike in the back of my nose, and then sneeze several times in quick succession, so loudly that passers-by recoiled in alarm – or I'd sit at the traffic lights, twitching and gasping and grimacing as I felt a sneeze coming on, and worrying that people crossing the road would think there was something wrong with me (which I suppose, in a way, there was). It is, I discovered, impossible to keep your eyes open while sneezing, so this added another element of risk to proceedings, and I learned to examine the road ahead of me even more carefully, knowing that some of the oncoming potholes and pedestrians might have to be navigated in momentary blindness. Several times a bristle lodged in my throat and I rode along hacking and retching, and once or twice I walked into a reception or post room, opened my mouth to ask for a package, and was suddenly convulsed with coughing, unable to contain it for even a second, holding up a hand in feeble apology as I and various confused receptionists waited for the storm to pass.

Ash, who had taken a few days off to build a website for someone, didn't see what all the fuss was about.

'Ah, come on, it's only hay fever – some people go through this every year!'

'I really don't think it is – I've never had anything like this before. And anyway, it's still horrible.'

By the end of the week she was back on the road, and had completely changed her tune.

'I've never had allergic reactions to anything before – isn't it weird?'

'I don't know how anyone could not,' I replied. 'I don't really think it's about allergies – I think anyone would cough and sneeze if you blew millions of tiny tree particles into their nose and mouth and eyes. It was like a snowstorm on Fitzroy Square. And on Park Lane.'

'Oh, my God, and Bayswater Road this morning! Russian Embassy pre-book was even less fun than usual.'

The Russian Embassy pre-book was a new development. Ash had finally found herself a job at one of the more respectable courier companies – Reuter Brooks – about which we were both pleased: her because she was finally earning a decent wage, and me because Reuter Brooks used the same radios as Pink, which meant I didn't have to carry my bulky charging unit around in my bag all day if I was planning to spend the night at her place in Walthamstow.

She had been given a daily pick-up from a big company in EC2, shuttling visa applications back and forth to the embassy, all the way across town, beyond Hyde Park and into Notting Hill. This journey, I realised, would inevitably take her all along the northern edge of the park, where Bayswater Road was overlooked by ranks of lofty plane trees, with their mottled bark and intricate patterns of leaves, speckling the flagged pavements and wandering tourists with thin shafts of sunlight, and gently rustling beneath the roar of the traffic. I wasn't often sent out that far, but whenever I rode that way, Gerard Manley Hopkins's lines would pop into my head – 'Glory be to God for dappled things!' – and I'd rummage haltingly through what I could remember of the first stanza, until I got to 'all trades, their gear and tackle and trim', and then, with some satisfaction, I'd consider my own newfound trade, and all its associated paraphernalia – the bulky bag; the radio aerial poking up over my left shoulder; the taut, grubby track bike – and my mind would wander to all the other tradespeople I saw around me – the window cleaners with their ropes and carabiners; the police with their truncheons and radios; the street cleaners with their trolleys and spades and litter pickers – and I'd line myself up alongside them with a pleasant sense of being part of it all, of being in place. And then I'd turn my thoughts to wherever I was going next, usually a right turn onto Queensway, or onward into the mansions of Notting Hill, and Hopkins would be left behind on Bayswater Road, for me to pick up again next time I passed that way and was struck afresh by the pied beauty of the plane trees.

Except these days I was mostly struck by their fluff, which scoured my eyes so that by the end of the day they'd be sore and bloodshot, and caked onto my sweaty skin so that my face throbbed and itched, no matter how often I furtively sneaked into office bathrooms to wash myself down. The brisk May wind didn't help matters, and I found myself longing for it to rain, so that the fluff would be flushed from the air and stuck to the pavements and washed down the gutters.

'One even got down my top,' said Ash, and I ignored what might have been one-upmanship, partly out of sympathy, and partly because I was so glad that she finally agreed with me.

Lukasz was a more regular co-complainant, since we covered the same circuit, and were thus more likely to run into each other on the arteries between major clients, or in their loading bays and receptions. Plus, the man loved to complain, and would often cycle rapidly through several discrete bugbears during one momentary encounter. We met in Falconberg Mews one sweaty, itchy Friday afternoon and ranted cathartically at each other about *these fucking plane trees*, before lapsing into more subdued grumbling about the controllers, knowing that our joint outburst hadn't made a modicum of difference, but somehow also that it had.

Andy had gone on holiday for a couple of weeks, and we were feeling slightly abandoned, left to the tender mercies of Paul, and Mark, the well-meaning but ineffectual office manager, who had almost no controlling experience, and whose radio voice had a slightly put-on quality, as if he were trying to be one of the lads and not quite succeeding. It wasn't until we had to work without Andy that we understood how good a controller he was. Without him the circuit stalled and stuttered, work would build up as we cooled our heels in parks and on street corners, and then we'd be given unwieldy, badly planned runs that took us all over the city and kept us out beyond the time at which we'd normally be turning towards home. Where Andy would handle the evolving workload lightly and capably, as an experienced courier surfs through the traffic, in Paul's and Mark's hands it took on the guise of a wild and temperamental animal, constantly threatening to break out of their control. They would certainly have no time for a courier with a bit of plane tree in her eye. It wasn't necessarily that they were unsympathetic – just that they had far too much on their hands as it was. Andy, intolerant though he was of moaning, had been a courier himself once, and while he might not remember the precise seasonal cycles of pollen and pollution, he at least retained a sense of the way in which a rider's mood and inclination might be affected by external circumstances, and despite his impatience with the lazy and accident prone, never lost sight of the fact that it was our legs and lungs rushing the packages from one end of London to the other.

I'm sure I wasn't the only one who sometimes felt a little wistful when he signed off at five on a Friday afternoon, often thanking the fleet for its hard work – 'especially the pushbikes; you've been *blinding* this week'. If chance and workload allowed, I would try to deliver my final package just before he went, then radio in before the handover and say, 'Is it alright if I knock off now?' If I got the timing wrong, whoever took over from Andy might ask me to stay out longer, or just send a couple more jobs down to my Xda before I could get a word in edgeways to excuse myself. The other controllers, usually ex-motorbikers or van drivers, didn't fully comprehend that 'just one more job' might involve an extra half-hour or more of pedalling, in the wrong direction, when the courier was already in agony with saddlesore, or aching knees, or wet shoes, and desperate to get home and recover.

'I feel kind of sorry for Mark,' said Lukasz. 'He's basically out of his depth. It's all zero-seven Emily, one-four Lukasz." (One of Mark's most frequent failings was that he mixed people's numbers up, especially those of myself and Aga. He seemed to consider us, as the only two women on the fleet, interchangeable.)

'I bet they can't wait for Andy to get back either,' I replied.

'I know! It's pretty funny though. I was on my way home last night and Rob – you know, zero-six – texted me and was like, "Turn your radio back on." And it was fucking chaos! I just went home and made a cup of tea and sat there and listened to it all kicking off.'

We called POB on each other's radios, just for the hell of it, wondering if they'd notice, giggling as we did so. Mark's reedy, slightly nasal voice issued from the radio in response.

'Zero-seven, zero-seven Lukasz! Nice one, mate, nice one. Now once you've dropped the Haymarket, can you head over to White Cube Hoxton Square, head over to White Cube Hoxton Square, rodge, pick up their post run.'

I caught Lukasz's eye, knowing that his face would mirror my own aghastment. Summoning a rider from Haymarket to Hoxton Square was effectively commanding him to ride from one end of the city to the other without a job on board (not to mention the fact that this particular run would then bring him all the way back to sw1). This was known as a 'slap' – a term I always assumed had evolved from the Yiddish schlep, since it served a similar function – and was one of the least popular chores a clueless or vindictive controller could inflict on his riders. 'My controller was slapping me about all over the place today' was a complaint you'd sometimes overhear at the Foundry, and although this wasn't as physically violent an experience as it might sound to the uninitiated, it tended to command a similar sympathy. It seemed highly unlikely that Lukasz was the closest empty rider to Hoxton Square. In fact, since he first had to go west to Haymarket, he was probably the furthest away.

'Rodge,' he said shortly into the radio, evidently deciding that he wasn't going to dignify such an insult with anything greater than contempt, and probably resolving to stop at Fullcity en route for a lengthy session of coffee and bitching with Lawrence (with whom he now seemed to be on as close terms as I was), knowing that there was nothing Mark could do about this – in fact, also knowing that Mark would be unlikely to notice that the job took half an hour longer than usual, but that it would restore a little bit of his own wounded pride.

We looked at each other blankly for a moment, Lukasz and I, then burst into unexpected laughter. After all, we'd expect nothing less of a controller who wasn't Andy, and since I had been there to witness it, the ill fortune that Lukasz would otherwise have stewed over for the rest of the day was instantly elevated to a good story.

'How long do we actually have till Andy's back?' I asked, as our mirth gradually subsided.

'Next week, I think? Hope so, anyway. Not sure if I'm going to survive much longer.' He gave a theatrical sigh, swung his leg over his bicycle and settled his face into its customary scowl. 'Anyway – back to Emin's crotch.'

I took my usual back route towards Holborn, flicking left onto Litchfield Street as soon as I'd cleared Cambridge Circus, and then following Long Acre and Great Queen Street through Covent Garden, crossing Kingsway into the peace and quiet of Lincoln's Inn Fields, and then taking a little shortcut I'd only just figured out, which took me the wrong way along Whetstone Park (which sounds like it should be a leafy avenue in w11 but is really just a narrow alley that runs along the northern edge of the square, its buildings facing outwards into Lincoln's Inn in one direction, and outwards onto High Holborn in the other), and then through a tunnel that appears to be a loading bay, but leads out onto High Holborn itself, and is used by taxi drivers and the occasional cycle courier to avoid the unwieldy and time-consuming one-way system.

As I emerged from the tunnel, halting momentarily to check for oncoming traffic before I bore down on my right pedal, dropped my right shoulder, and felt myself swing into the eastward turn towards the City, I spotted Ash's orange jacket weaving in and out of the traffic that was piling up at the Holborn interchange to my left. As I watched, she switched lanes, disappearing behind a cab, and then reappeared as she hopped the kerb – a new trick of hers – continuing along the wide pavement for a few seconds before ducking back into the road as she reached the lights. I debated giving chase, reckoning that I could probably catch up with her as we crossed the top of Kingsway, but through a combination of my existing momentum, and reluctance to lose ground by putting myself on the wrong side of a one-way system, decided to carry on the way I was already planning to go. As I sped past the turning for Red Lion Street, I noticed I was smiling to myself.

It was Friday afternoon and within a few hours Ash and I would be riding – in blessed daylight, since it was now almost summer – back to Walthamstow, where, she assured me, she had already taken the Lidl sausages out of the freezer and stocked up on mushy peas. We would take it in turns to shower while the potatoes cooked, and then, after eating, curl up together like kittens and fall asleep by ten o'clock. The following day, Ash's friend Alex was arriving from Dublin, in town for a job interview. I was slightly nervous of meeting Alex. She and Ash had originally been lovers, but that hadn't lasted and they had ended up becoming close friends instead, with Alex taking on something of a big-sister role, since she was about fifteen years older than Ash and, what's more, had spent a year working as a courier in London in the early 1990s. This was the first time I'd met any of Ash's family or friends (at least, the ones she'd had before she met me), and I had uneasy suspicions that I would be judged, and possibly found wanting, especially by someone who had been a courier herself, so was unlikely to be under any illusions as to the menial nature of my job.

Alex had left London long ago, had various cycling adventures in the US (which included working as a courier in San

Francisco for a couple of days, until the hills defeated her), and finally settled in Dublin, where she trained as a yoga instructor and eventually met Ash. Because of her magnitude in Ash's life, I had expected her to be taller than me, and more generally imposing, but she was small, lithe and energetic, with big curly hair, a slight squint, a ready smile, and the ghost of an Irish accent. She didn't remember the Season of Perpetual Sneezes, as I had taken to calling it, but she commiserated knowingly over the endless grey drizzly days that stretch out between October and March.

'I started in winter,' she recalled, sitting cross-legged at one end of the zebra-print-covered sofa in Ash's kitchen, while Ash did something with bikes on the back patio and I kept half an eye on the flapjacks I'd just put in the oven. 'And I was totally clueless. Didn't have proper waterproofs or anything like that. I was just wearing this pair of baggy culottes, which was all I had, and big NHS glasses, and a denim jacket with the shoulders worn out, and I used to get absolutely soaked to the skin. I used to go to the underground toilets at the end of Carnaby Street – are they still there? – and use the hand driers there to get the feeling back in my fingers.'

I hadn't thought of that. I told her about my favourite hot-air vents, and my occasional habit of finding a Sainsbury's and lurking guiltily next to the rotisserie oven, worried that at any moment a security guard would come and move me on. She told me about a run-in with the police on her first day.

'I was totally lost, and panicking a bit – you know, "have to get there, have to get there, have to get there" – and I ended up going the wrong way up Tottenham Court Road, and I got stopped by the police. And I was trying to engage them in conversation, you know, to try and charm my way out of it. So I said, "Why's your car red then?" And he just looked at me and said, "Because we're armed." And that's how I found out that the police in the red cars are the ones carrying guns.'

This was news to me. As far as I'd known, the only armed police were the ones you'd see lined up at the entrance to Downing Street and outside the Houses of Parliament. A few months later, a regular w1–w2 job would take me through Connaught Square every couple of days, and I'd exchange nods with the bored-looking officers wielding semi-automatic rifles outside Tony Blair's townhouse.

Later on, she had been headhunted by another courier company, specifically because a female courier had been requested to deliver Princess Diana's mother's shoes from Gucci on Old Bond Street to her Mayfair residence.

'I remember getting into the lift – I think it must have been the first time – and I was circled by models, who were all about twice my height, and I'm standing there, all grubby, with my Jewfro, and they were *literally* talking over me, and they were all elegant, and clean, and beautiful, and I remember thinking, "Turn your radio down, turn your radio down", and just wishing the floor would swallow me up.'

I recalled a delivery I'd had, just a couple of weeks earlier, when I walked into a studio and was faced with a man and woman sitting behind a desk, as if they were about to audition me.

'Erm, are you here for the casting?' the man had asked, sceptically.

'No – I just need you to sign for this,' I'd said, handing him the package and my Xda, and he'd looked distinctly relieved. As I left the building, I almost walked into a small knot of incredibly tall, incredibly thin women, all of them pale and tired-looking, with dark circles under their eyes. The contrast between their willowiness and my short, stocky, sweaty self was so absurd that I couldn't help but laugh as I pedalled off, and hoped I'd run into Ash that afternoon so that I could tell her about it.

Meeting Alex felt a little like discovering a missing link, between the job as I knew it today and the long-distant, mostly forgotten early days of the industry. It was a history few had bothered to record but which I had, to my delight, stumbled upon in a story called '5½ Charlotte Mews' just weeks before. The short story opened with a volley of radio-speak, and was quite clearly about a young female cycle courier (much like myself), who had a minor crush on her controller (which I didn't, though I could see how easily it might happen). I read on, burrowing into the machinations and minutiae of the 1980s courier world, which Anna Livia drew as vividly onto the page as if she were sitting opposite me, nursing a pint and holding forth about how things had been in her day. I discovered that, in the early days of the industry, radios were too expensive to give out to just anyone, so most couriers started off on pagers, until they had worked their way up to an average of twenty jobs per day. Of course, all a pager told you was that someone wanted to speak to you – 'To find the pick-up you had to dismount, locate a functional phonebox, wait your turn in the consequent queue, and ring base.' Suddenly my repeated stops to check my Xda and flick through the A–Z for an address I thought I'd already committed to memory seemed much less tiresome. Back in the day, all information was given over the radio – or over the phone, once you'd queued outside the phonebox – and couriers would have to listen intently, and then remember four or five addresses for long enough to write them down on a day sheet, because the controller would be too busy to slow down and spell things out for the hard of hearing. I doubted I'd have had the brain capacity to survive back then, especially in my Thursday afternoon haze of exhaustion, and reflected with a mingled sense of regret and relief that I had come into the industry at its flaccid tail-end, where machines did most of the work for us, and where there was far less work to begin with anyway.

The story is of a bristly young courier called Lizzy, desperately racing against the men to 'break the twenty-a-day barrier and achieve a radio. Get up to thirty like the longtermers. Prove she could do it.' I identified with her immediately, and realised that it wasn't that different a world after all. Women were still expected to fail, cabbies were still the enemy, and there were still the occasional funny drops: 'a piece of liver for the ICA, green test tubes for Regent's Park Zoo'. I wondered if the ICA was still in its current spot on the Mall, back in 1986. If it was, then I could picture exactly where you might take the liver – to the shiny modern entrance at the front, where a fresh-faced intern from Roedean or Francis Holland would regard liver and courier with equal suspicion, or to the less imposing back door on Carlton House Terrace, where I once spent a good ten minutes dripping rainwater on the tiled floor while a confused security guard and an equally confused young man in a crumpled shirt and a lanyard dithered over what on earth it was I might be supposed to pick up.

And there was still the mutual admiration between a fast courier and a skilled controller. Singing Andy's praises, JP had once joked that not only could he direct you turn by turn to the delivery entrance of every building in London; he could also tell you which floor you wanted once you were in the goods lift, the code for the back door into the office, and the exact desk to stop at once you got there. Lizzy holds her own controller, a husky-voiced woman named Kit, in similarly high regard: 'Taking directions from Kit used to be pure joy. So beautifully accurate, lyrical almost. "South along Berwick. West Noel. South Poland. East Darblay. Right at Portland Mews. Yellow doorway, left arch, top buzzer."' And it's all still there – the only thing different today is that Poland Street's now one way, running south to north, meaning that to get to Portland Mews from Oxford Street you'd ride straight down Berwick, right on Livonia Street and right again. Come to think of it, that might have made more sense back then as well, but maybe Livonia Street wasn't open in those days. Or perhaps Anna Livia (on whom I confidently assumed Lizzy was based) just hadn't figured that shortcut out yet.

I became slightly obsessed with Anna Livia. It was clear from the detail and accuracy of her story that she had been a courier herself, ten years before Alex's time and over two decades before mine, when I was still staggering around in nappies. I imagined that some day I might track her down, make friends with her, listen while she told me her stories of the road, tell mine in turn, and marvel at how similar, and yet how different we were. It was only when I came across an obituary that I realised I'd missed my chance. In her mid-thirties, Anna Livia had finally grown tired of the London scene, and moved to Berkeley, California, where she eventually became an academic and a translator. She died suddenly, aged only fifty-one, about a year before I became a courier, leaving behind her partner, her twin children, and a series of short stories that I gradually discovered, in collections and anthologies, published by outfits such as Onlywomen Books and the Women's Press, languishing in bookshop bargain bins and hiding on the shelves towards the back of the shop, where 'women's interest' and 'gay & lesbian literature' were almost invariably found. Her writing was transparently autobiographical, and I got to know her through the heartaches that had characterised my own early days in the city – the precariousness of accommodation, the unreliability of lovers, and the drudgery of working day in day out in jobs you'd picked up through sheer desperation, since it's hard to be picky when there's the rent to pay.

In 1983, while Hollinghurst's privileged and promiscuous young heroes were snorting cocaine, cruising at the Corinthian Club, and enjoying one last golden summer untainted by the looming tragedy of the AIDS crisis, the real -life Anna Livia was working long shifts at a cafeteria till. For her the lines of beauty were 'a butter wrapper neatly folded so my hands don't get greasy when I clear up'; '4 sandwiches and 8 teas which cost exactly five pounds when I have no change in my till'.

Love and romance were by no means dead, but they flourished as weeds among the uneven paving stones of living and working and eating and sleeping and commuting. The ambiguous attraction between Lizzy and her controller is persistently quashed by the dynamics of the job – no time to flirt when there are hundreds of jobs a day to cover, clients barking down all six phones and twenty riders all cutting in over each other on the radio. At the beginning of one of her other stories, Livia's narrator describes a slumped figure asleep on the District Line, and then slowly realises that it is the woman she has had a crush on for weeks – except that this woman seems fairly crushed herself, so exhausted by her long shift that she sleeps through her stop and has to be taken home, fed, gently undressed and platonically put to bed.

Reading this, I couldn't help but remember my own early days in London, trying to scrape myself off the bottom of my overdraft by working as a receptionist during the day and a barmaid during the night, and somehow managing to fit a few flings into the nooks and crannies of this punishing schedule. Taking the last tube back to my damp, unfriendly flat share in Ealing, I'd note with dismay that it was already after midnight, and I had to be back on the train in just under seven hours, and I wasn't even home yet, let alone in bed. I'd make myself a list of things to do when I got in (wash tights and hang them up to dry, because you're down to your last pair and too short on money to buy any more; pack one pair of clean pants (maybe two?) because you'll probably stay out on Thursday night; shave legs; lay out clothes for the morning; remember a spare shirt (for work on Friday) and a sparkly top (to update outfit for the evening); buy Red Bull on way to station, and hope you left those cheap ear-rings in your desk drawer), so that I could be asleep as quickly as possible, tiptoe into the darkened flat trying not to wake my flatmates, and then be out the door before they were up in the morning. A lot of the time I was living out of my handbag, bouncing off my supposed home only every couple of days, rushing in and out of the flat only for long enough to pack some clean clothes, wash the ones I'd just worn, so that they'd be dry by the next time I was in, and snatch a few hours' sleep in my cold damp little bedroom.

I sometimes brushed shoulders with the heirs of Hollinghurst – they were the privately educated people I'd been friends with at Cambridge, now living with their parents in Barnes and Fulham while they did their internships and had their affairs and planned out their lives, and occasionally invited me round for dinners for which I was both grateful and guiltily resentful, since they inevitably reminded me of my drudgery, and made me wonder whether I was getting something wrong, and whether, if I really got my act together, I could have had their successes and opportunities.

If I had read '5½ Charlotte Mews' back then in my pre-courier days of desk jobs and bar work, no doubt I'd have envied the glamour and freedom of Lizzy's job – her fighting it out with the men in rainy 1980s streets while I watched the world go by from my over-heated reception in 2005 – but felt it was a world so far beyond my reach that there was no point aspiring to it. But reading it during my first winter on the road, it felt as if the world I had now tentatively stepped into had suddenly been enlarged, given a history and a heritage and a family tree, as well as a curious sense of commonality that meant that the next time I rode through Portland Mews myself, I looked out for a yellow arched doorway and almost imagined Lizzy with her old racing bike and her spiky hair, screeching to a halt in front of me and greeting me with a smile or a scowl before clattering up the stairs to her next pick-up.

I once mentioned the story on the blog I had started to write about my life as a courier, and caught the attention of Zero, a grizzled South Londoner who had been a courier since the dawn of the industry. He was so fascinated that within a week he'd bought the anthology, read the story, and confirmed that 'Kit – the controller with the husky voice – is a close match for Anthea(?), the controller at Hand'n'Deliver (in Charlotte Mews), who did indeed start their riders off on bleepers.'

I shivered with amazement as I read this. Here was a character who had been known briefly by the author, almost thirty years previously, captured in prose, published, and who had then lain dustily on the shelves of second-hand bookshops for decades – until I discovered her, and then just happened to find that we had a friend in common. It felt almost as if a dead and dried-up flower had fallen from the pages of a book, magically taken root in the earth and come back to life again.

Who knows what happened to Kit/Anthea? In the days before the Internet, it was easy for people to lose touch once their lives moved on, and never find each other again. Back then there was little sense of connection and community spirit among couriers, and the vast majority of the industry's characters and personalities will have disappeared as soon as they retired or changed jobs. Most of the people who were couriers in the early 1980s are still alive today, of course. But their lives will be very different now. If you care to search for them, there are lists online of some of the celebrities who worked as couriers, back in the grubby, impoverished days before they made it big. Jennifer Aniston is the most improbable. I've asked around over the years, and no one remembers a courier called Anna Livia (though she might have had a different radio name, as Lizzy does in the story). Somehow the fragility of her memory made it all the more precious, all the more compelling. Few people will have bothered to record the modest and mundane tribulations of the women who operated tills, answered phones, cleaned offices and delivered packages all those years ago, and who, at least in some cases, went on to greater and better things. And much as I remain fascinated by the beautiful and the doomed; the antediluvian glamour of all those gay men in their brief golden era in between legalisation and AIDS – I am less like them than I am like Lizzy, hungry and sweaty, pedalling exhaustedly through the rain towards Charlotte Mews, where there is no longer a 5½, if indeed there ever was.

8

Alex flew back to Dublin on Sunday evening, sending Ash a text from the airport that read, 'She's lovely! Nice one babe.' We regarded it with respective pride and relief, and I set out for w1 the following morning feeling far more contextualised than I had when I arrived in Walthamstow on Friday evening. Not only had I been acknowledged and legitimised as part of Ash's constellation – I also had a more nebulous sense of having found something to identify with that wasn't the typical male, tattooed, aggressive bike messenger of popular imagination. And I enjoyed the tenuousness of it all – of having just about grasped something, through a chance meeting, or on the shelves of a second-hand bookshop, that might otherwise have slipped out of reach and been lost for good.

Perhaps this was one of the many reasons I loved being a courier so much – since couriers, like women, tend to exist in the margins of the world as it is generally seen. Mainstream history and the literary canon are dominated by men, but women are always there if you know where to look, not always hidden away in the margins – sometimes, in fact, electing to sit there quite happily and deliberately. For isn't it the business of marginalia to comment on, and expand, and contest, and subvert whatever is written in the main text? In some ways it's a privileged, though rarely a powerful position.

A courier never expects to be able to change the world. Usually, she is obliged to accept the ways it changes around her, and occasionally changes her, such as when a taxi driver decides to turn right across her path and she has no option but to swerve, brake or die; or when the council removes the park bench she used to daydream on between jobs; or when the security guard who used to let her in the front entrance tells her that the rules have now changed and she has to go round the back, down the ramp, through the scanners and up in the goods lift to deliver her package.

Sometimes I know that my life, like that of Anna Livia's determined and exhausted heroines, and despite its geographical proximity to the decisions and enactments that will fill tomorrow's history books, will continue in its narrow plodding course ad nauseam, ad absurdum and ad nihilum. And even though I can claim to have been in a neighbouring street when something happened – well, so were a thousand other people. London's a big city, and the closeness of significant and utterly insignificant events is inevitable, and thus entirely unremarkable. We all remember where we were when the Twin Towers fell, when the bombs went off on 7/7, and when certain parts of London exploded into riots in the summer of 2011, but even though some of us might have been close by, or have passed that way days or weeks previously, we didn't see anything, nothing touched us, and we discovered what had been going on only long after it happened.

But at other times I had the strong sensation of being right there in the middle of it all, of witnessing first hand what people all over the world were watching on television screens. I delivered an envelope from the CBI to David

Cameron, on the day he became prime minister. To my great surprise, I wasn't immediately sent round the block to a boring delivery entrance, or even directed to a special post office several streets away, as often happens with government buildings. (The US Embassy, being especially paranoid and/or unpopular, will accept deliveries only from approved courier companies, although that doesn't stop a few unscrupulous companies accepting the booking, picking up the package, sending the courier to do a couple more jobs, and then returning it undelivered and demanding a fee for the return journey as well.) Instead, the policemen at the gates of Downing Street ummed and awwed, and then waved me through into a security hut where I was scanned and searched, and then directed by a fatherly officer in his sixties up to the big black door of Number Ten itself, where 'my colleague over there will sort you out'.

I virtually tiptoed up to the door, trying to ignore the phalanx of photographers and film crews across the street, and convinced that I'd somehow still made a mistake, and was about to be told off and sent round the corner to the door the policeman had really meant.

'Er, am I in the right place with this?' I asked, nervously, showing my envelope to the policeman on the door.

'Yes, you are,' he reassured me, and knocked on the door, which was immediately opened by a uniformed flunkey, who let me in and closed the door behind us while he took the package, told me he was called Benjamin and waited as I typed his name into the Xda. The entrance hall was a typical and unsurprisingly Georgian interior, with a black-and-white-tiled floor and gilt-framed portraits, very much like some of the embassies and hedge funds I deliver to in Mayfair and Belgravia. And it was all over in less than a minute, and I accelerated back up Whitehall towards Soho, delighted by my newly minted anecdote, and wondering who I'd get to tell it to first. The following day, every front page showed Cameron beaming on that same doorstep, one hand resting proprietorially on the enormously pregnant stomach of Mrs Cameron, and I recognised the door and the steps and the policeman, not only because of all the thousands of times I'd seen it on television and in the newspapers, but also because I'd crossed that threshold myself, within hours of the photo being taken, while the same policeman was on duty and the same photographers were peering down the same lenses.

I couldn't always claim to have been there, like Forrest Gump, inadvertently stumbling into history at every turn. But we couriers often feel ourselves displaced by the ripples of more noteworthy events, as in late 2010, when we felt the tension mount and watched the traffic slow to a halt and more police than any of us had ever seen flush through the streets as fifty thousand students marched on Parliament to protest the removal of the cap on tuition fees. It fucked up our day's work – even on a bike, it was impossible to get between W1 and SW1 at anything other than tourist pace and a lot of the streets were closed altogether. And a month or so later, the magistrate's court on Horseferry Road (since demolished and replaced with luxury flats) was surrounded by a huge crowd of press photographers, TV reporters with the badges of various foreign news channels on their microphones, and vans covered in satellite dishes, waiting to beam the resulting footage to Doha and Tokyo and Washington. I managed to edge and barge my bicycle through the loitering crowds, wondering what might be going on, and found out just a couple of minutes later, as I strolled into the reception of 89 Albert Embankment, and saw on their big Sky News screens that Julian Assange was being refused bail.

I saw it from the street; I saw it on the screen. Perhaps the receptionist of 89 Albert Embankment had spotted me wading through the crowds a minute or two beforehand, and been surprised when I then walked into his building in the flesh, though I doubt it.

A few years later, my life overlapped again with Assange's, this time rather less fleetingly. By this time he was living in the Ecuadorian Embassy behind Harrods, in a tiny studio flat, formerly someone's office, with only an Internet connection, a treadmill, a sunlamp and an erratic stream of visiting celebrities to maintain his grip on reality and connection with the world outside. I was back in London after finishing my voyage across Asia and chasing couriers through the streets of Tokyo, and was now riding for Creative (where I answered to number seven-eight), controlled by the estimable Buffalo Bill, who sent me down to the western fringes of sw1, one grey and drizzly autumn afternoon, to pick up three envelopes going to a couple of production companies in Soho, and DreamWorks Studios out in Hammersmith. For some reason, it had been booked as a cash job, which meant that, although I received the same electronic docket on my Xda, payment would be handed to me directly by the client, rather than going through the courier company's billing system (and arriving on my payslip a week later in much diminished form).

Assange had recently aired his indignant disapproval of a film DreamWorks was about to release, in which he was played by Benedict Cumberbatch, so it wasn't difficult to imagine what the envelopes might contain.

'And do you mind,' asked the smiley young receptionist, in almost unaccented English, 'delivering the Soho ones first?' She was counting out the money onto the polished wooden podium behind which she stood, and which took up most of the tiny hallway, and pointedly placed an extra five-pound note on top of the pile as she asked this. Not that I wouldn't have done it anyway, I thought, as I nodded thank you at the armed policemen flanking the entrance and pedalled off through the aimless hordes of wealthy tourists who clog up the streets around Harrods. True, it would have made more sense to go west to Hammersmith first, so that I'd then call in empty back in Soho, where there were far more likely to be further jobs, but the general rule was always to deliver things in the order the client wanted, since they were the ones who actually put money into the company, unlike couriers, who often seemed to be treated more as a tiresome drain on profits than the essential resource they actually were.

So I rode back along Knightsbridge, through the tunnel that runs under Hyde Park Corner and along Piccadilly towards the two drops in Soho, before turning round and going back more or less the way I'd come, all the way out to Hammersmith, where pushbike couriers rarely tread. We weren't really supposed to be sent out that far, but I rarely minded when it happened. These longer jobs often came up on quiet afternoons, when the controllers took pity on couriers who'd otherwise be sitting around killing time and buying too much coffee, and borrowed work from the motorbike circuit to keep them moving. Not only would these jobs pay more – they'd also take you out of your normal orbit, give you a chance to explore far-flung corners of the metropolis, like Deptford and Acton and Wimbledon, and mean your legs and lungs could settle into a long ride for once, rather than the perpetual stop–start–sprint of central London.

Today, though, I'd have preferred to be sitting in a cafe, watching the world go by and the rain come down. The drizzle I'd ridden into during my morning commute had thickened implacably into a steady shower that seemed to hold within it all the grey promise and presence of an impending November. Everything was wet. My socks squelched as I pedalled and my gloves squelched as I steered. My shorts clung damply to my legs, chilling the skin underneath, and my hair and cap were saturated, leaking fat drops of grimy water down my forehead and occasionally into my eyes. And despite my eternal optimism, London rain doesn't clean or refresh you, at least not if you're cycling. My ankles were already rimmed with dark grey tide marks where the filth that splashed up from the road had seeped down my bare legs, and whenever I dismounted, I saw that my saddle (and no doubt also the seat of my shorts) was coated with sand and grit, flung up from the puddles and potholes by my back tyre. There was no point in trying to get or stay dry, and my main concern whenever I stopped was trying to find some part of me that I could wipe my fingertips on, so that I didn't end up soaking my Xda, or handing envelopes over covered in damp fingerprints.

And DreamWorks seemed no longer to be based in Hammersmith; '45 Beadon Road', said the envelope, but I couldn't find it. Some addresses jump out at you – the road is quiet, meaning that you can ride slowly along the length of it (without invoking the wrath of the driver behind you), looking at all the numbers of the houses, which are helpfully displayed in a large font on each of their (regularly sized, regularly spaced) doors, and alternate nicely, the odd ones on the left and the even ones on the right, so that you don't get halfway along and then have to go all the way back to where you started to find number 159. Beadon Road was not one of these. For a start it was one way, which meant that once I'd cycled the length of it and failed to find what I was looking for, I had to dismount and walk back the way I'd come, scrutinising each building all over again. And there weren't even that many buildings. Fifty years ago, Beadon Road might well have been an orderly suburban street with fifty or sixty terraced houses – but progress has a habit of hacking away at streets like this, so that you'll find just a few remnants of terrace, here and there, their numbers starting confusingly at 26, since the other things on the street are now a warehouse and a supermarket and a car park.

There weren't anywhere near 45 buildings on Beadon Road. At one end there was a Victorian redbrick with minicab offices and florists' kiosks downstairs and what looked like cheap office space upstairs. Halfway along an incongruous towerblock overlooked a sprawling building site, whose hoardings encroached onto the pavement so that pedestrians brushed shoulders as they walked past, and glared pointedly at my bicycle, which they clearly felt was taking up more than its fair share of space and ought to be on the road. (If I stepped into the road, passing drivers would glare at me with exactly the same contempt.) And at the far end the entrance to the road was flanked by two stout and fairly ugly office blocks, one clad in brownish glass, one whitewashed and functional. I stood outside each in turn, scanning the boards that listed their tenants – DreamWorks was definitely not among them. I walked slowly back down the road, and then back up again, checking every door, and looking up at every building for the telltale logo. I walked back again, checking round all the corners, as I knew only too well by now that a business whose address claims it is on one street is often almost entirely located on a slightly less desirable neighbouring street. I went into the receptions of the two ugly office buildings and asked if anyone knew where DreamWorks was, or whether it had ever been here. (Quite often, you'll try to deliver a package, only to be told by the receptionist that this company hasn't been here for four years, and yet we still get their mail, and no I don't know where they've gone.) No one could help.

'Seven-eight, seven-eight?'

'Seven-eight, go ahead.'

'Having trouble locating DreamWorks. I've been here about fifteen minutes now.'

'Ah, seven-eight, se-e-e-e-e-e-e-ven-eight.' This was Bill buying time, going back into the docket on his screen, trying to remember who I was, what I was carrying and where he had sent me, and then to come up with a useful response. 'Seven-eight. You're definitely on Beadon Road?'

This was not a useful response.

'Roger-rodge.'

'And no sign of DreamWorks?'

'Negative.' I could have told him of my fruitless and frustrating treks up and down in the rain, wrestling my bike along the narrow pavements, hopping in and out of the road to let people pass, getting in their way again as I paused outside buildings to scan their windows and doorbells for any sign of what I was looking for, but he'd doubtless heard it all before – and been there himself. He didn't need to know.

Bill let out a noisy sigh, which sounded as if it issued from the very base of his soul and contained all the anguish of the last twenty years of unreliable clients and unlocatable addresses (though in reality, he sighed like that almost every time a problem came up with a docket, and problems seemed to come up with at least half of the dockets we were issued).

'Seven-eight, stand by. I'll get back to you.'

Knowing that it would take at least five minutes for someone in the control room to get through to the client, explain the problem and ask them for further instructions, and suspecting that Assange's cronies were unused to this sort of thing and would take a while to figure out what to do, I found myself a corner under the dripping eaves of the brown-glass building, got out a sandwich and watched people walking past in the rain, more for something to do with my eyes than out of any genuine interest.

There was a momentary kerfuffle as two hooded teenagers on BMXes jostled a middle-aged woman in a waxed jacket.

'Fuck you!' they responded to her exclamation of outrage.

'You fuck off!' she shouted back at them, surprising herself as much as anyone else.

'Sorry!' she announced, to anyone who might have over-heard. 'It's just, you know, these cyclists, they were on the pavement, and, oh . . .' And she realised that, on top of swearing publicly, she was now effectively talking to herself in the street, and covered the rest of her embarrassment with indignant middle-class muttering, shaking her head sorrow-fully at the now distant teenagers, who had probably already forgotten about the incident, and were disappearing around the corner onto Glenthorne Road.

I carried on with my sandwich, half listening to other jobs being given out, riders calling in POB, queries being taken. As I suspected, it was a long time before Bill got back to me.

'Uh, seven-eight, seven-eight?'

'Seven-eight.'

'Seven-eight, I'm afraid DreamWorks has *moved*.' I could have told him that. 'They're now saying it's at 18 Soho Square. Can you take it back to Soho? Uh, sorry for the dead miles.'

'Roger-rodge,' I replied cheerfully. I could quite legiti-mately have guilt-tripped him by injecting just the right amount of weariness or annoyance into my voice, but it was far more in my interests to remain unconcerned, and my cheerfulness would, in its way, be just as much of a guilt trip as if I'd sounded morose.

So I spent the next twenty minutes pedalling back into central London, package still on board (and by now slightly damp around the edges from the rainwater that had begun to seep through the fading Cordura of my five-year-old bag; belatedly, I stopped and wrapped it in a bin liner someone had given me a couple of weeks back).

DreamWorks wasn't at 18 Soho Square either, and after a lot more dithering on their part, and a lot more waiting around in the rain on mine, the controllers told me to bring the package into the office, where they'd hold onto it until they'd either managed to locate DreamWorks, or received further instructions from the client (which were usually, in my experience, to return the package to whence it came, because they had decided to give up on the idea).

By the time I got to the control room, Bill had disappeared and Lisa was on the box – not by any means a regular occurrence, since she was one of the owners of the company, and usually had much more important things to do than move couriers around the city. But she filled in on the radio from time to time, partly, I assumed, because she was one of the only people in the company who had any experience of controlling, and also, I guessed, for old times' sake, since when the company first got going in the early 1980s, she had run it with only one other person, from a tiny office at the top of Wardour Street. I imagined her as having been much like Anna Livia's Kit, sitting at a rickety desk heaped with paper dockets and overflowing ashtrays, a telephone receiver wedged between ear and shoulder as she fielded enquiries and abuse from clients while simultaneously barking instructions down the radio and sifting through the piles of dockets with the deftness of a cardsharp. Now, three decades later, she was a handsome woman in her early fifties, with an accent that sounded as if it had once been cut glass, but which had been pummelled and smoothed into Cockney vowels by her years among the blokes of the courier industry, the same way a rock will gradually be rounded by the river that runs over it.

I was always happy when Lisa came on the radio. As far as I knew, she was the only female controller in London – the countless couriers I'd shared park benches and street corners with over the years had all had a male voice, usually with some sort of London accent, issuing from their speakers – and she was married to a woman who worked on the sales side of the company. Somehow, despite yawning discrepancies in our age and economic status, I felt we had much in common.

But today I approached the control desk with a certain amount of nervousness, aware that everyone was now heartily fed up of this never-ending docket, and not knowing Lisa well enough to be sure that she wasn't the sort of person to shoot the messenger. And the edges of the envelope were now so damp that it was beginning to dissolve at the corners. I made a great show of unwrapping it from the bin liner, hoping that she'd notice the fact that I'd tried to keep it dry rather than the fact that I'd failed, and placed it on the overnights desk, far enough away for there to be a chance that someone else would deal with it and it would never even fall into her hands.

I needn't have worried. Lisa looked up and smiled warmly at me as I walked over to the control desk to ask where I should go next.

'Hello, Emily! Sorry about all that, my love. I'll try and make it up to you this afternoon.'

Emboldened by her friendliness, I decided to push my luck and ask for more money. Usually, if a courier is obliged to take a package on to a forwarding address, or back to where it came from, or even over to her company's depot, the controller will add an extra drop to the original docket for the unexpected journey, and it'll automatically be billed to the client. But this was a cash job – the client had already paid, and extracting any more from them would involve either going back down there in person, or belatedly asking someone for their credit-card details.

Lisa frowned when I asked her, trying to think her way through the problem rather than because my request had annoyed her.

'Hmmm, yes. Leave it with me, love. I'll see what I can do for you. Now, I've got details in EC1, if you want them?'

I turned tail and headed round the corner to pick up a job that would take me back into Soho. Lisa was as good as her word, and I spent the remainder of the afternoon constantly on the move, which is the best way of passing the time when it's raining – as long as you keep cycling, your wet clothing warms up through contact with your skin and you stay reasonably comfortable. It's only when you stop and get off the bike that the segments of fabric that have been hanging off your body in the cold air suddenly start sticking to it clammily and you wish with all your heart and soul for the hot shower and warm pyjamas that await you, many hours and many more miles hence.

I didn't see Lisa for several weeks after that, and when I attempted to chase down the extra money with one of the other controllers, he said they'd try to find out what was going on, and eventually presented me with the mobile number of someone who'd said they could give me an extra ten pounds, if I would go down to the Ecuadorian Embassy to collect it. The phone was answered by a brusque woman whose schedule for the rest of the week contained only small gaps that didn't coincide with any of mine. We agreed that I'd call her again the following Monday, but she never answered her phone, and after a few attempts I gave up, embarrassed by how money-grabbing I must have seemed (even as I insisted to myself that I was quite right to demand payment for the extra work I'd done at their behest). I never found out where DreamWorks had moved to. And Julian Assange still owes me a tenner.

9

It wasn't long before Lukasz and Lawrence fell out. Or maybe Lukasz fell out with Lawrence. Or maybe Lawrence was at fault. I tried not to find out too many of the details, being too invested in my friendship with each to believe one over the other, and dismayed that a friendship I took partial credit for had foundered so soon. It was something to do with a bike that Lukasz had been going to buy from Lawrence's shop (to replace his old one, which had so much wrong with it that it wasn't worth fixing). I gathered that the bike had turned out to have an undiagnosed flaw, which Lawrence had endeavoured to fix, lending Lukasz another one to ride down to the workshop in Putney to pick up a part. And when Lukasz got there the workshop had been closed. He rode all the way back to Clerkenwell in a major huff, threw the borrowed bike back at Lawrence and never darkened that door again. There were no doubt more details, and at least two differing sides to the story, but I preferred to keep out of it. It was easy enough to maintain friendships with both parties, since Lawrence was rarely seen outside Fullcity and Lukasz no longer went there, so there was very little chance of running into one when I was in the company of the other.

Fullcity was starting to feel like home for me. Since I was habitually an early bird, I'd often be waiting when Lawrence arrived, leaning against one of the empty market stalls as he rolled up on his Pinarello, waiting for him to raise the rattling metal shutter and switch on the coffee machine, and helping him shift a few of the bikes outside. And more and more regularly, I was one of those who would swing by on the way home, either to shout farewell to anyone of interest who might be gathering there, or to stop for a couple of cans of beer, or to join a crowd that would eventually roll onwards to the Foundry, a couple of minutes' ride along Clerkenwell and Old Street.

I was no longer afraid of the other couriers. In fact, up close, I was beginning to find out we had much in common. Chiefly, it was the constant level of slightly manic energy couriers have to maintain if they're going to get through the day. And the closer you get to the end of the week, the less real energy you have to rely on – once you've burned off the weekend's sleep, the large plate of pasta you ate the previous evening and whatever you managed to force down for breakfast, all you have left is the energy of sheer motion itself. And, much like the lines we improvise through the moving traffic, if this falters, it can never be regained. If you're tired, which you often are, the best thing is just to keep on riding. If you're obliged to stop, then you try to keep yourself going however you can. For the couriers who hung around Fullcity this took the form of constant unstoppable talking and laughing, and even singing – and we all fed off each other, with the delight that comes of meeting someone who understands the experience you're having, rather than looking at you as if you're crazy. (Though admittedly, Fullcity's civilian clientele tended to treat us with something between admiration and polite curiosity. We were another layer of local colour on an already colourful street.)

It wasn't always jovial though. People would also come to Fullcity when something terrible had happened – be it a patronising receptionist or a murderous driver – in order to vent their anger to someone who would understand, and to feel that they were among friends. A blond, dreadlocked courier called Kris, who was known (and faintly celebrated) for being a bit dodgy, once screeched to a halt in front of the shop, theatrically glancing to all sides as he dived into the scrum of bikes, and started stripping off his clothes.

'Mate, has anyone got a hoodie I can borrow?' he demanded, holding out a frantic hand at no one in particular as he shuffled his jersey over his head. Someone flung him a sweatshirt and after reordering his layers of clothing he put it on, tightened the toggles and tucked away the last strands of his hair with the scrupulous vanity of a teenage girl.

Now he relaxed, and realising that his dramatic entrance had won him an expectant audience, decided to explain at length what had brought him here.

'Yeah, man, it was the cops, those ones on bikes – they stopped me on the Strand and I don't know, I stopped, and they were gonna give me a fine, and then I just legged it! And they were chasing me, so I went down – you know, that one? Adam Street, whatever, and kind of hid from them, and then I doubled back, and I've been going round in circles for a bit, making sure I've lost them. But I reckon they'll all be looking for me now. That's why I got to change my clothes – they think they know what I look like, but now they ain't gonna spot me.'

'You want a coffee, my man?' asked Lawrence.

'Yeah, go on then,' said Kris, and the shop swung back into life, as the mechanics turned back to their work stands and Lawrence switched on the grinder, and one or two couriers who had poked their heads round the door to see what all the fuss was about went back outside and relit their rollies.

I had never been chased by the police, but Fullcity was just as much of a refuge for me in other ways. It was somewhere to stand by when it was raining, or so cold that sitting in parks was impossible. It was the guarantee of friendly faces on those days where it seemed that everyone, controllers, cabbies, receptionists and pedestrians alike, had it in for me. It was where I went when things went wrong, on my bike or with the job or with my life, knowing that I'd be looked after.

The most obvious thing a courier can do wrong is lose a package. But I almost couldn't imagine how I would ever do this, since it seemed so simple not to. The package goes into your bag, you tuck it in carefully, close the flap and do up the buckles, and then it comes out of your bag again when you get to the destination.

It's not that simple, of course, because of the thousand-and-one variations that might occur with any given job. One courier I know nipped into the client's toilets on her way out of a reception, placed the package she had just picked up carefully on the cistern, and then walked out, cycled off, and left it there. Reconstructing other couriers' ups and downs from the one-sided discussions I heard over the radio, I once gathered that one of the Pink fleet had lost a package, which turned out to have found its way into another package in his bag (a large open bag of shoes or clothes, going to one of the magazines based in the Blue Fin Building at 110 Southwark Street) and been delivered to the wrong place. (I had no idea how the control team might go about retrieving it, and never managed to find out.)

Buffalo Bill had a fantastic, and characteristically superlative, story about the early 1990s, when On Yer Bike – the original pushbike courier company, where 'all the fastest, coolest and best-dressed London bicycle messengers worked' – was bought out and forced to merge with Security Despatch, a much more traditional motorbike company, run by former cabbies, who generally considered cyclists the scum of the earth. The rivalry and tension in the control room and on the circuit took an enjoyable twist one day when one of the motorbike couriers lost a package, somewhere in the ten miles between Hammersmith and London Bridge, that turned out to be an irreplaceable financial bond worth £10 million. If it was not found, the client would sue Security Despatch for the loss, and put everyone out of a job. So every available rider was sent out to search for it.

'All along the Embankment, from Westminster Bridge to London Bridge, they searched. Birdcage Walk, Constitution Hill, Knightsbridge, Brompton Road and, I guess, the motorbikes must have been covering Cromwell Road down to Hammersmith.'

In the control room, the controllers paced and panicked. After a couple of hours, one of the pushbike couriers found the package under Blackfriars Bridge, next to a bench full of winos, and the whole city breathed a sigh of relief. No one will ever top that.

I read this story on *Moving Target*, soon after I started couriering, and of course, I vowed that I would never be so foolish as to lose a package, and of course, it was only a matter of time before I did.

It happened on one of those interminable grey Thursday afternoons, where the hour between 2 p.m. and 3 p.m. seems to stretch out to infinity, and I'd been feeling awful for a couple of days, weighted down by exhaustion and hormones, suffused with a sort of negative energy that threatened to pull me into the ground if I gave it the chance. It was a fatigue beyond the usual end-of-an-honest-day's-work, looking-forward-to-the-pub tiredness. If I had a ten-minute break between jobs – or even sometimes waiting in a warm reception – I'd notice my body trying to put itself to sleep. Even if I wasn't struggling to keep my eyes open, I couldn't muster the energy to read, or even really to think. I just stared into space. Sometimes, Andy had to call me two or three times over the radio before I heard him. ('Nice of you to join us, one-four.') The world seemed to be at more of a distance than usual, and I moved as if surrounded by thick grey fog, constantly misjudging gaps, tripping over kerbs, bumping into people on my way through doors, forgetting where I was going and having to double back. Really, it was a recipe for disaster.

At about 2 p.m., I was given two pick-ups in the West End, heading out towards EC1. As I picked up the second one, I noticed with embarrassment that I hadn't changed the status of the job on my Xda, to show that the first was POB, and hurriedly updated it, hoping that no one else would notice, because I really wasn't in a fit state to be told off for running late. I crawled over to Fetter Lane for the first drop, parked the bike, and found myself staring into an empty bag, with the same horror I sometimes experience momentarily when I emerge from a building and discover that my bike isn't where I left it (except in that case the horror is always momentary, as I quickly remember that I actually left it somewhere else).

With a terrible sinking, shrinking feeling in my chest I leaned the bike against the building I should have been delivering to, put my bag down on the pavement and begun to hunt meticulously through all of its various compartments, knowing all along that this was pointless, that I'd only ever have put the two packages in the main compartment, and if they weren't there, they weren't anywhere. I eventually found one of them, tucked in next to my A–Z (and remembered only belatedly that, of course, I sometimes put the smaller envelopes there to stop them being crumpled by all the miscellaneous junk I carried in the rest of my bag). The other one was gone.

And then suddenly, heart-stoppingly, I realised that I had never picked the package up in the first place. I'd just ridden straight past the address on Dean Street where it was waiting, where the receptionist was probably even now phoning up Pink to complain that this was an urgent package, and why wasn't the courier here yet? It wasn't the first time this had happened, but every other time I'd noticed my mistake within a minute or so, made a swift U-turn, and got the package on board before the receptionist had time to think anything was amiss.

There was no way I could do this now. I was already at Holborn Circus – it would take me far too long to get back to

Soho, and by the time I'd ridden there, retrieved the package, placated the receptionist and raced back out to Old Street, I'd be over half an hour late delivering the package, and Andy would have questions to ask (assuming he hadn't already noticed I was taking so long and enquired as to my whereabouts, or fielded an angry phonecall or two from the client).

So I had no choice but to tell him. My head was buzzing with panic, and my chest was so tight that my voice sounded raw and hollow, even to me. Not only did I have to admit that I'd forgotten to pick up the package – I also had to explain how I had somehow ended up updating my Xda and calling POB, and I couldn't really. I don't know what I was thinking. In fact, I wasn't thinking – I was just plodding along, suffocating under the grey fog of exhaustion and pain and blankness.

To his credit, Andy was a lot less annoyed than he might have been, given that my mistake was most definitely his problem. And that was just as well, because as soon as I'd dropped off the remaining package, I fled up Hatton Garden to Fullcity, threw the door open and collapsed into sobs of frustration, unconcerned by the mechanics, who all suddenly hunched over their work stands, each inexplicably fascinated by a sprocket or bottom bracket or whatever else was to hand that was easier to repair than a crying woman.

Lawrence was not embarrassed. He gave me a backslapping hug, and then went over to the coffee cart and started making me a cup of tea as I told him what had happened, and railed with impotent anger against the hormonal surge that I was convinced was to blame for my day's doldrums and disasters. Why, I stormed, must I put up with this when none of the men have to? Why, when I try so hard and so constantly to be good at my job, am I so regularly let down by my own body? (I had recently had to break a long-standing rule of mine and take a day off every month, when my cramps became so painful that even the motion of cycling couldn't soothe them.) Why, if something must go wrong with me, could it not be something like a sore knee, that the controllers could understand and sympathise with? Why do I have to suffer in silence, when the job is so much harder for two or three days every month?

Not that I was suffering in silence any more. The mechanics carried on earnestly polishing their cranks and chain rings, more diligent than I ever saw them before or since. My sobs began to subside, and I apologised, lamenting ruefully that I seemed to be fulfilling the stereotype of the hysterical woman, ruled by her hormones and unable to contain her emotions. Lawrence gave a don't-mention-it wave of his hand.

'Girlfriend, we all get like this from time to time. It's just, if you're a man, you're not allowed to cry about it, so you end up getting involved in things like wars, or football, instead.'

'Or driving black cabs,' piped up one of the mechanics, and we all laughed. A minute or two later, another courier walked in, and immediately my career-ending mistake became social capital.

'Oh, you'll never guess what I just did!' And then I told him, and then he told me a few of his own fuck-ups, and we marvelled at how we'd managed to keep our jobs for so long, and then Andy called my number over the radio, sending me off to a pick-up in Lincoln's Inn, and we swung our legs over our bikes and rolled off in opposite directions, him weaving his way between Leather Lane's idling shoppers and swinging racks of handbags and cheap summer dresses; me ducking past the fruit stall and the pie shop, along Portpool Lane and out onto Gray's Inn Road.

These courier refuges were increasingly under threat though. A couple of months later, to everyone's dismay, the Foundry closed its doors for good, making way for an eighteen-storey Park Plaza 'art 'otel'. It had been on the cards for a while, to the outrage of London's couriers and hipsters – there was no way such a prime location was going to be passed over indefinitely. The elegiac note with which we acknowledged this loss set the tone for the mingled anger and resignation with which we greet every new encroachment of the faceless, soulless, heartless 'prime location mixed-use developments' that are sweeping the capital as swiftly as they can wangle planning permission.

Of course the Foundry was going to fall prey to developers sooner or later. If I were in the business of building luxury hotels, I'd have built one there. It was on a major junction (with enough space around it for the building to be visible all the way from the Old Street roundabout), right in the middle of Hoxton, which at that point had just the right edgy/arty/hipster vibe, while also being conveniently located on the upper edges of the City. If I were flying in from my TriBeCa loft in New York for a breakfast meeting with my shareholders, Hotel Hoxton would make me feel perfectly at home. And, as people had been pointing out for quite a while now, the artists and squatters stopped moving into Hoxton years ago, and were all now heading for Camberwell and Tottenham, priced out by the start-ups and media professionals, who will in turn be diluted by the pinstripes ebbing out from the City. A ten-minute morning stroll down to Exchange Square for your Pret sandwiches and professional engagements, then a lazy cab back to Old Street in the evening, freshen up at the hotel, and cocktails and sushi in Hoxton Square. Nice, if that's your sort of thing.

But the Foundry was such a loss to us all. Ride past it on any evening of the week, from about six, and you'd see dozens of battered, stickered bikes (hundreds on a Friday) locked all along the railings outside, as half the city's couriers came home to roost, packed onto the big wide pavement, still bristling with radios and bags, guzzling cheap lager from the bar (or cheaper cans from the off-licence over the road), glowing with the euphoria, exhaustion and sweat of a day on the road, breaking off from conversations for a cheer or a slap on the back as someone else pulls up, shooting flamboyantly into the crowd and swinging their leg over the saddle as they skid to a halt inches from someone's pint or toes, stumbling or darting in and out of the hordes on a mission to round people up for an alleycat, or borrow a fiver, or find out if that rumour is really true about how . . .

The Foundry was home, family, our own place. After you'd spent the whole day being shouted at by pedestrians, cut up by cabbies, undertaken by mopeds, ignored by controllers, patronised by receptionists and hit on by security guards, the Foundry was where people would be on your side. They'd ask how your day went, and sympathise, and understand, and care when you told them. You'd be the protagonist in your own story again, rather than just the small, soft, insignificant cyclist being hit by a car in one corner of the big picture – like Bruegel's Icarus, tumbling unnoticed into the sea while the world carries on around him. And there'd be mutual respect and admiration, rather than the contempt, pity and plain confusion with which most people seemed to view our job. Fellow couriers judge you by the standards you want to be judged by – rather than commenting on my arse or my accent, like every other van driver and security guard in town, people at the Foundry would remark that they'd seen me going bloody fast down Holborn today and where did I find that tailwind, or that I'd done well in that shouting match with the van driver on Oxford Street.

And of course, we all reflected, out loud and in private, this solidarity would transcend mere geography, and just as easily alight on Fullcity, or the Duke of York, a short ride down Clerkenwell Road, which actually pre-dated the Foundry as a courier pub. We'd take ourselves elsewhere. But we also knew that, as the scaffolding and tarpaulins went up, and half the junction was blocked off, and the whole thing was pulled to pieces, the bulldozers would be pulling up the anchor of a huge sprawling web of collective experiences and memories that, yes, would continue to exist, but without the physical underpinnings that brought them together in the first place. Perhaps they'll be all the stronger – after all, nostalgia is a powerful and compelling thing, and the days of the Foundry would now pass into legend. One more thing to taunt the newbies with: 'Back when we were at the Foundry . . . oh, sorry – before your time.'

The Foundry looked something like the bastard child of a well-trodden local pub and a squatful of art students. Most of the furniture was decades old and might well have been salvaged from skips. There were strange junk sculptures and banks of old flickering TV screens around the place. People who know more than I do about such things spoke very highly of the music. But the best thing by far was the graffiti. Along with big names like Faile and Banksy, countless patrons had left their mark over the years, and over the top of those that went before. The women's toilets were a rainbow riot of wit, profanity, absurdity and beauty, with not a single empty bit of wall – the perfect physical manifestation of how a place becomes imbued with the images and ideas and memories (and in this case the drunken reveries) of those who have passed through it.

In a hundred years or so, no one will remember that there was such a thing as a cycle courier, and that people who pursued this improbable career used to congregate at a pub called the Foundry. And if some record does survive, will it really matter to anyone any more? Or will they pass over us, turning the page to something more interesting, unable to conceive of the great richness of friendship and suffering and hilarity and mythology that these people shared?

The Foundry stood empty for a few months after it closed. Someone removed the O, the N and the D from above the door, so that it read F U RY. Couriers defiantly continued to congregate outside on Friday nights, and the building was even squatted for a while. Eventually, people drifted back to the Duke on Clerkenwell Road. Later that summer it too changed hands, bought out by a restaurant group who reinvented it as a smart gastropub called the Clerk & Well. Four years later, there's no sign of the Park Plaza art 'otel on Old Street. What was once the Foundry is now an unremarkable coffee shop.

10

One hot sunny day at the height of June, I was riding north over London Bridge, that doleful conveyor belt shovelling commuters into the furnace of the city, and I swear that just for one elusive second the scent of roses drifted past me, blowing sweetly from some unseen garden or roof terrace or flower stall across the river. By the time I'd filled my lungs a second time, wanting to confirm and savour the fragrance, it was gone, and my airways were scorched once again with the sour taste of road fumes.

I noticed smells more in my first summer. In winter they're contained in layers of clothing and deadened by the cold air; in spring the streets are freshened by breezes and washed by rain. But in summer the air is thicker and the streets fuller. There is far less space to breathe, but breathe you must.

Riding past a crowded pavement on a hot day, swallowing consecutive gusts of perfume, sunscreen, cigarette smoke, and sometimes even halitosis, you realise just how help-lessly intimate we all are in this city, uncomfortably close, crowded up together whether we like it or not (and mostly we don't), sharing the same air, inhaling the vapour that rises from other people's skin, along with the effluence of exhaust pipes and the dust whipped up by millions of feet tread-ing through the same parks and streets, carried to and from distant corners of the city by the commuter trains, fanned through the streets by the traffic, settling and smudging in the sweat on all of our seething skin. No matter where the dust came from and what colour it started out, it inevitably ends up the same dark grey. I have ridden through countries where the soil was red and brown and golden; stuck to my sweaty skin, it was always dark grey. London contains people of a thousand different colours, what each of them puts into and onto their body is unique, yet we all cast off the same dark grey dust. It's a memento mori, a miniature death that is – or should be – a continual reminder that, no matter what our differences, we'll all go the same way in the end. Dust to dust.

It's not only the people. There are days when the Albert Embankment smells puzzlingly of toast. The cluster of Japanese restaurants at the western end of Brewer Street, where Soho begins to fray into Piccadilly, gives you two warm, nutty breaths of cooking rice as you ride between Regent Street and Glasshouse Street, and the waffle stall at the southern end of Wells Street wafts a deceptive cloud of sweetness (deceptive because waffles and crêpes never taste as good as they smell, and you might as well not waste your money) at you as you leave Fitzrovia. There was one afternoon back in 2009 when Great Eastern Street smelt of decomposing flesh (I actually checked the news that evening, to see if some builders had stumbled across a mass grave or charnel house), and one morning in 2011 when Parliament Square smelt exactly like an old man's breath before breakfast.

It's a subtler filth than the open sewers and unsealed roads of two centuries ago, but it's filth nonetheless. Arriving home after a hot summer's day on the road, pouring with sweat, I'll find myself covered with dark-grey smears – the patches on my bare forearms where I slid down the sides of buses in order to balance myself through some of the tighter gaps; the rock-chick shadows under my eyes that make it look as though I'm ill-advisedly wearing make-up to work; the tide marks on my ankles that merge with my tan lines, so that I'm never quite sure when to stop scrubbing them. No matter how often I wash my hands during the day, they are always black with dirt – it collects under my nails, settles into the folds of my knuckles and ingrains itself in tiny mosaics in the cracks of my calluses. Ten minutes after I send a whirlpool of grey water down the sink of someone's office restroom, my hands are as grimy as if I hadn't washed them all day. From time to time, if a pair of worn-out gloves or unfamiliar handlebars has given me a new callus, or worked the dirt into my skin a little harder than usual, the black lines and shadows on my palms don't even disappear when I stop cycling at the weekend, and I wonder if they're now a permanent feature that I'll one day show to my grandchildren, like the small blue-grey line on my left elbow, which looks like an amateur tattoo, but is actually a memento of that long-ago day, the summer before I started couriering, a few weeks after I met Ash on the road to Dunwich, when I wrote off my Surly outside Richmond Park, grazing myself in various uncomfortable places, and absorbing more grit than the nurses were able to tweeze and scrub out of me. I don't really mind things like this. I like the fact that the road has left its mark on me, that I've absorbed some of the molecules of London (which, in all likelihood, have passed through many of its other bodies before mine), and kept them, and made them part of me. That in this great heaving transitory city, there is at least some permanence.

Becoming a courier meant losing my squeamishness about dirt. Every now and then, one of the guys on the corner will drop half his sandwich on the ground and hesitate over picking it up, until someone reminds him that the pavement of Broadwick Street probably has no more germs than any other outdoor surface in central London, and is at least washed once a week (by hi-vis council employees, who scrub and sluice it with an industrial cleaning fluid that smells like bubblegum). Unlike our courier bags, for example, most of which are washed once a year, if at all. And each of us must, at numerous points in our career, have pinched our tyres to check their pressure, and then minutes later picked up an apple or opened a bar of chocolate or dipped a finger into someone else's tub of hummus, completely forgetting where our fingertips (and tyres) have been. It doesn't seem to have done any of us any harm, and even those who fastidiously pluck off the corner of their baguette after a fly lands on it will swallow two of the fly's relatives on their post-lunch run down to sw1, and survive, and indeed, continue to thrive. For all their aches and pains and moans and whinges, couriers generally appear to be in rude health, especially in the summer – blooming like weeds on street corners, billowing jauntily through the streets like dandelion seeds, glowing with the invincibility of youth and strength and a high metabolism and an immune system that's exercised as regularly and rigorously as their bulging leg muscles.

Many of us stink, of course. You couldn't really expect to spend a day cycling at top speed through London traffic without sweating and, like our post-work exhaustion, the uniquely pungent courier odour is exacerbated by the continual stop–start–sprint of courier cycling, each successive wave of sweat drying and then reanimating as another wave of sweat follows in its wake. The sweat attracts the fumes and flies and filth that float about the streets of London, looking for things to stick to. It coaxes the sediment of long-forgotten rides from the folds and seams of your clothing. During my first winter, I became used to the strong salty stench that would drift out whenever I unzipped my jacket; in summer I get to know the ripe reek of fermenting armpits, nudging itself insistently through deodorant and synthetic jerseys, so that I try to keep my limbs close to me when sharing a lift with people who don't know what it is to sweat for a living, uneasily suspicious that they'll still exchange disgusted glances as soon as my back's turned, because we now inhabit nasal worlds that are a long way apart. I'll inhale the scent of a receptionist as she rises from the desk to escort me to the lift, or of a suit as he lifts an arm to hold the door open for me, and marvel at the beautiful synthetic cleanliness of them, knowing that this is a smell carefully curated, the skin primed with gels and scrubs and cleansers, dressed with lotions and balms, and finished with a perfume carefully selected both to charm the beholder and to complement the rest of the wearer's arsenal of chemicals. On top of that, add underwear that matches, that isn't stained, or yellowed and frayed after too many washes, that will be thrown out long before it's in danger of harbouring any smells; add a camisole washed with fragranced fabric softener and folded carefully into a hardwood chest of drawers, add a crisp shirt, white or pink or chambray, fresh from the box or the drycleaner's, add shaving foam and hair mousse and the warm oily scent of lipstick, which distantly reminds me of furtive rummages through my grandmother's dressing table when I was a child.

I used to smell like this. I remember how much I cared, and how my first thought on waking would often be which of my collection of shampoos I'd use, and how somehow it had to be just right for whatever was going to happen to me that day, even though I never ever, in hindsight, recalled a conversation or task that could have gone better had my hair smelt differently. It's not that couriers lose all sense of hygiene – more just that their parameters are narrowed to 'clean' and 'unclean', and they quickly lose sight of 'how clean'. When I commuted eight miles by bike between West Norwood and Bloomsbury, I would shower assiduously at either end. Nowadays, I quite often ride into town and back on my days off, and in comparison to a day of courier work, feel as if I've hardly broken a sweat. On these occasions, it doesn't seem worth having a shower before bed, particularly if I'll be back on circuit the following day. Whereas the showers that follow a day of work are occasions of almost religious ecstasy – the delicious sensation of hot water on tired skin, stickiness giving way to smoothness, the gratifying sight of a whole day's filth swirling past my feet and down the plughole. Afterwards, I feel purified; cleaner than I ever was back in the days when I was always clean. But during the day, I am dirtier than I ever would have thought possible. Sometimes, catching sight of my blackened visage in a mirrored lift, or glancing down at my dust-and-sweat-and-oil-stained trousers, I tell myself

I have ventured into a mostly unexplored country; with my loss of inhibition discovered a whole new register of bodily potential. I had never allowed my armpit hair to grow longer than a couple of millimetres, ever since it first sprouted, or breathed in the pheromonal stink that it conducts out into the atmosphere. Some people probably never will. I had never experienced the way that dirt will emphasise the contours of one's face, highlighting the wrinkles of the eyes and the creases of the lips, and darkening the shadows under the cheekbones. I had never sweated so copiously that there was no longer any point trying to staunch or conceal it; never stood in calm and close proximity to other people with beads of salt water pouring down my face and neck and arms, soaking into my jersey and dripping from my nose and fingertips onto the floor.

Few of the people around me will ever have let themselves get this dirty, and most would be disgusted at the thought of it. From the other side of the Rubicon, I could tell them that it's really not so bad, that you get used to it, that your standards slip remarkably quickly, that you lose the shame, forget the discomfort and ignore the indignity. That it's somehow liberating, to discover that your fears were unfounded, that life continues much as it always did, and that no one really notices or cares about the additional grime. Or maybe they do. I occasionally worry that I've lost all perspective on odour. Perhaps I really do stink, and everyone's too polite to tell me. I often flinch, and pre-emptively apologise when friends try to hug or air-kiss me when we meet after work. This is one of the many reasons, I suspect, that couriers congregate together in the evenings, preferring to form a majority where sweatiness is the norm, rather than be the smelly one in a group of clean people; enjoying the sense of all being in the same boat.

One summer day I rolled up at the corner to find Gertie sitting there, his LCEF (London Courier Emergency Fund) jersey unzipped to the waist, displaying a skinny ribcage not all that dissimilar from those of the Tour de France riders I'd been watching in a cafe earlier on, struggling up the Tourmalet, open jerseys flapping in the wind, their bony white chests contrasting improbably with their deep brown arms. He looked flushed and flustered, and his hairy forearms and shaven legs were beaded with sweat. Gertie probably isn't the oldest courier on the London circuit, but he's certainly been around the longest, and remembers the days before GPS tracking, electronic dockets and LED bike lights. He's never done any other job, and never will. ('Well, unless I can persuade someone to pay me to drink tea, listen to Radio 4 and do the *Guardian* crossword!')

'Bit warm?' I asked. His face instantly animated into its usual toothy grin, a parabola of wrinkles stretching up his cheeks to his eyes, showing just how regularly this grin had been deployed over the last couple of decades.

'Ah, yeah, I suppose you could say that!' he agreed, with a slight tilt of the head to indicate my similarly frazzled appearance, acknowledging our discomfort and laughing it off in the same gesture. For once there was no real need to complain any further, or to explain to each other what we were both already well aware of – that the heat was making our job more of a struggle than usual, but that we were getting by. He lit up a cigarette and turned his attention back to the crossword; I fetched my bottle from my bike and took a long tepid swig, deliberately letting some of it dribble down my chin and neck and onto my jersey, through which several litres of sweat had doubtless already seeped and evaporated that day.

A few feet away a group of bored tourists was being told the story behind the Broadwick Street pump, by an earnest young man who was standing up on the pedestal that surrounded it, in order to be seen by his flock. We couriers know the tale of the pump extremely well – it's the water source to which Dr John Snow traced Soho's 1854 outbreak of cholera, proving that it was a waterborne rather than an airborne disease – and could tell you all of the little variations and errors written into the story by the various tour guides. (My favourite is the tale of a mother and daughter who contracted cholera despite having moved from Soho to Hampstead, since they preferred the taste of the water from the Broadwick Street pump, so had it specially delivered to their house.) I have even seen Gertie take on the role of a tour guide and recount the story to individual tourists who have followed their guidebook to the pump, just as if it were part of his job, along with the other unofficial courier roles of giving directions and lighting cigarettes. Most of the time, though, we just ignore the tourists, or shuffle reluctantly aside as they dutifully photograph the pump and its plaque. It's our corner – Creative Corner, Moaners' Corner, or just the Corner, as it's known in the business. For years couriers have sat there, eating, smoking (or trying not to), snoozing, gossiping, flirting, ranting, checking out passing talent, judging passing hipsters, complaining about the lack of work, recovering after a hairy encounter with an Addison Lee driver, reminiscing about the Good Old Days, or just staring into the distance. Like any subculture, or indeed any family, we have our own mythology, with all of its larger-than-life characters, all its in-jokes, all its feuds and rivalries, all its endlessly repeated anecdotes.

Two wheels entered my peripheral vision from the left, and half a second later, Lima halted in front of the pump, swung his leg over and leaned his bike against one of the bollards that ostensibly keeps vehicles on the cobbles and off the pavement, but in actual fact needs to be replaced or repaired every few months when some careless driver knocks it over or rips it from its foundations. Lima is one of the few South Asian couriers I've seen on circuit, and if you ever get talking to him he'll tell you very enthusiastically about how long he's been studying wine, and how he has plans to set up his own vineyard, either in Slovenia, where land is cheap and wine has room for improvement, or in his native India.

I was halfway through our usual enthusiastic greeting when I realised that, for once, Lima wasn't smiling. He looked as overheated and bedraggled as Gertie and me, but didn't seem to be as amused by it. Giving us a morose nod, he stalked off across the street towards Pret à Manger, and I watched his back, laden with a bulbous low-hanging courier bag and two roomy pouches clamped to his belt, obscuring each buttock so that all that was really visible of him was bare arms, muscular calves and the back of his head. I remembered how Lima had spent most of the winter riding around in shorts and a T-shirt, arms rigid with goosebumps, his mood never faltering. When I asked him whether he wasn't cold (I underdress in winter myself, but never to his extent), he'd shrug, and smile, and say, 'Oh, you know, I just . . . I don't know really!' I had never seen him looking as angry as he did today. Like Gertie, he seemed to be one of the few couriers who acknowledged the stresses of the job, yet was never seriously affected by them.

He returned, a paper cup of water in one hand, stomping back across the cobbles with a cursory rightward glance for any oncoming traffic that might dare to impede his passage.

'How's it going?' I asked, more to give him a chance to offload his woes than as a greeting or a query.

'I've just *had* it,' he huffed. 'I've had it with all of this – with sitting around for two hours waiting for one *poxy* job, and then busting a gut to make two pound fifty, and all these kids taking the work who just thought it'd be a cool thing to do in their summer holidays and'll've *fucked* off again by autumn.'

That was enough. He flopped down onto the step next to us and lapsed into aggrieved silence, gulping from his cup of water as if it were a flask of whisky. Gertie and I, after a moment, went back to reading and rehydrating. The radios buzzed on, and we ignored them just as they appeared to be ignoring us. There's not really much you can say – any professions of sympathy are already taken for granted, and couriers know better than to suggest solutions, because we know that the only real solution is to get out. We chose this job, after all, and we could choose to leave. It doesn't do to think too much about how things might be changed, because you'll either realise that they can't, or that they can (and then you'd have to do something about it).

I felt slightly guilty as well, having spent twenty minutes earlier that morning getting to know one of these summer interlopers, and finding him perfectly pleasant. It hadn't occurred to me that he might be any less of a courier than I was (though I hadn't seen him before, so he was probably newish), partly because he looked a lot more like one, with his tattoos, high-end steel frame and grimy singlet fluttering from broad tanned shoulders. These were the guys who would be stopped by street photographers several times a week in summer (though admittedly I sometimes was too, because of the perpetual fascination with any woman seen to be 'making it in a man's world'), and whose image would be fed into popular culture to perpetuate the cult of the young, handsome, surly, virile, hyper-masculine messenger, in comparison with which a girl like me, or an old-timer like Gertie, would only ever be projected as an alternative, or a curiosity, or an anomaly. Now I recalled part of our conversation – we'd been discussing our commutes, and his was, at ten miles, slightly longer than mine.

'Oh – whereabouts do you live then?' I'd asked.

'Uhm, Wimbledon,' he'd muttered.

Of course. It made sense now. He was still living with his parents.

Mind you, I myself now lived in increasingly upmarket Stoke Newington, lured there by its reputation as London's lesbian village, as well as a friendly landlady who was going to charge me only £300 a month for my room. It didn't turn out to be exactly as I'd expected it – the wholefood shops were full of yummy mummies buying organic chia seeds, rather than sensibly shod middle-aged dykes weighing out aduki beans as I'd hoped – but I was now closer to Ash's place, lessening the feeling of being stranded at the far edge of London when either of us spent the weekend at the other's house, and Alex had got the job she interviewed for, and was hoping to move back into the area, where she'd lived during her original years in London.

We met up one Saturday afternoon at the Blue Legume, during one of her visits from Dublin to look at flats. Ash was fixing bikes up at the climbing centre, and I felt as though I hadn't seen her for weeks, though in actual fact I'd ridden past her twice the previous day. Since Alex was now back, staying in Walthamstow while she househunted, we'd agreed that it made more sense for me to spend Friday evening at home for once, and we'd all meet up the following day. Over our coffees, Alex told me with great excitement that she'd walked down Riversdale Road on her way to meet me, stopped outside a house she used to live in, laid her hand on the gatepost, and felt past and present draw themselves closer together. After her many years of wandering, she was returning to the closest thing she had to a home – to where she had spent a happy year of her youth, and where, even longer ago, her Jewish immigrant grandmother had put down roots in a new country.

'I see Ash still isn't a morning person,' she remarked, and we both laughed as she told me how she had got up, helped herself to a pot of coffee, climbed back into bed and set it down a couple of inches from Ash's nose, forcing her to wake up. I envied Alex's courage, having developed a fear of Ash's morning grumpiness, which, unless I trod carefully, would often manifest itself in snappish exchanges that cast a pall over my otherwise joyful commute.

'Oh, hang on, I've just spotted there's a noticeboard behind you – going to go and check if there's any room ads!' Alex disappeared up to the front of the cafe for a moment, before bounding back to the table and picking up her jacket from the chair. 'Sorry. I'm just making sure I leave no stone unturned at the moment – I saw one place this morning that I found online, and I'm asking all my friends, seeing if they know of anything coming up. I've given myself a week to find somewhere! Anyway, shall we head out? I'll show you a bit of my Stokey.'

We paid up, crossed Church Street and strolled into Clissold Park, which was as busy as a London park ever gets, the parents and pushchairs that populated it during the week joined by well-dressed wage-slaves snoozing and picnicking through their hangovers, and all manner of people out for their Saturday stroll, or bike ride, or skateboard. On a previous walk, I'd noted with amusement that the same woman passed me three times, trundling placidly along on her mountain bike in her work-out gear, and wondered if for her this counted as an exercise session – wondered also whether, for me, just a few years ago, it might have felt similar.

'Oh, this is nothing like it was!' exclaimed Alex. 'It used to be – I mean, it was always a great park, because it had the aviary, and the river running through it, but it was kind of shabby, not like this. There used to be a massive carved wooden totem pole over there, as you came in, and that cafe – is that still a cafe? That used to be where everyone hung out. And it was kind of – not quite greasy spoon, more jacket potato and beans, you know what I mean?'

We stopped in our tracks as a couple of six-year-olds on scooters shot past, and then ambled over to take a look.

'Oh, yes, here, this was all run down back then,' continued Alex, and I had the impression that she was talking as much to herself as to me, bringing her memories back to life as she laid her eyes on where they had taken place. 'And all of the outside, all of the inside, it was just full of people with dreadlocks. Everyone seemed to have a dog on a piece of rope. I mean, it sounds like such a stereotype now. But it was all communities of people who had dogs, and hung out there, and loads of us were couriers, loads. And everyone was beautiful, in my eyes, and it was – well, for me it was a really great time.'

We walked a circuit or two of the park, and she told me how she had taken a year out of Oxford, suffering from emotional difficulties, and not having anywhere else to go, had thrown herself on the mercy of a friend who was squatting in Hackney.

'It was one of those big old Victorian houses on Rectory Road.' She waved a hand in the direction of the High Street. 'And I don't know what percentage of the houses on that road were squatted, but it was a lot. This whole area was, back then. I could probably walk you down that road and point out where all the squats used to be. And it wasn't just crusties. There was a guy in my squat who was an electrician, who had fallen on hard times. And there were couriers of course. And a lot of artists. In fact, some old friends of mine – we've lost touch now – they were squatting while they saved up money for a deposit, and then they bought a place just off Church Street. I wonder if they're still there now.'

I tried to picture Alex, almost twenty years ago, scrawny and miserable, standing nervously in the corner at a squat party and eventually getting into a conversation with a woman who turned out to be a courier with Metro.

'So I ended up working for Central Despatch. I don't know how. I guess I must have called them, from the phone-box on the corner of Rectory Road – because of course this was before the Internet.'

'You know, that's an element of psychogeography we don't have these days,' I mused. 'I mean, I always know where the nearest toilet is, and all the benches, and bins even, but there's no need to register phoneboxes any more.'

'Yeah, phoneboxes were a thing we knew back then. Because we needed them. You know, if your radio went down – and they sometimes did, because the battery packs wouldn't always last till the end of the day – then you'd have to find a phonebox and call in, and then cycle back to base to get another radio.'

She reminisced for a while about old haunts, former colleagues and half-remembered jobs, breaking off occasionally to ask me if the Passport Office was still on Petty France, or if the American Express offices were still at the bottom of Haymarket.

'I never had a female controller. And Bill was on the scene back then. Buffalo Bill? This was before he became a controller. I remember – I remember seeing him coming down past the Angel, Rosebery Avenue, something like that. And he was rolling a fag.'

'Riding along?'

'Yep. And I don't think I made that up – you know, heard

the stories and turned it into a memory. I remember seeing him, and thinking – blimey!'

We wandered down to the eastern end of Church Street, past all the boutiques and organic bakeries, planning to pick up a picnic lunch in Fresh & Wild (which Alex insisted on calling 'Fresh and Wildly Expensive') and share it with Ash when she finished work. Every few minutes, Alex would exclaim over something that had or hadn't changed since she was last in the area. She was evidently delighted to be back, despite the fact that, by her own admission, she had spent little more than a year living here.

'You see, for me that was probably one of the most important years of my life. Because it saved me. I wasn't in a good place, and what I found here was a whole community of outsiders. Before that I didn't fit in anywhere. I didn't fit in Oxford, I didn't fit in my family – I was gay, so I didn't fit in society. I didn't even fit in the gay community, because they were all so . . . terrifyingly butch, and I wasn't like that. I didn't socialise much in the courier community, but when I was working, people were friendly. It gave me the tiny little toehold, so I could start to fashion an identity and a level of self-esteem from which I could grow the rest of my life.'

I think I had been sceptical, at first, of Alex's sense of Hackney being her home, even though the other thirty-nine years of her life had been spent elsewhere. But now I saw it for what it was – the place where her personality and identity had finally taken root; the moment at which she recognised herself; the point of stability from which she grew.

'Maybe if I'd ended up in a squat in Waterloo, I'd have ended up feeling this way about Waterloo. But I don't think so. Because Hackney's also where my nan's from, and this whole sense of Jewish East End identity. I was looking for some roots, however fantastical – you know, I was looking for a story to tell, to explain myself to myself. And this is where I found it.'

Several years later this conversation would come to mind as I sat at Nhatt's kitchen table, drinking Turkish coffee and discussing my recent return to the city, and her imminent departure from it. After more than a decade in London, she was going to try her luck in her home country for a while, and had booked a one-way flight to New York the following week. It had only just occurred to me that she might consider herself a Londoner, despite what her passport and accent might say to the contrary.

'I don't have a lot of family,' she mused. 'I've always felt like I needed to be somewhere where I was surrounded by people who just accepted me and were welcoming, and that's one of the things that the courier scene does really well, is that it picks up waifs and strays like me and makes them feel less . . . waify or strayey.'

I agreed with her, still slightly surprised by how readily I'd been accepted by the other couriers, despite my gender, accent, lack of tattoos and obedience of traffic signals. I remembered the over-confident, privately educated young men who had persistently shouted me down at Cambridge, and who, even though I had eventually learned to shout back, had instilled the firm conviction in me that this was *their* place, *their* culture, *their* rules. The degree I'd come out with was ultimately no more than a language I'd learned to speak, however fluently, whereas couriering was something

I'd built from scratch, and owned as much as anyone else who had ever strapped a radio to their bag and scraped a living in the streets.

Alex and I walked back towards the park, with our cartons of quinoa salad and roasted vegetables, her in her yoga pants and me in my Indian skirt – looking for all the world like we belonged in Stoke Newington. And then Alex stopped in her tracks, pointing frantically at a handsome crescent of houses overlooking the park on its southern edge. They were the typical north London mix of brickwork and stucco, with wrought-iron balconies on the first floor, and five broad steps leading up to the columns that flanked the front door.

'Oh! This whole row was squatted, back in the day. I actually lived there, in the one at the end, for about a week, at one point. And that was around the time that the Criminal Justice Act was going through, that was going to make squatting illegal. It was actually them trying to contain a whole social movement – they also wanted to make it illegal for people to gather over a certain number. And it was rave music, that was the music of the time. So they were trying to say that music above a certain number of beats per minute, you couldn't play. And ludicrous stuff like that. Anyway – what happened in Hackney was that they started hiring private security firms to evict people, even though it wasn't yet illegal to squat. And so basically what you had were a bunch of thugs, who would forcibly enter your home, and attack people, and this was happening all over Hackney, and the people in this crescent barricaded themselves in, and it became this massive siege, for ages. Was just after I left actually.'

'You had a lucky escape then!'

'I did.'

We stood and looked at the crescent for a moment, seeing it illuminated by Alex's reviving memories, imagining the boards and the barricades, wondering if the families who now lived here had any idea of their houses' history.

'We'd better get moving – Ash'll've finished work by now,' I said, suddenly realising that it was after three, and she'd be wondering where we were. Alex somehow sensed an anxiety I was only half aware of myself.

'You shouldn't put up with Ash's crap as much as you do,' she said, and then, perhaps noticing my dismay, added, 'She does really care about you, you know.'

But I needn't have worried. A minute later Ash strode into sight, instantly visible to me with her green T-shirt and cut-off jeans and auburn hair, her pace quickening as she spotted us, and her face lighting up as she realised we were carrying food.

11

I had always been surprised, since Ash spent most of her weekends smearing herself with bike oil, that she didn't hang out at Fullcity during the week, since she could probably have ruled the roost with her engineering background, not to mention substantially increasing the likelihood of our paths crossing during the working day. But she insisted there was something shady about Lawrence, and that he was an appallingly bad mechanic.

'Besides,' she told me, 'I went to buy a coffee there once and this guy walked in and started claiming that this Dolan in there was his, and he could name every single dent on it. He was really kicking off, threatening to call the police right then and there, unless they gave it back to him.'

'What did Lawrence do?' I asked.

'He wasn't there,' she replied. 'Just that American guy –'

'Jim?'

'Yeah, Jim. And a couple of others. That guy with the teeth. And they didn't really know what to do. They ended up just giving it back to him. So, yes, I kind of think they must have some hot bikes in there.'

I felt a vaguely proprietary embarrassment, not sure whether to defend Lawrence, who could quite plausibly have bought a bike from some reasonable-seeming person without realising it was stolen. He had once, I remembered, told me the story of how a girl had come in to sell a Charge Plug, and as he was checking it over he'd noticed a nick on the frame that could only have come from a pair of bolt cutters.

'I'm afraid I can't buy this,' he'd told her, pointing out the mark and explaining that the bike had almost certainly been stolen.

'But I asked!' she'd protested. 'I got it off Gumtree, and the guy promised me it wasn't stolen.'

I laughed along with the mechanics, though I did wonder afterwards how anyone could possibly know the provenance of every second-hand bike in the city. Several of mine had been acquired from people on the Internet who seemed perfectly genuine, but who was to say they weren't just good liars, hiding behind the assumptions people will make about nice white middle-class women and well-spoken bearded men? And even if they themselves hadn't stolen the bike, how could I be sure that someone further along the chain hadn't? True, the chances of a former owner spotting and claiming the Dawes Giro I'd exchanged £75 in cash for on St Albans station were remote, but I was unsettled by the bad karma that might hang around a bike with this sort of back story. Ridiculous to care about such things, I told myself – but still, when the bike's energy and my own seemed so intertwined, it didn't seem entirely impossible that I might somehow be affected by its history; that its fate might not somehow become entangled with my own.

I had a word with Lawrence, suggesting that he at least cover his back by asking for ID from anyone selling him a bike, and keep track of the frame numbers of the bikes that passed through his hands. He agreed that this was a good idea, though I'm not sure how often – or even whether – he implemented it. It wasn't hard to see why. If you happened to walk past Fullcity half an hour before closing time, you'd marvel at the apparent chaos that burst out of the warm golden light of its windows – commuters returning to pick up their bikes for the homeward journey, picking their way nervously through the crowds of couriers who were beginning to assemble on the pavement outside, rolling their end-of-day cigarettes and running back and forth to the off-licence two doors down for cans of beer, heading inside to where several mechanics laughed and gossiped, and ducked smoothly as, one after the other, the bikes were lifted down off the wall and passed overhead towards the door where their owners were usually being talked into staying for a coffee, or maybe even something stronger. Lawrence was immediately friends with everyone, flattering the man with the steel road frame, nodding patiently as the Pashley rider dithered over one colour of bar tape and another, sympathising with the courier scraping together enough cash to pay for a tyre; somehow everywhere at once, never quite busy enough not to hail you loudly as you walked in, and switch on the grinder before he'd even finished asking whether you wanted a coffee.

'Of course,' I remarked, 'there's always the risk that someone went in when Lawrence was there, checked the bike over, and then waited till Jim was in charge before going in and, you know, "identifying" it.'

'That's what the guy with the teeth said. He was kind of slagging Jim off, didn't like him. But Jim was saying that the Dolan wasn't actually very good, so if you were going to do that, you'd have chosen a better bike.'

'Well, some people like Dolans.'

Ash rolled her eyes, as if to say that she couldn't imagine why, but there was no accounting for taste.

'I don't think I'd get into trading second-hand bikes myself,' she said. 'You just can't regulate it.'

'You could a bit,' I argued. 'At least, you could cover your back by documenting where the bikes come from. And the same if you find your stolen bike there – you should have to prove it's really yours before they just give it back. I think they need more than just someone's word.'

'Well, if the guy had to jump through too many hoops, he might have gone and made a big fuss online, and made things worse for Lawrence.'

'Well, maybe, but I think it would be fair enough for Lawrence to say that he wouldn't buy a bike just on the verbal assurance that it's not stolen, and therefore, he's not going to just hand one over on the verbal assurance that it is.'

'Yeah,' agreed Ash, reluctantly. 'But I did wonder, when Jim handed it over like that, that maybe he didn't trust that it wasn't stolen.'

'Jim's not much of a bike person though – maybe he was erring on the side of caution.'

'He's nice though, isn't he?'

The conversation turned to Jim's personal merits, mechanical shortcomings and ongoing visa problems. It turned out that both of us had offered to marry him at one point or another, in my case almost seriously. (He had said no.)

'He makes the best coffee there, definitely,' said Ash.

'Oh, I don't know – Lawrence's is stronger.'

'That doesn't mean it's better.'

'It does if it's a Thursday afternoon.'

'Eh?'

'I always have wooden legs on a Thursday afternoon.'

'It's because you insist on riding fixed, isn't it.'

Ash had finally put her money where her mouth was and converted her precious 1984 Olympic replica Raleigh (christened 'Sir Walter', usually shortened to 'Wally'), back into a road bike, 'as God intended'. She was now almost as evangelical about the benefits of a freewheel as most other London cyclists were about a fixed gear. She was also now capable of beating me up Pentonville Road on our way home, to my annoyance. The only thing I liked about this new state of affairs was that her extremely noisy Campagnolo groupset made it impossible for her to creep up on me when she spotted me waiting at the lights.

'Why don't you borrow Wally for a day or two? I guarantee you'll love it.' She gave me a sly grin, knowing by now exactly which of my buttons to press. 'You'd be so much faster . . .'

'Ach, Wally's far too small for me. What is he – a 49?'

'51!' said Ash, with a short person's ready indignation.

'Still. It'd feel like riding a clown's bike.'

'There's not really that much difference. I have him set up really tight is all. You'd just have to get a longer stem from somewhere. I bet Lawrence would have one lying around.'

'Hmm,' I said, deliberately stalling the conversation. It had been several years since I rode a bike with a freewheel and gears now struck me as unnecessarily complicated. And I was reluctant to compromise my increasing virtuosity on fixed by starting again at the beginning.

But a couple of weeks later the decision was taken out of my hands. The morning after a long rainy August afternoon my lock seized up, leaving my bike shackled to the balcony outside my flat, where I kept it when I wasn't riding it. After a fruitless twenty minutes of trying to force the key to turn, raising two blisters on my right forefinger in the process, I admitted defeat, called Andy to explain the situation, and wandered off down Church Street, to see if either the fire station or the bike shop there would be able to help me out. They weren't, but when I got home it turned out that Nhatt had responded to what I had assumed would be a fruitless Internet plea, offering me both a spare lock and the use of one of her own bikes – of which she now had several, since she had recently left couriering behind for good (or so she claimed), and was working as a mechanic in Brixton Cycles, taking advantage of the staff discount to augment her stable with eccentricities such as a Salsa cyclocross bike (the first non-mountain-bike I had ever seen with disc brakes and knobbly tyres), a pink and orange Brompton, and a Surly Steamroller set up with moustache bars and a rear coaster brake. The first time I saw her on the latter, freewheeling down Stamford Hill with no visible brake, I was so shocked that I almost steered into a bus.

I was terrified by the coaster brake, and worried that the untried ferocity of disc brakes would send me straight over the handlebars the first time I attempted to stop; so that left Nhatt's precious Jack Taylor track bike (which I'd long admired, loving the way the curved down tube followed the line of the rear wheel), and her Orbea road bike. And the Jack Taylor didn't have a brake at all, so that left the road bike.

I was slightly nervous about this, not having ridden with a freewheel for almost four years, but the only other alternative was twiddling my thumbs at home while I waited for a solution to present itself to my lock problem, and I had the rent to pay. So I wrenched the pedals off my Condor, stuck one in each pocket, swung my bag onto my back and walked over to the old house on Shacklewell Lane that Nhatt shared with two cats, several other couriers and more bikes than anyone had ever bothered to count. Half an hour later, I rode away nervously on the Orbea, trembling ever so slightly, and repeatedly reminding myself to brake with my hands, just as earnestly as a novice fixie rider will remind herself to keep pedalling, don't stop pedalling, don't try to freewheel or the bike will kick you right off.

'Nice bike,' said a passing cargo bike rider, as I rested near the Old Street roundabout that afternoon.

'It's not mine!' I exclaimed.

'I know.' He laughed, from which I concluded that he must know Nhatt – and, presumably, since he didn't immediate try to wrestle me to the ground and retrieve the Orbea, that she had lent me her bike.

'Oh – haven't you met my boyfriend?' she asked when I related the episode to her. I hadn't. Like Nhatt, Selim was progressively distancing himself from the industry, trying his utmost to do fewer and fewer days on the road, in the hope that eventually he'd be down to none. Many of the people I'd seen on the road during my earliest days, or whose names had been tossed to and fro on *Moving Target*, were now getting out, into bike shops, postgrad courses, parenthood, community projects and, in one case, a black cab, and I had a mournful sense of having just missed out on a golden era. Had I started just a year or two earlier – or back when I very first moved to London – these people would have been my peers, and I would have been known to them as they were to me, and perhaps even ended up living in the house on Shacklewell Lane. As it was, I watched them slip away into their future, only slightly disappointed, still almost entirely wrapped up in my own present.

Gradually, some of the skills I had unconsciously developed during my fixed-gear years began to cross over to the road bike. I learned I could buy myself extra fractions of seconds in slowing traffic by shifting my weight backwards, or tighten a curve ever so slightly by leaning into it, crumpling my head and shoulder and elbow and hip together and stretching out the other side of my body so that the bike couldn't help but turn. I came to understand the brakes better – although I never entirely trusted them – and learned how to control my velocity by feathering them lightly, tapping them gently as I eased into a corner, using them to prolong a pause just long enough for the bumper ahead of me to pull forward so I could swing into the gap it left.

After a few days of this, I finally found a friend of a friend with a pair of bolt cutters, who came round to the flat and freed my bike within thirty seconds, to my moderate alarm. I just hoped no bike thief would ever bother to climb up to the third floor of my block, or consider my slightly rusty Condor worthy of stealing. (I had met a bike thief once, hanging around among the post-work crowds at Fullcity. He claimed to be reformed, but still didn't seem very sympathetic when I started trying to tell him how much people's bikes meant to them, and how heartbroken I'd be if any of mine were stolen. 'They should have insurance,' he said, dismissively, and went outside to join the smokers.)

'I see you're giving fixed a try,' said an older courier whose name I didn't know, as we waited for the lights to change on Holborn the following morning. I didn't bother to correct him, since I had got used to having this conversation now and then even before my brief flirtation with a freewheel. Typically, a courier I knew by name, but not much more, would nod towards my rear wheel and say, 'On a fixie now, are you?' or 'How you getting on with fixed then?' and I'd shake my head in bewilderment, and explain that not only had I been riding almost exclusively on a fixed gear for the past few years, but furthermore, that I had never couriered on any other bike, so I didn't know where he was getting his ideas from.

The most obvious (and only imaginable) explanation for this was that they were surprised to see a girl riding fixed, and just somehow assumed that she must be new to it – even though most of the female couriers on circuit were riding track bikes. Even now, when men come up to me in the street to start conversations about my bike, they'll often ask whether I know it's dangerous to ride a single-speed with only one brake, and when I tell them it's actually a fixed gear, will raise their eyebrows in surprise and ask me how riding fixed is going for me. But maybe it has nothing to do with gender. Maybe I just look like the sort of person who would be riding a road bike.

And if this does betray some small vestiges of sexism on

the part of my male colleagues, I'm happy to let that slide because, as Nhatt pointed out to me during my first year on the road, despite the sexism that bounces off us all day, from the van drivers who ogle (and occasionally slap) our arses, to the post-room guys who breathe their ham sandwiches over us as they try to help us wedge the package into our bag when we're perfectly capable of doing it ourselves, to the various stand-in controllers who would foolishly try to ingratiate themselves with me by addressing me as 'babes' over the radio – *despite* all this, couriers themselves tend to be mostly gender-blind. If you're putting in nine hours a day on the bike, if you can carry ten kilos on your back, and if you smell of several different vintages of stale sweat, then you're a courier, and whether you're male or female is largely irrelevant.

Nhatt was missing this, now she worked in a bike shop. Her colleagues were mostly accepting, but quite often, when I dropped in after work to buy a brake cable or a new inner tube, or just to pass the time of day, I'd witness a long line of customers waiting for Nhatt's male co-workers, while she hung around at a loose end, occasionally shouting, 'Can I help anyone?', to which the people in the queue would generally shake their heads, and say no, thanks, they were waiting to speak to Lincoln, or Barney, or Billy.

'Couriers just treat you like a courier,' she sighed. 'I mean – I know this wouldn't make me very popular, but with a lot of the male couriers, that doesn't apply to any woman who isn't a courier. You know, people still have sexist views, but at some point you transcend all that to be just a courier.'

She was right, as ever. I had sometimes felt distinctly

uncomfortable, wobbling on one of Lawrence's aluminium chairs among a gang of male couriers, listening to their appraisal of passing buttocks and bosoms – but at the same time, I never felt any fear that this gaze might be turned on me. And I was touched by how quickly – or at any rate, how much more quickly than I'd anticipated – the other couriers seemed to have accepted me as one of their own.

'Oh, come on,' said Nhatt when I admitted I had finally stopped feeling like a fraud when I told people what I did for a living. 'It's not rocket surgery. You get told where to go, you pick up a package, and then you go and deliver it. Most of the time no one even cares how fast you are – your company's much more concerned with you not losing packages, or yelling at security guards when you're in a bad mood. They just want you to be reliable. And as long as you pick up packages and deliver them in a reasonable amount of time, then you're a cycle courier. Ninety per cent of it is just giving a fuck. Like I said, it's not rocket surgery.'

It was somehow slightly ironic – but also entirely obvious – that one of the most well-known perpetrators of the courier mystique should be so disillusioned by it herself. For me, on the other hand, the perpetual nostalgia of the older couriers, along with a growing sense that I was floating on top of a long history that went all the way back to the dimly remembered days of phonebox queues and paper dockets, meant that most of what it had long meant to be a courier was beyond my grasp, and that I had to make do with a leaner workload, an impoverished circuit, and constant reminders that the good days were behind us. Still, as the days began to shorten, the year rolled downhill from the dazzling heights of summer, and I realised I would be spending another winter on the road, I started to feel that I was now treading on familiar ground – that I knew what lay ahead.

12

That autumn brought with it rain, the familiar smell of last year's winter jacket, and a succession of anniversaries. It was a year since I'd floated out from the comfortable berth of academia into the uncharted waters of manual labour. It was a year since I'd turned on my radio and started following Andy's voice to and fro across the city. It was a year since my first date with Ash. She celebrated by dumping me.

It was and wasn't a surprise. I had just returned from Delhi, where I'd watched an old friend get married and caught up with the dwindling number of acquaintances I'd held onto from the days I worked there. This unavoidably expensive trip had preyed on my mind all year, especially on those torturous summer afternoons where the radio lapses into silence and you tot up the jobs on your Xda and realise you're still only in single figures. But I'd made it, just a few pounds from the end of my savings, and while I was out there had done the first few shifts of a new freelance job I'd acquired, remotely monitoring an editorial platform for a European investment bank (hilariously outsourced to India, and then re-outsourced to me back in London), every Sunday, from 5 a.m. to 3 p.m. This antisocial shift would eventually add an extra third to my income and, although worrying had become far too ingrained a habit to lose entirely, effectively end my financial worries. (In direct contrast to couriering, my editorial job paid an hourly rate, and often involved no more than a couple of hours per day of actual work.)

Ash came over for dinner the night before I left, and I served her sausages, and lumpy mash that tasted of soot, because I'd let the steamer boil dry. We ate side by side on the balcony, in the dark, unable to pretend that the food was enjoyable, but too hungry not to eat it. I cringed with suppressed apology, feeling that the harder I tried to make her happy, the more I'd instead end up irritating her. Every time I thought of something to say, I'd immediately decide against it, already anticipating her disagreement or criticism. Eventually, all that was left was, 'Do you want to break up with me?'

'Em!' she said, and put down her knife, and took my hand – something she rarely did, so it exacerbated my fears, rather than comforting me as had probably been her intention. It was too dark for me to make out her exact expression, but she turned towards me and I could see the translucent darkness of her eyes contrasting with the pallor of her skin. She shook her head slightly, and we sat there in silence for a moment.

'I don't know,' I began. 'I just feel like – like I'm always annoying you, and I don't know what to do to make it alright.'

'I'm sorry,' she said. 'I think maybe I haven't been very nice to you lately.'

'No – no, it's not that,' I said, even though really it was. 'I don't know – am I doing something wrong?'

'No. I . . .'

There was another long pause, and we both stared out into

the night, through the branches of the plane trees, towards the lit-up windows in the block opposite, idly registering the Liberty wallpaper on the fourth floor; the windowboxes and wind chimes on the third; the fleeting shadow of someone passing behind net curtains.

'I don't know,' she concluded. 'I think neither of us is really thriving at the moment, you know? We're not making the best of ourselves. We should be doing more with our lives than this.'

We ended the conversation, threw out the rest of the potatoes, swapped her radio for mine in the charger, and went to bed. I was going to work for a few hours of the morning, before heading to Heathrow. Ash was monosyllabic as we unlocked our bikes from the balcony and upended them into the lift, but this worried me less than it had last night – she was almost always less energetic than I was in the mornings.

'Why don't we stay in bed?' she said suddenly. 'Come on, why don't you just call in, tell them you're not coming in, and we'll go back to bed?'

'I can't do that! They're expecting me. I said I'd work this morning. I need the money. I can't just call in sick. They'd . . . they'd know I was lying.'

'Oh, come on!' Her expression was almost triumphant, as if she already knew I was going to turn her down, and I was somehow proving her point.

'Ash, I really can't.'

'Fine. Alright then.'

She stalked out of the lift doors ahead of me, got on her bike, and rode off without a backward glance. I followed her anxiously into town, unsure whether she was expecting me to ride with her, or wanting me to leave her alone, wondering if she'd be angry if she turned round and saw me there, or angrier if she later realised I'd gone my own way.

'Bye then . . .?' I called, as we approached Theberton Street, where I'd turn right, following Tolpuddle and Amwell down into Clerkenwell, and she'd head east, towards the City.

'Yep. Bye.'

We made friends again over email while I was away, but the evening I got back, laden with block-printed cotton bedding for her and the Thai fisherman's pants that Alex had requested from Pahar Ganj, she met me at the flat, sat quietly beside me on the bed, held my hand, and said, 'Emily . . .', and I knew she'd decided to end it, and that nothing I could do or say would persuade her to change her mind, or to stay with me for one more night, knowing that no one else could possibly comfort me.

Going back to the familiar and all-absorbing routine of couriering helped me to keep going, because there was no option but to keep going, because the exhaustion very effectively anaesthetised my mind, and because I spent most of my courier life alone anyway, so in some ways it didn't feel all that different. The gods of the circuit were kind, and I didn't run into her for the first week, though I often wondered where she was, and whether she was thinking about me. Andy welcomed me back when I first called in over the radio, something I'd never heard before, and Lukasz beamed at me when we met in a loading bay in EC2, reminding me of the pub crawl we'd planned to celebrate our first year on the road, since we'd started within a couple of weeks of each other.

'Yeah, I was thinking one drink in each postcode? Start off with W2 and NW1 maybe, get those bad boys out the way first. Maybe Edgware Road – what do you think? Then work our way over to the City, finish off at the Foundry.'

We considered the next few Fridays. He was keen to do it right away, but Ash wanted to see me at the end of that week, for what I assumed would be the customary exchange of belongings and post-break-up post-mortem, or even an expression of regret, and a hope that we could somehow work it out.

We met at an Irish pub just south of King's Cross, and managed to make small talk for the duration of two pints and a shared plate of chips. I was reminded bizarrely of our first date, where for a whole night we had carefully avoided addressing the real reason she had flown over from Dublin.

Since we'd met on a long bike ride, and each been delighted to discover another woman as obsessed with bikes as we ourselves were, we had quickly come up with an incredibly over-ambitious plan for what we weren't yet admitting was going to be our first date. As I stewed over my going-nowhere thesis, and she whiled away the extraordinarily long notice period at the digital agency she worked for in Dublin, and both of us wished we were out on our bikes, we noted that it was about three hundred miles from where I sat in London to where she'd get off the ferry in Holyhead, if she crossed from Dublin.

'Meet you in the middle one day?' she asked me, with a little typographical wink that showed either that she wasn't serious, or that she was very serious indeed, depending on how I chose to interpret it.

And so a plan was hatched, and so the plan developed, both of us giddily nervous about whether we'd actually make it, and whether we'd be in any state to hold a sensible conversation when our paths finally crossed, somewhere along the A5, having cycled a hundred and fifty miles apiece, and (secretly) whether we'd actually find each other as attractive as we had during our few passing encounters on the road to Dunwich. And then the plan fell apart, two weeks before we were due to meet, when I took my precious Surly Steamroller out for a Sunday morning spin round Richmond Park, hoping to release some of my pent-up energy and clear my head of mystifying concepts like Spivak's 'parasubjective matrix', skidded on the Priory Lane roundabout, and went straight into a lamp post. I survived the crash, merely losing a little skin and gaining a few chunks of tarmac that are still visible under the scar tissue on my left elbow, but the bike was a write-off, and the unfriendly black Condor I'd recently acquired from Lawrence looked as if it would have to become my main ride.

Ash sympathised sincerely, and suggested we modify our plans, working around my injuries and the fact that I'd be riding a slightly less comfortable bike. (The Surly Steamroller, despite having been designed as an urban fixed-gear ride, had turned out to work very well over longer distances, and after a few short but successful tours on mine, I had decided to equip it with a rack and panniers, and devote it to weekend riding, keeping the nippier, twitchier Condor for my commute, whatever that might turn out to be after my degree ended.) She booked a flight to Gatwick, the day after my thesis deadline, and we conspired to cycle to Brighton together, eat dinner, and then ride back to London.

The frantic anticipation with which I'd looked forward to seeing her again melted into calm on the twenty-mile ride to the airport, and I parked myself and the Condor next to the barrier, wondering whether she'd have remembered exactly what I looked like, but reassuring myself that, since there were no other dark-haired women with bikes in Arrivals, at least she wouldn't have trouble picking me out.

And as soon as she emerged, I knew this had been a good idea. She was slightly smaller than me, pert and wiry, with boyish auburn hair and pale skin that on a less healthy person might have been pasty and mottled, but in her case glowed with a summer of cycling and – possibly – the anticipation of meeting me. We greeted each other with broad smiles and an awkward hug, and wheeled our bikes over to the nearest coffee shop, where I ordered a couple of espressos and she made last-minute adjustments to the frankly tiny amount of luggage she'd brought over for what was currently an open-ended trip. We had avoided talking about how far its ultimate length depended on me – quite comfortably so, since we were both at stages of life (her post-job; me post-degree) where the future was entirely undecided, and far too gleeful over our new-found freedoms to have any real concerns over this. A bulky Carradice saddlebag sagged over her back wheel, held in place with a homemade confection of metal struts, which I later found out she'd salvaged from an old child seat. She wore a small backpack over her green cycling jersey, and otherwise that was it. The old three-speed handlebars she'd fitted on her Raleigh frame didn't allow for any sort of bar bag, and nor did its seat stays have any braze-ons for a rack. She introduced me to Wally with transparent pride and affection, and I marvelled at what a good fit they were (both small, red, well built and born in 1984) and watched the muscles shifting and rippling under the skin of her forearms as she hoicked the saddle up a couple of centimetres, tightened the bolt with her multitool and then snapped it closed and dropped it smoothly into her pocket.

We arrived in Brighton, leg-braking our way down the hill towards the beach, in time to meet another of Ash's Internet friends, who had just finished work. 'We've been chatting a bit lately,' Ash had explained a couple of days pre-viously, then added 'though not as much as you and I have been chatting, eh'.

Tiff was pale and skeletal, her face dwarfed by an enor-mous nose-ring and her shaven head etched with tattoos. She was waiting for us on the stones of Brighton beach, watching as twilight slowly fell over the burnt-out pier, a BMX leaning against her leg like a tired dog. Until she saw us, her expression was solemn to the point of hostility, but as we approached her she broke into a nervous smile and hailed Ash with a warm fraternal handshake.

'Shall we go and get a drink then, matey?'

'I think we're going to need to eat,' replied Ash, and I lis-tened to her voice subtly change its register with something already approaching a proprietary curiosity, noticing how her Irish accent thickened slightly in response to Tiff's northern one. We discussed our options, three near-strangers, not yet sure of each other's preferences and proclivities.

'There's an OK Thai place just over there a bit,' offered Tiff, waving a skinny hand back towards the beachfront, where the lights were beginning to come on in the buildings and along the promenade. 'Should be vegan-friendly for me, and I think they do quite big portions.'

We bumped our bikes back across the stones of the beach and spent a couple of hours demolishing enormous plates of food, discussing our ride from the airport, Ash's abandoned web-design career and my lapsed academic one. Tiff, originally a nurse from Lancashire, had been in Brighton for a couple of years, working in a body-modification studio that offered anything from piercings to tongue splits, though her speciality was scarification. She wasn't making anywhere near enough money out of it though. The BMX had been a lucky charity shop find, and most of her clothing had seen better days. Without even needing to discuss it, Ash and I picked up the bill, and Tiff looked guiltily relieved.

'Thanks, mate – tell you what, I'll get you dinner when I'm back up in London. I want to move up there, got a few friends in town. Thought I might try and get a job as a cycle courier.'

I yawned happily at her, delighted to have helped, but concerned that the meal had been a little too good. I'd been awake since six, and already cycled over fifty miles, and now, sitting in a warm restaurant with my belly full of food, it seemed that the only thing that could possibly follow was a slow, snoozy descent into unconsciousness. Getting back on the bike and cycling another fifty miles back to London seemed impossible, but giving in and buying a train ticket was unthinkable. I had no idea how Ash was feeling (maybe she'd be relieved if I proposed we truncate our ride still further and head over to the station), but to give up now felt like a betrayal of the adventure we'd planned together, and of our excitement about each other. I wanted to be, in Ash's eyes, the sort of girl who would come up with a hare-brained idea like cycling to and from Brighton on our first date, and then stick to the plan and make it happen, rather than admitting that perhaps it had been a little over-ambitious; perhaps we hadn't really been serious about it after all; perhaps we weren't really the people we had hoped. The spell would be broken if we gave in now. What would we talk about on the train on the way home, under the unfriendly fluorescent lights, shifting our limbs about to keep ourselves from falling asleep?

So we got back on the road, and headed back up the hill, reluctantly at first, with heavy legs and heads – and then ecstatically, as our lungs sucked in long cool draughts of sea air, and it washed over our tired skin, and ran through our hair, and we were magically revived, and settled into the steady push-push-push rhythm of climbing, nothing to be heard but our breath, and the slight grinding of my over-tightened chain. As we neared the top of the hill, the streetlights came to an end, and nothing lay ahead of us but a vast darkness, stretching out across the South Downs and Sussex, hiding within it a thousand solemn and somnolent villages, fields full of slumbering livestock, and hedgerows bustling with their nocturnal populations of rodents and mustelids, whose eyes reflect the light of an approaching cyclist with a glimmer of accusation as they scuttle propri-etorially across the road. We paused for a minute or two on the brow of Ditchling Beacon. She photographed her bike propped up against the fence and I savoured the realisation that I was about to descend a hill I'd only ever climbed – and wondered if this was the moment I should kiss her. And then we got back on our bikes, as yet unkissing and unkissed, and pushed off into the great darkness that lay ahead of us.

'Cheer up, girls!' shouted a passing man.

We glared at him over our empty pint glasses, somewhere between hostility and disbelief.

'You both look really miserable!' he added, with a slight note of self-righteousness, as if he was only trying to help. We continued to glare wordlessly at him, and he eventually turned, shook his head, and disappeared around the corner towards King's Cross.

'There's something I've got to tell you,' said Ash. 'The day after I saw you . . . I . . . something happened between me and Alex.'

She stopped there, and after a few seconds I realised it was my turn to say something.

'I'm not surprised,' I told her, in a voice that sounded shockingly like my own, given that my throat and jaw were suddenly clenched so tight I thought I might stop breathing. And I wasn't surprised, although it hadn't occurred to me until she said it that this might happen. 'OK then, I'd better get going.' I didn't want her to tell me anything else.

And I stood up, and walked past her, over to the ivy-covered wall across the street where my bike leaned against hers in the twilight, bent down to open my lock, stood up, flicked it round my waist, caught the loose end in my left hand, closed the padlock on my right hip, let the key ping back against my wrist on its elastic, concentrating on these familiar movements as if my life and composure depended on it, which at least one of them did. Ash stood next to me, watching me, waiting until she could reach her bike, maybe also waiting for me to say something.

'How about a hug?' she said, as I turned to face her.

'Not this time,' I replied, and swung my right leg over the bike, and clipped in, and turned to face her one last time, vaguely aware that her face was taut with concern. 'Good luck,' I said, gruffly, and rode off without looking behind me.

Thank goodness for Pentonville Road. I have probably never ridden up it faster than I did that evening, filling my lungs with filthy London air and my leg muscles with lactic acid, desperately straining to displace grief with pain, to crowd out the sobs that would otherwise engulf me. I don't think I ever cried over our break-up. I just kept on riding.

13

Soho seems to capture better than anywhere else the sense of a city awakening. The air is still and fresh, not yet stirred up by all the hordes of people who will suck it in and out and swirl it about themselves as the day heats up. The streets are not empty, but they somehow feel it – everyone is busy; nobody loiters. Commuters stride along the well-trodden paths that lead them directly from tube station to office, no reason to hesitate or deviate or even look about them. (Many of Soho's offices and studios don't open till 10 a.m., so a lot of its workforce will be still in bed at this point.) Street cleaners plod behind their wagons. Dustbin lorries growl along the gutters, hazard lights flashing, and every now and again shatter the silence, the eardrums of passers-by, and a thousand empty bottles as they pour from two upended dustbins into the lorry's open mouth, with an almighty roar. There's an elusive (and possibly illusory) sense of order that I know will evaporate as the sun comes out, the streets heat up and the day takes hold. Soho in the mornings is like a pristine, immaculate double bed, all hospital corners and starched white sheets, the chambermaids flicking the last motes of dust from the room as they bow out, leaving it to the mercies of whoever's booked it for the weekend. And within a couple of hours all their work is undone: the sheets are crumpled and stained, the pillows flung every which way, and the bed reeks with filthy humanity – much as Soho does after its nightly excesses.

My day begins as the chambermaids disperse – the street sweepers hurry the last few cigarette butts into their pans; the road cleaners fussily rinse away the waves of piss and puke that wash up on Soho's pavements overnight and stagnate like rockpools in its alleys. On Old Compton Street, the cafes are already lined with ranks of sturdily handsome men in their forties, with close-cropped hair and manicured beards, ogling passing twinks over the first latte of the day. I am all the more keenly aware of their gaze because it does not fall on me – in this economy of attention, with its currency of winks and nods and raised eyebrows and backward glances, I am bankrupt and invisible, as is the short-haired barista with the Grecian profile. She and I exchange our own glances, though I have never yet engaged her in conversation, or managed to make her smile. So I direct my gaze outward, casting it over the oblivious commuters: the blond girl on the green Giant road bike, slightly hunched as it's too small for her; the short, chic woman who works for one of the fashion magazines headquartered at 33 Broadwick Street, and whose long hair is always styled elaborately, and differently from the day before; the pretty dark-eyed girl with the nose-ring, striding off towards the Crossrail site on Soho Square in her overalls and steel-toe-capped boots; the man with Michelangelo's David tattooed on his left calf, who always locks his bike up next to mine. I know the last few metres of their journey to work as well as they do themselves, though where they've come from remains a mystery. I once found myself following the green road bike into Soho via Covent Garden and Shaftesbury, and felt strangely guilty, as if I were spying on her. But there must be just as many people who notice me, day after day after day – for whom I am 'the girl on Stockwell Road', 'the woman on the yellow bike', or 'the courier in the red cycling cap'.

To some people I am an intrinsic feature of Soho's wild-life, like the colourful tramps, the craggy, loud-mouthed market traders on Broadwick Street, the strutting boys in white singlets who take over Old Compton Street in the early evening. There are characters I noticed again and again during my first few weeks on the road, eventually realising that our repeated encounters were not mere coincidence – they were at home in these streets, sometimes literally. There was the curious gentleman I often saw riding his bike around Fitzrovia, wearing a broad-brimmed hat that for some rea-son had grey synthetic fur sprouting out of its crown, and with massive pumped-up arms and shoulders that suggested he must spend much of his life lifting weights in the gym. I sometimes tried to make up stories about what he might be up to – perhaps he rode around flashing his enormous biceps as a rolling advertisement for the gym he frequented, in return for free membership. Perhaps he just lived locally and ran a lot of daily errands. Or perhaps, like the gym bunnies down on Old Compton Street, he was cruising for talent. At any rate, he didn't seem interested in even making eye contact with me, let alone making friends.

And there was the man with the shopping trolleys. He was tall and upright, with sturdy boots and a long coat, grey hair and a well-cropped beard, and the first time I saw him manoeuvring four trolleys full of bags along Mortimer Street (laboriously parking two a few yards up the road while he went back for the other two), I assumed that he must work for one of the fashion companies in that area, and be moving garments over to their studio for a photo shoot or a sample sale. But I saw him again and again, and eventually real-ised that he just spent his days endlessly moving his worldly goods around Soho and Fitzrovia.

One day, a couple of years into my courier career, I sud-denly remembered that I hadn't seen him for months. I wondered sadly what might have become of him, aware that I'd almost certainly never know. Maybe he had somehow managed to get himself off the streets, and into a halfway house or a job, or he'd died, or gone to prison. Then, not long after he'd popped into my head, I saw him again, downsized to one shopping trolley, pushing it slowly down the cycle lane on Bury Place. I'll never know where he went, but I was pleased to see him again, and I doubt I was the only one who noticed he'd gone.

For weeks after Ash and I broke up, I dreaded running into her in the street. While we were together, a chance sight-ing of her red bike and orange jacket, or the deerstalker hat she wore in cold weather, would make my heart leap with excitement, and I'd swing the bike round and give chase, or race ahead and park my bike where I knew she was head-ing to lock hers up, or turn around and just happen to be walking down the street towards her, smirking helplessly as I waited for her to notice me. But now the leap of my heart was closely followed by the crashing remembrance of what had happened. If I didn't see her, I could sometimes manage to forget for a few hours. If I did, then I'd spend the rest of the day turning it over and over in my head, and then even not seeing her was torture because I'd then wonder where she was, what she was doing and with whom, and what she must be thinking, and planning and looking forward to, without me.

When I did catch a glimpse of her, I'd immediately refocus my eyes, gazing intently at the road ahead, or looking in the opposite direction, or letting my face settle into the thousand-yard stare common to couriers, which results from the heavy concentration needed to take in every possible obstacle in the immediate vicinity, the middle distance, and the very edges of the rider's peripheral vision. She wouldn't be fooled by my pretending not to see her, but in my moments of panic on spotting her, I couldn't think of anything else to do. Once, I came round a corner and found myself staring her straight in the face, and we nodded awkwardly, each with a little tightening of the mouth that was nowhere near a smile, and I wondered what she was thinking, whether she was embarrassed to see me, or sad, or worried about me, or irritated by the intrusion of what she had now left behind her.

After a week or so, I realised I was getting the same treatment from Lukasz. It took three or four encounters before I really noticed he was blanking me, having initially assumed that he either hadn't seen me, or hadn't had the spare attention to be able to acknowledge me. After all, couriers know better than anyone that sometimes the road is just too complicated to be able to take your eyes off it for even a second. Often, I'll be able to greet a colleague with only the tiniest twitch of my chin, even though I'm well aware they're passing me, because I don't dare take my eyes off the gaggle of indecisive pedestrians a little way up the road, or divert my attention from the wobbly commuter cyclist who I suspect is about to turn right without signalling, and the unidentified vehicle behind me whose uneven revs suggest that the driver might be thinking about overtaking.

But, passing just a couple of feet from him on our respective ways east and west along Theobalds one afternoon, I was forced to conclude that he was ignoring me. He was a habitual frowner, exuding contempt at all who crossed his path, but I was used to his face lighting up as he spotted me, or at the very least to the conspiratorial wink or eyebrow twitch that told me the frown was for everyone else, but not for me. At first I concluded that he had taken umbrage over my continually postponing our pub crawl – our last text on the matter had been my explanation that I had just been dumped, and could we possibly not do it this week after all? 'Dumped YOU?' had been his gratifying response, and I'd thought little more of it, wrapped up in my exhaustion, and grief, and the grey autumnal clouds that had settled over London as I dismally began my second year on the road.

Mysteriously, and mercifully, my sadness over the break-up seemed diffuse and somehow fractured, seeping persistently through my awareness like a bad smell, rather than hitting me like a thunderbolt as had happened with previous girlfriends. Maybe it was the ever reliable courier exhaustion, which dims your senses and bossily elbows aside any more sophisticated sensations. I would occasionally torture myself with reminders that this sadness was one-sided, that everything I still felt for her she was now feeling for someone else, knowing that sooner or later I'd tire of the pain and move on to apathy, or even to being happy for them. But mostly I just felt tired and grey, unable to care much about whether I had offended Lukasz, uninterested in seeing any of my friends, on or off the circuit. I even avoided Fullcity for a while, knowing that Lawrence's bubbliness would only grate on my nerves, and that I'd be unable to muster the joy (real or feigned) at seeing him that he would inevitably display on seeing me.

My grief, which I was beginning to think I had avoided, hit me unexpectedly one afternoon on my way through Lincoln's Inn Fields, precisely at the moment when I turned left off Newman's Row onto the cobbled entrance to New Square. I don't know why that particular section of road would have brought Ash so strongly into my mind – as far as I could remember, we had never shared any moments, significant or otherwise, in Lincoln's Inn Fields. Instead, she had been subtly injected into my consciousness by some forgotten thing I'd seen or heard a few minutes previously, and the resulting train of thought had led me, circuitously and quite unexpectedly, to the crashing realisation, 'I've lost *Ash*!'

I had, until then, been absorbed only with the immediate indignity (and incidental agony) of being dumped, and then swiftly replaced. But now an unexpected tide of memories poured through my head. Ash grinning at me in my untidy bedroom at the end of a rainy afternoon where all either of us could think about was being warm and dry and together. My pride as Ash sat at my parents' kitchen table with a cat on her lap, charming my mother over a bottle of red wine. Ash and I riding home drunk one summer's evening, stopping halfway up Camberwell Grove for a rest, trying to kiss, but repeatedly missing and collapsing into giggles instead. Ash lying on her kitchen sofa, with her head in my lap, fingers laced in mine, saying out of the blue, 'It's amazing that we met.' Our habit of taking a bottle of wine to see us through the excruciatingly crowded Friday-night train journey when we went to visit my parents – and fellow passengers' amusement the time she picked up a £1 box of real wine glasses in one of the Tottenham Court Road furniture shops on her way to Euston. Ash fixing bikes at the climbing centre, in her element, smears of grease all over her bare arms and legs. How sometimes, when she was in a bad mood, she would kiss me quite suddenly, as if to assure me that it had nothing to do with me. I remembered how she hated getting up in the mornings, so I always had to make the breakfast and sandwiches, even when we stayed at hers, and how I secretly didn't mind, because I loved looking at her sleeping face with its slight frown, her straight nose and her wry mouth, and pink creases from the pillow, which were the only flaws I ever saw on her skin.

'I've lost *Ash*,' was all I could think, as I rode past the Lincoln's Inn security guards, who didn't care, and the handsome clerks, who didn't care, and the bare trees above the square, who had seen it all before, out onto Chancery Lane and up onto Holborn, further and further into a world that no longer contained her.

Eventually, I stopped seeing Ash around London, and a few months later, she emailed to tell me that she had accepted a job as a mountain-bike guide in Spain. By then I had reached the third or fourth stage of post-break-up grief (promiscuity), and was indulging womankind's new-found interest in me, since during the time I'd been dating Ash, I'd metamorphosed from a dowdy student into a sharp, confident and fairly muscular cycling machine. As I started to notice women again, I also noticed that they were noticing me, much more than they ever had done before. I contracted various overlapping affairs that winter: a recent Cambridge graduate who gave me lengthy post-coital seminars on Wittgenstein; a sound engineer who spent half her time in New York and would text me about the cycle couriers she could see riding through Times Square as I sat watching the snow fall in Mayfair; a veteran courier who was as unassuming as a sparrow until she had a bike between her legs, whereupon she became a falcon, soaring through the streets, utterly fearless, the only person I had ever seen who could ride through a busy junction at top speed, judging the gaps between moving cars so minutely that it was as if the traffic were pausing and parting to let her through.

I also realised that I'd become friends with Andy, having very belatedly got over my fears that he was going to sack me at any moment. I was not, after all, I discovered, the slowest courier on the fleet.

'Ah, one-four Emily – you've been our highest earner three days in a row!' he announced one afternoon, as I stepped into the control room down in Vauxhall to drop off an over-night job that was going up to Manchester. 'You even made more than some of the motorbikes yesterday.'

This surprised me, since several times a day I'd run into some fellow courier or other, and we'd say, 'How's it going? Busy?', and he'd complain about how he'd only done twenty-two jobs so far, and it wasn't a patch on the good old days. For me, twenty-two jobs was a pretty good day, so I had long assumed that I must be one of the slow ones, and wondered how these guys were managing to fit such a large amount of work into the same amount of time, and worried that the controllers were just giving me fewer jobs because I was a girl or something. Now I realised that everyone else was just bluffing about the amount of work they were doing.

Andy was reputed to be fond of female couriers, and a lot of his former favourites, about whom he occasionally reminisced when I passed through the control room, had been women. But his penchant was more precise than this, I realised, as I listened to what was evidently the tail end of some hapless girl's courier career over the radio one afternoon (she'd lasted just under a week, and apparently, made mistakes on almost every job, to Andy's mounting displeasure). He was a man who not only took great pride in doing his job well, but who enjoyed as much as I did the sense of the circuit being a well-tuned machine, with so many parts that something was almost bound to go wrong but, just occasionally, didn't. Couriers tended to come and go very quickly – after only a year I was already one of the most senior members of the fleet – but there were moments when Andy would find himself working with ten or so reasonably reliable riders, and his satisfaction was like that of a bike mechanic who gets her hands on a perfectly machined groupset, and knows that all she needs to do is index it accurately, making sure everything's in the right place at the right time, and let it get on with the job. He liked people who knew what they were doing, and got on with it.

'The thing I always say about a good courier' (he always said) 'is that you can't tell by their voice what the weather's doing.' Which was not to say he preferred us to be cheerful. He seemed to be fond of Lukasz simply because he was *always* miserable.

''E's like a shark,' he said once. 'You almost feel that, if 'e gives you a smile, that's when 'e gets really dangerous. And you know, working with some of these guys', he glanced furtively towards the far end of the control room, where the van controllers, with their beer bellies and football shirts were slumped in front of their screens, 'I'd be grumpy too.'

Lukasz had stopped talking to him too, a fact that made me feel simultaneously slightly better about the situation, and slightly worse. Neither Andy nor I could work out why he had suddenly taken against us, though he had his suspicions.

'I reckon it'll be a bit too much of this,' he speculated, miming someone toking on a spliff. 'I've seen it 'appen. Shame though.'

I missed Lukasz. He certainly wasn't the only misery-guts on circuit, but he was by far the most entertaining, and after the wit and fluency of his complaints, the predictable gripes of Fullcity's regulars seemed disappointingly pedestrian. I still regularly dropped in to trade hugs with Lawrence and insults with Arsen, but occasionally, if there was a big crowd outside, I'd keep cycling, knowing that all I'd be listening to would be endlessly rehashed accounts of unreasonable drivers and unreliable bicycles, and having to deal with quite enough of that already.

14

'Bugger. Bugger. Bugger.'

I never used my back brake and it wasn't even connected – but I had foolishly (well, lazily) failed to remove the calliper, and when some forgotten impact knocked it out of place, I didn't notice for quite some time that it had begun to rub against the rim. By the time I'd spotted it and straightened it, it was already too late, and a few hours later, as I was riding through the busy tunnel that runs under the elevated section of Westway, on my way to deliver a package to the fire station on the Harrow Road from a law firm in Soho, fast traffic roaring all around me and above me too, I suddenly felt something change in my back wheel – I couldn't even tell what – and got off the bike, cursing, thinking I might have a puncture, only to see the tyre bulging unnaturally like a snake who's swallowed a piglet. As I watched, there was a silvery *ping* as the rim ruptured, and a split second later, the tyre exploded with a massive echoing **boooooooomm**, amplified and distorted by the tunnel, and so loud that my ears rang for several minutes afterwards. A few cars swerved. They must have thought a bomb had gone off.

'Bugger,' I said again, infuriated by the sudden descent from swiftness to helplessness, and hoisted the bike up onto my shoulder, hoping the cars would give me a wide berth until I was out of the tunnel.

'One-four, one-four?' I called, as soon as I was back in signal and a gap had appeared on the airwaves.

'One-four Emily – is that POB, rodge?'

'Uh, yes and no. I've got them both on board, but my rim's just blown out. I'm about two minutes from the Harrow Road drop, but I'm afraid I'm not going to be able to do the other one.'

Andy gave a hearty sigh, which managed to convey very clearly that his exasperation was entirely with the unreliability of bicycle wheels, and the vacillations of Fate that had brought this mishap into his life, and had nothing whatsoever to do with me.

'Roger-rodge, one-four, these things 'appen, I'm gonna send someone to get that off you.'

And a second later, I heard him calling one of the motorbikes, telling him to head over to the Harrow Road to pick up a package from one-four Emily, who's having mechanical problems.

I've told this little story to quite a few people since it happened – to my flatmate when I got in that evening, and to my father when I spoke to him at the weekend. A few days later, I ran into Andy in the control room and filled him in on the gory details that he'd missed over the radio. Every now and again, it'll come out as I sit on a street corner with other couriers, or in a pub with my cycling friends, swapping stories of our most irritating or hair-raising mechanical failures. After the initial dramatic explosion, I tell them how I phoned Lawrence, asked him if he had a spare back wheel I could borrow or buy, and whether he'd be willing to stay open long enough for me to get over there and pick it up (I was about as far from Fullcity as I could get within the scope of the normal courier circuit), and then spent the next hour wearily trudging across W1 and WC1, top tube wearing a groove in my shoulder because I couldn't even wheel the bike (the rim was so badly cracked that the wheel no longer went round). When I finally arrived at Fullcity, the day had ended and couriers were gathering outside the shop, drinking cans of Stella and Kronenbourg from the off-licence two doors down and revelling in the post-work glow. Light spilled out from the open door, through which I could see Lawrence and Liam, the latest addition to the workforce, putting the finishing touches to the day's repairs.

And I was absorbed into the friendly bosom of my people – people who knew exactly how infuriating it was to blow out a rim on the Harrow Road with two jobs on board, and who sympathised, and shared their own stories, and applauded when Lawrence finally presented me with my rehabilitated bike, once again a magic carpet that would transport me smoothly up the dark hill to my house.

But what I don't usually tell people is how this anecdote intersects with one of my other stories – one I also drag out from time to time, but in different conversations, with different friends. It's the best illustration of how rarely certain parts of my life coincide, and how surprising it is when they do.

A few minutes after my tyre had exploded, I plodded grumpily into the forecourt of the fire station, wondering if there'd be anyone around to sign for the package – because this was a semi-regular delivery, and half the time when I turned up, the place would be deserted, and I'd pace circuits of the building, wandering in and out of locker rooms and up and down staircases, calling, 'Hello-o?', and wondering whether I was technically trespassing and about to be told off.

But this time I was in luck. Two large gleaming fire engines were parked in the forecourt, doors and windows open, hoses protruding from every orifice, rumbling and snorting like sleeping elephants. A stocky man in his forties leapt down from the cab just as I approached, and when I proffered the envelope, with my standard line, 'Am I in the right place with this?', he glanced at the address, and told me to, 'Head round the front, and the lady there'll sign for it.'

I carried on round the side of the fire engine, my curiosity predictably piqued by the thought of a female firefighter. Since I became a courier my taste in women had changed – or just accelerated in a direction it was already going – and I was now less interested in curvy femmes with long eyelashes, and more and more taken with muscular tomboys who fixed their own bikes and went their own way. But such women were curiously hard to come by. A lot of the female couriers caught my eye at first, with their biceps and undercuts and piercings, but they would always mention a boyfriend within a couple of minutes of my starting a conversation. And many of the women I'd picked up online, in my post-break-up binges, loved it when I turned up outside their offices with my sweaty Lycra and bulging calves, but gave me little chance to enjoy the meeting of minds and muscles I was hoping for and have since found more reliably among rugby players than cyclists (indeed, cycling is a very straight sport).

Round at the front of the engine, a person, broad-shoul-dered and short-haired, in voluminous heat-proof trousers and a snug navy-blue T-shirt, was bending down, tidying up something on the ground. Could this be the lady he meant? I cleared my throat, and then watched with great interest as she straightened up, noticeably changing pace halfway, as my cycling shoes and bare shins caught her eye. She wasn't what I'd expected, I most certainly wasn't what she had expected, and it was far too late to hide our reaction to each other.

I could feel my lips tightening in an involuntary smile that was reflected perfectly by hers. We were delighted to see each other. Here was a young, glowing cycle courier, with fresh sweat visible along the lines of her triceps and shin-ing on her forearms as she held out the package. And here was a tall, handsome woman somewhere in her late forties, with a soft black crewcut and tanned skin that was smooth across her muscled arms and delicately crinkled around her eyes and on her hand as she reached towards me to tilt the envelope, so that she could read the address.

'Yep, that's me,' she said, nodding, with a knowing smirk, as if I were the only one to notice a secret she had been hiding in plain sight. Her hand dropped back to her side, and I instantly wanted to step closer to her, to bring myself back into her orbit.

I'm not normally so smooth when talking to women I find attractive, especially not when they're older, and taller, and better looking, and have evidently spent the last twenty years rescuing damsels from burning buildings. But her gaze was steady, and she looked me up and down with approval and a flicker of amusement. For once, the mutual attraction was so perfectly, tangibly, inescapably obvious that there was just no point entering into the usual pantomime of evasion and disavowal. So when I answered her, it was with a confident purr, quite unlike the usual staccato squeaks that usually emerge when I'm nervous or wrong-footed.

'Well, in that case, I'll need to get you to sign.' I held her gaze as I fished the Xda out of my pocket, then clicked through to the signature screen, and asked for her name. As I typed it in, she took half a step towards me, swivelled so that we were standing almost shoulder to shoulder, and watched my hand as I typed. It briefly crossed my mind that it was hypocritical of me to enjoy this so much – the men I deliver to will quite often stand over me to look at the Xda, or worse still, grab my hand in order to read its contents for themselves, as if they don't trust me to have got it right. I've got used to flinching, frowning and stepping back to maintain my personal space – but with this woman I was leaning towards her, doing all I could to get closer. Her scent drifted over me, clean and warm, not at all like the floral perfumes that reek from the city's receptionists, or the sweat that pours from its couriers, and thinking of this, I realised that she must also be able to feel the heat radiating out of my body.

'Do you, uh, want my rank as well?' she asked. I suspected she might be stalling as much as I was, aware that this was an encounter that would typically last less than a minute, and wanting to string it out as much as possible.

'I'd *love* to know your rank,' I drawled sultrily in response (wondering all along where I was getting this from, which corner of my psyche this persona had been hiding in and why this woman had suddenly brought it out of me), 'but no, I just need your signature.'

And I handed her the Xda, and she stepped back and signed with a flourish, and for just an instant, two of her fingertips pressed against my hand as she passed it back.

And then that was it. 'Thanks,' I said, and we grinned at each other for another moment or so. Nothing more to say, and we both knew, I think, that it would go no further than this. Later, when I described the encounter to my queer friends ('Oh, my God, it was like the start of two porn films at once! Sweaty cycle courier arrives with an *important package*, meets tall butch firefighter *wielding her mighty hose*.'), most of them asked, 'So did you get her number?', and seemed surprised that that hadn't even occurred to me. But I have never regretted leaving it as it was – it would have been very hard for any further contact to live up to that first breathless encounter. Had I got to know her any better, I might have discovered she had a wife and teenage children, that she read the *Daily Mail* and believed asylum seekers should all go home, that she was irreconcilably different from me, or simply very dull. We might have gone on a date or two, she might have taken me to a bar I didn't like, we might have drunk slightly too much to make up for the slow conversation. She might have patronised me; I might have irritated her. She might have expected me to be a princess once she got my clothes off – or she might have become one herself. We'd share the embarrassment of failing to live up to our first encounter, but we'd never acknowledge it. Fantasies aren't supposed to come true – and when they do, it's best not to push it.

My fantasy gave me a wink as I stepped past her, and turned to watch as I strode self-consciously back towards my bike, grabbed the top tube and swung it onto my shoulder with a flourish that was entirely for her benefit. And then I stepped back into the other story that was going on – waiting beside the Harrow Road for the motorbike to come and collect the remaining package, the long trek across town with the bike on my shoulder, the light and warmth of Fullcity, Lawrence's shout as he hugged me, chips, and a new back wheel. Few of the lads outside the shop were ever going to be trusted with the firefighter, though I retold the tale of the exploding wheel several times that evening, and listened to theirs in turn. And when I recounted the fire station episode in all its winking, smirking, sizzling detail, my listeners were rarely the sort of people who would be interested in something going wrong with my bike, even if it did involve an explosion in a tunnel. This is, in fact, possibly the first time I've told the two stories as they happened, interlaced, entwined, interlocked, just like the rest of London is, whether we're able to notice it or not.

A few months later, a similar encounter slipped me unexpectedly from one of London's worlds into another I hadn't known existed. I had just crashed my bike into the back of someone's car – partly her fault, since she had braked very suddenly as she spotted a parking space in St James's Square; and partly mine, because I really should have been paying more attention to the traffic, and not thinking about whether I might squeeze a sandwich break into my next run of jobs.

This time the damage was to my head rather than my bike – although, as a matter of fact, the rear windscreen of the car came off worse, and I slid down onto the tarmac of St James's Square in what looked like a shower of diamonds. I wasn't badly hurt, but no one takes any chances with a bump to the head, so someone called an ambulance, and the driver whose car I'd ridden into fussed maternally over me until it arrived. As we waited, I called Andy on the radio, explained that I was going to have to go to hospital, *but that I was completely fine*, and he wasn't to worry, but he should probably send someone else to pick up the job I was on my way to. Hours later, when I strolled into the office, after spending the afternoon snoozing in an A&E cubicle while a succession of medical students confirmed the existence of various imaginary bumps on various parts of my skull, I found the control team in a state of agitation and despair. Concerned that I was downplaying my injuries, and unable to contact me on the phone or over the radio, Andy had used the GPS tracker on my Xda to locate the hospital they'd taken me to, and spent the afternoon harassing their switchboard for information on my condition, being told repeatedly that I wasn't there. Had this gone on any longer, I suspect he'd have started phoning round the morgues. He and Mark and Paul and the van controllers virtually cheered when I walked in, and when I pulled my Xda out of my pocket and noticed for the first time that I had smashed the screen when my right hip hit the car, they assured me that they'd replace it, and I wouldn't be charged for the damage, and there was no need to worry.

But what few of them ever found out was that, the previous day, sitting there on the kerb between parked cars, cradling my ringing head and waiting (with practised patience) for the adrenalin to drain out of my system, a shadow fell over me and I looked up to see the spiritual sister of the butch firefighter – a tall, handsome paramedic, with short hair and long eyelashes, gazing speculatively down at me. I couldn't help but break into a grin, and had to quickly duck my head and pretend to be overcome by a new paroxysm of trembling to hide my amusement. 'Life,' I thought to myself, 'appears to be even stranger than fiction. And a lot less subtle.'

The paramedics immobilised me with a neck brace and strapped me to a stretcher. And as I lay there in the ambulance, unable to look at anything but the ceiling, feeling myself pressed in one direction and then another as the ambulance went round corners, and trying to guess where I was and which hospital they might be taking me to, I overheard them chatting about what they'd been up to that weekend, and found that I recognised the names of most of the bars.

'It's such a shame Ghetto's gone, isn't it?'

'Yeah. Well, it's moved to East London – you knew that, right? – but it's not the same. We're all just hanging out in Ku Bar now.'

I cleared my throat.

'Umm, is this a gay ambulance?' I called out, slightly nervously.

The paramedics were momentarily wrong-footed, and then both laughed. 'Yes – yes, it is,' said the man, who was keeping an eye on me while his colleague drove, and we all fell into hilarity for a minute, delighted by our new sense of camaraderie.

'Well, this is quite a find!' I said. I felt like Harry Potter, being swept up onto the Knight Bus and finding myself unexpectedly among friends.

'Oh, there's quite a few of us,' they told me, and started to gossip about various people in their industry who Were, or who Probably Were.

'Those guys on the bikes –' said the man.

'Oh, I know them!' I interrupted excitedly. 'I see them around Soho all the time. There's one who always parks up on Frith Street in the morning.' Pushbike paramedics had been introduced to central London at around the same time I started couriering, and proved a runaway – or rather a rideaway – success. I had read somewhere that they were so quick in response to 999 calls that most of the time they arrived on the scene while the call was still in progress.

'Yep, I think that must be Phillip. He's having a great time – spends half his day sitting in Soho Square, topping up his tan.'

'Is *he* gay?' shouted the woman from the front.

'Oh, I don't really know,' said the man, in a tone implying that he nonetheless had his suspicions, and possibly even concrete evidence. 'I think he likes the attention though. You know, like the policemen at Pride? You see them – they're lapping it up. I've heard that the mounted police – those guys on the horses? – they're all really keen to do Pride, and then you see them, sitting up there above the crowd, looking all sexy in their short-sleeved shirts and their aviator shades . . . Oh, yes, they're loving it.'

I giggled.

'What about your lot?' asked the driver.

'Ha – my lot!' I was enjoying this – the sensation of translating between two worlds of which I was equally a part. 'Less than you'd think. Or maybe more than you'd think, but it doesn't really get talked about much.'

I was surprised, I'll confess, not to come across more queer couriers. Somehow I'd imagined that we'd be a sub-culture unto ourselves, yet one more counter-cultural group among all the squatters and vegans and ravers. But for a long time the only other gay courier I knew was Ash. The girls who looked the most promising were all straight, and if there were any gay men on circuit, they kept it to them-selves. It wasn't till I'd been around for well over a year that I started coming across people – and it was never the ones you expected. The first one I met was Maria, a slightly surly Brazilian girl whom I'd passed many times on the bike with-out ever getting more than a curt nod. Naturally, I assumed this was because I was beneath her, because she didn't talk to other couriers until they'd survived at least two winters, because I was wearing the wrong sort of jacket, or riding the wrong sort of bike – or just because I was a bit scruffy, because she herself was immaculate, always dressed head to toe in black, or in well-fitted navy-blue waterproofs, riding a modified Charge bike that looked as if she spent most of her evenings cleaning it.

I finally met her outside a loading bay on London Wall, stepping through a doorway in the huge metal shutter that covered the entrance just as I was locking up my bike. She approached me without a smile, and without preamble, said, 'My bike was stolen. Have you seen it?'

'Oh, no!' I replied, noticing how wholesome she looked

with her fresh pink skin and slightly plump cheeks, and wondering whether she was younger than I'd assumed. 'What happened?'

'It was in Covent Garden, at the weekend,' she drawled, and I caught a flash of anxiety in her eyes as they met mine. 'Oh my goodness, she's shy,' I thought, suddenly seeing her gruffness for what it was – the closest she could get to a show of confidence – and realising that her forcefulness might just be a way of taking control of conversations so that she didn't have to try to understand the mumbled and accented English of the other couriers.

'I was in a shop, with my girlfriend, on Long Acre' (I recognised the microscopic hesitation as she mentioned her girlfriend, the almost imperceptible gauging of the other person's reaction, as she studiously continued in exactly the same tone of voice) 'and when we came out it was gone. I locked it up, but they cut through my D-lock.'

There wasn't much I could do, beyond wishing death on all bike thieves, and promising to keep an eye out – though she probably knew as well as me that there were hundreds of Charge bikes on the road in London, and it was very unlikely that hers would ever turn up again.

'Have you had a look on Brick Lane?' I asked. Brick Lane was where everyone went to flog the bikes they'd stolen during the week, and if your bike was stolen it was customary to spend a few hours there the following Sunday, inspecting what was on offer, and either buying back your own bike, or summoning the police to sort things out with the person selling it.

'Yes, we went there on Sunday. Didn't find nothing. OK, I

got to go.' She held out an arm, and bumped shoulders with me in an awkward approximation of a hug. Where other couriers occasionally reeked of stale sweat and bad breath, she smelt of nothing but soap powder.

'See you!' I said brightly, hoping to provoke a smile in response, as if that would somehow seal our friendship, but all I got in return was a mournful nod, as she swung a leg over what was evidently a borrowed mountain bike, and pedalled off towards Moorgate.

Maria and I slowly became friends over the next couple of years, and once she found out I was gay too, she would sometimes flirt clumsily with me in between girlfriends. And, over time, I found out about others, most of them long gone, only vaguely remembered by people who'd crossed paths with them briefly in the overlap between one career beginning and the other ending – and surely many more had been forgotten entirely, or never even noticed. After all, being gay has always had to be something fairly private. Until about a decade ago, you didn't talk about it for fear of punishment. Now you don't talk about it because half the time when you do, someone will point out that homophobia doesn't exist any more, and no one cares about your sexuality, so why make such a fuss about it?

Over the years, I'd learned mostly to keep it to myself, sometimes slightly intoxicated by the secrecy of it all – the sense of speaking a language few other people understood, of being able to see things that were invisible to most ordinary passers-by, of the knowing glances and nods I'd occasionally exchange with other dykes as we passed each other in the street, of the ongoing, never-consummated, are-you-aren't-you tension with the barista on Old Compton Street. A later courier girlfriend remarked that she suddenly got a lot more flirtation from receptionists when she started carrying her keys on a rainbow lanyard she'd picked up at Pride, as though all of this had been lying dormant, and just needed to be unlocked. I remembered when I'd been a receptionist myself, and no one had suspected. I'd always been rather sceptical of the fantastical queer urban land-scapes painted by writers like Edmund White and Alan Hollinghurst, with their language of lingering glances and loaded backward looks, furtive impromptu orgies in public lavatories and hook-ups with everyone from policemen to the doctor at the STI clinic. But while no receptionist has ever invited me into the stationery cupboard, I very gradu-ally began to capture a comparable sense of there being a lot more simmering under the surface than most people would ever suspect, visible, audible and tangible if you knew what you were looking for, but non-existent if you didn't.

As well as the people I ran into (sometimes literally, as with the brown-eyed van driver who cut me up on Buckingham Palace Road, and managed, to my amusement and infuria-tion, to charm her way out of it, speeding off with a wink once she'd won me over), many of the coordinates on my personal map of the city were the sites of dates, assignations and arguments, of chance meetings and first kisses and last goodbyes. Although gay women don't share the historic communal landmarks of cruising, like Clapham Common and the Broadwick Street public toilets (which the courier boys would sometimes visit with exaggerated reluctance), we still have the South Bank, where I have piled up so many memories over the years that strolling from the National Theatre along to the London Eye is like jostling through a crowd of ex-girlfriends and lovers.

I joked, when I first moved down to London from my small university town, that I was Dyke Whittington, expecting to find streets paved with lesbians. But rather than paving the streets, they often appeared to be hiding in the woodwork, camouflaged expertly against the backdrop of normal life, and it took a trained eye to be able to spot them. A trained eye, that is, and personal contacts.

Because one of the great unsung advantages of being gay is the additional facet of social mobility it gives you. There are times when the gay scene seems fairly pointless, populated with people with whom you have little in common beyond the broad brushstrokes of your sexuality – but the flipside of this is that, like cycling, it can be a way of slicing through a cross-section of society, connecting people across social and generational boundaries that ordinarily ensure they'd never meet. Through cycling, I've ended up with a large number of straight white male friends in their forties and fifties – people with whom I'd otherwise have almost no meaningful encounters. And through my gay circles, I find I have all sorts of unexpected connections to the bankers and lawyers and receptionists and waitresses and actors and dancers and other people I come across in the (extra)ordinary course of my life. It's now rare for me to find another gay Londoner with whom I don't have at least one friend in common, and quite often at parties there'll be a minor explosion of mirth as I get to know a friend of a friend and discover we share an ex-girlfriend, or are similarly connected by an improbable and mostly unmentionable chain of liaisons. We're one of the city's unseen networks – much like cycle couriers, in fact.

The morning after my ride in the gay ambulance, I overheard a one-sided conversation with one of the motorbikes over the radio – 'Yeah, she's fine. No long-term damage, and she's back on the bike today' – and I smiled to myself, riding through the leaves and sunlight of the Mall towards Trafalgar Square, comforted by the concern of people whose faces I might never even have seen, even though they would only ever know half the story.

15

The woman in St James's Square had been kind, much more concerned about the state of my head than about who was going to pay for her shattered windscreen. I already knew that this was unusual, but the day I realised how helplessly vulnerable and visible I am to drivers bearing a grudge was one of the most frightening of my career; a loss of innocence I have never quite recovered from.

It was three days, actually – a series of events connected only by their coincidence. On Tuesday, I was overtaken by a cab going south on Charlotte Street; a fairly pointless manoeuvre on his part, because there were two cyclists and a van approaching in the opposite direction, and the street was too choked with parked cars for two vehicles to be able to pass easily, so the moment he'd passed me he had to swing back in to the left, very nearly pinning me against one of the parked cars in the process. I acknowledged this piece of idiocy with a swift, open-palmed slap on the flank of his car, mainly (I would respond if questioned) to let him know I was there, since perhaps he'd failed to check his mirrors when he turned left – but also as an efficient and harmless means of expressing my displeasure. The problem is, for a lot of drivers, a perceived attack on their vehicle might as well be an assault on their person. Forgetting all about whatever headway he was making, the driver braked sharply, leaned back in his seat (I was roughly level with the rear passenger window) and launched into a torrent of invective so fluent and so shockingly obscene that it seemed as if all the anger he had ever felt against cyclists, road restrictions and other people in general was pouring out of him in one long helpless gush. The young man's two passengers sat motionless and silent in the back seat, making eye contact with no one; not sure what to do.

I'd been on the road a couple of years now, and was at the stage of my road-rage policy where I carried a camera, easily accessible in a front pocket, partly so that I could record drivers' misdemeanours, but mainly so that I could intimidate them into calming down and pushing off. There wasn't a great deal of room between the cab and the parked cars, but I managed to wrestle myself and the bicycle round to the front, fished the camera out of my pocket, and started taking pictures. The cabbie was still roaring abuse – I'm amazed he was able to keep it up for so long; the only words I remember were 'stupid fucking bitch, don't touch my car', though admittedly, these were repeated several times, in several permutations. By now passers-by had begun to notice what was going on, and several had stopped to gawk or were hovering on the fringes, wondering whether to intervene.

'You OK?' said a voice at my shoulder. I half turned to look, and found that it was the man with the enormous muscles and the fluffy hat. But now was no time for pleasantries. 'That's right, good,' he encouraged me. 'Make sure you get a picture of his number plate.'

The driver seemed even more incensed; his shouts rose a key or so, and he rolled the car slowly forward so that it bumped into my bicycle and legs. I staggered back slightly, and the car stopped. The man with the muscles put a reassuring hand on my shoulder blade. The driver, seeing that we weren't moving, slammed his vehicle into reverse, executed a swift and jerky three-point turn and accelerated off up the street. Just before he turned left onto Howland Street, he stopped the car, opened the door and half got out.

'Take this too!' he shouted, sticking his middle finger up at me. And then he was gone.

I don't remember what was said after that, or how the crowds dispersed. Certainly, I was back on my bike within a minute or two, carrying on down Charlotte Street and into Soho as if nothing had happened. And, I suppose, nothing *had* really happened. I knew that if I went to the police with this, or told a non-cycling friend, they'd listen sympathetically for a while, and then chime in with, 'Yes, but – he didn't actually do anything to you or your bike, did he?' Well, no, he didn't. At least nothing that could be photographed and presented as evidence. I was essentially unharmed, and I reminded myself of this rather sternly as I went about my business over the next few hours, the waves of shock and shaking gradually dying down as the tide of fear went out. There's very little point dwelling on the aftermath of an incident like this – unless it's possible to learn something from what happened – and doing so will merely pollute your concentration, poison your mind against other road users, upset your mood for the rest of the day and add to the victim complex you worry you might be developing. I resolutely put it behind me, got on with my day.

The following afternoon, just under twenty-four hours later, I had just delivered something to the Swiss Embassy in Marylebone, and was going through the well-oiled routine of unlocking my bike, adjusting my bag, and finishing off the docket on my Xda, when an unfamiliar voice said, 'Oh – hello!'

I looked up, and a tall, dark, slightly familiar young man was standing next to me, looking at me like a long-lost friend. I wasn't sure who he was, but it seemed likely that I knew him from some post room or other, and just couldn't recognise him out of context.

'It's me!' he exclaimed. 'In the car, yesterday. On Charlotte Street.' It was him, the cabbie, and I was as wrong-footed by his apparent friendliness as I was by his unexpected re-intrusion into my life, less than a day after he had sworn at me, terrified me, and driven his car into me.

'Oh! I've reported you to the police,' I bluffed, since I was still thinking about doing so, unsure of how seriously they'd take it.

'So have I,' he said, in a tone that suggested something done in the heat of the moment, and now affably regretted, forgiveness almost a certainty. 'And my two passengers – they were my witnesses. When you took your camera out, I thought you was pulling a gun. We all thought you were gonna pull a gun on us.'

'In London?' I asked, incredulously.

'You never know these days,' he responded, with a world-weary air of having seen things he'd rather not.

I didn't know quite what to say. I rarely do, until at least twenty minutes after I've lost the argument.

'Look, you need to be more careful,' I told him, trying to sound reasonable and calm, although for some reason my voice was shaking and my whole body trembling. 'You very nearly knocked me off when you overtook me like that. Where else was I supposed to go?'

'You need to be more careful,' he retorted calmly. 'You was right out in the middle of the road. How can I get past you? I ride a bike myself – I ride around here on my days off. You've got to keep in close to the kerb. It's not safe riding out there in the road. You need to learn to ride that thing properly.'

Five minutes after he'd walked off, I had the whole argument laid out in my head: how he was wrong, according to the Highway Code and the official training I've had; that cyclists are allowed – indeed, advised – to ride in the centre of the lane, for their own safety; how, in any case, Charlotte Street is so cluttered up with parked cars and slowly moving traffic that there isn't room to overtake a cyclist safely, nor even much point in doing so, since you'll immediately be held up by other traffic or at one of the numerous junctions and crossings, and she'll just sail straight past you again.

But in the heat of the moment, the best I could manage was a squeaked and garbled fragment of the above, which made no impression on him whatsoever. He lectured me a little further on my unsafe cycling, told me to take care, and then strode off, his point made.

I stood there and trembled for a while, and then the trembling began to concentrate itself in my jaw and behind my eyes, and I knew I was going to cry, something I once foolishly and futilely vowed I'd never do at work. So I did something else I thought I'd never resort to, and phoned my mother.

Luckily, she picked up, and even more luckily, she was in the mood to be comforting – just as well, since I was almost hyperventilating with fear and shock – and listened to what had happened, and made all the right noises, and expressed her outrage at 'the way people will behave when they're safely in their metal boxes'. And yes, that was part of the problem. I suspected that the reason the driver had been able to greet me so jovially was that he hadn't felt at all threatened or afraid during our encounter the previous afternoon, and nor had he been haunted by it for the rest of the day. So when we ran into each other again, his demeanour was rueful but unruffled, bearing no grudges, accepting that we'd both overreacted a bit in the heat of the moment, but no harm done, eh?

But after I'd calmed down and hung up and got myself back on the road, I realised that there was more to it than that. It wasn't just my residual fear, or my frustration at the driver's having verbally got the better of me in our subsequent encounter. It was that he had, however accidentally or inadvertently, found me again within twenty-four hours. Somehow, it had never occurred to me that that might happen. I had assumed, without ever bothering to think about it, that all my run-ins with drivers and pedestrians, angry or amicable, were essentially disposable, that they'd forget me within minutes (despite the fact that I was sometimes haunted by them for days, or even months), and that we'd never see each other again once our ways parted. Now I knew that wasn't true, the sunny summer day seemed to take on a dark and sinister edge, as though malevolent eyes were watching me from every corner.

It took me a while to realise that the driver had also been bluffing about taking it to the police. (Of course he was – why would his passengers have broken their journey to spend hours giving a statement about how they'd thought a cyclist was pulling a gun (if they ever really did), when it was apparent within a couple of seconds she was actually wielding a camera. And would they really have taken his side after hearing him hurl abuse at me for so long without being sure what I'd done to deserve it?) So I stopped at the Bishopsgate police station on my way home, fighting back tears as I explained to the officer on the front desk what had happened, and how I was afraid that I would now be prosecuted for an incident in which I'd thought I was the victim. He tactfully ignored my sniffling, and gave me some forms to fill in, and I cycled home by the back route, feeling glad that I was due to escape to Wales the following week, and wishing it were sooner.

The following day, I was cut up in a very similar way where Wigmore Street joins Cavendish Square – a van driver was desperate to overtake me so as to get through the lights before they changed, but then immediately had to swerve in front of me to avoid another vehicle. Again, almost automatically, I delivered a firm smack to the side of his vehicle as it sped past (he was so close that I barely had to extend my arm). A second later, he was stationary, mired in the slow-moving traffic that collects at the top of Cavendish Square where Wigmore Street, Harley Street and the western edge of the square all feed into it, and as I overtook his van, he leaned a long way out of his window, snarling something incomprehensible and brandishing a large wooden club that looked as if it might once have been the leg of a table.

I was getting more and more used to this. I swung round to the front of his van, got off my bike, and laid it down carefully on the road. Looking him in the eye, I took my camera out of my pocket, calmly photographed the front of the van and the number plate, then stepped round to his window and photographed him (the wooden club was no longer in evidence). He wasn't snarling any more. In fact, he didn't seem to know what to say. Stuck in a traffic jam, with my bike on the road in front of him, there was nowhere he could go, unless he opened the door and climbed out of the van.

'Are you going to show me that piece of wood again?' I asked, camera at the ready.

He grunted 'no', and then the traffic around us gave a slight lurch as the lights changed ahead and the queue began to press forward. I put the camera away, picked up my bike, and sprinted off along Cavendish Place, across Regent Street and into Fitzrovia, desperately racing towards the nearest police station as if my life depended on it, which at the time I felt it well might. The calm I'd managed to keep during the minute or so I'd spent with the van driver had dissolved into fear and panic worse than I'd ever felt, and my whole body was shaking so badly I had to grip the bars for dear life to keep the bike straight. After a brief, breathless exchange over the radio, to let them know roughly what had happened, and that I needed to go off the plot for a while, I pulled up at the police station on Whitfield Street, ignored the couriers sitting in the park opposite, and managed to explain to the duty sergeant that I had an incident to report, and about half of what had happened, before breaking down into uncontrollable sobbing, punctuated with intermittent apologies. The duty sergeant summoned a female colleague, who came out from behind the screen and sat next to me for ten minutes or so, handing me tissues and listening to the fragments of the story that I was able to get out between my bouts of crying. She sympathised expertly with how other people's anger and aggression can affect you sometimes, no matter how you try not to let it, and I realised – of course! – that she must be dealing constantly with exactly the same problems, with the embarrassment of reacting differently to male colleagues (who in my experience are usually more likely to punch a wall than burst into tears), and with the occasional days where it inexplicably all gets too much, and suddenly you feel afraid of the job you normally love.

Whitfield Street is only a transport police station, so I was directed over to the Holborn station once I'd stopped crying. The road didn't feel like home any more. I felt hideously exposed during the five-minute ride, not knowing who might be watching me, or from where, or what their intentions might be, and wanting to abandon my (bright yellow; very conspicuous) bicycle and slink along the pavement, flattening myself against the shopfronts like a cat to avoid being noticed. I couldn't forget about the man in the van, with his thick wiry grey hair, chunky fingers and face distorted by anger and then confusion, wondering where he was now, if he was thinking about me, if he could see me. Knowing that I'd effectively 'won' our encounter, by keeping my head and putting him in a position he couldn't easily argue or bully his way out of, didn't help me in the slightest. In fact, it made things worse – now he'd feel he had a score to settle. I thought of all the times that cyclists have been killed by vehicles on crowded streets and yet no witnesses came forward. If he spotted me again, in fast-moving traffic on Upper Thames Street or Park Lane, he could run me off the road and be out of sight by the time anyone realised what had happened. And, judging by how quickly my path had crossed with the cabbie after our first encounter, it was only a matter of time – and probably not very much time – before we'd meet again.

Devastated though I plainly was, the Lamb's Conduit police weren't going to set out in pursuit of the driver then and there; they gave me a handful of forms, explained to me that I had to fill them in, and that someone would be in touch about an appointment at the Paddington Green station, where I'd give a statement. I mournfully left the station and trudged across Theobald's Road, the fear and shock leaving me exhausted as they ebbed out of my body, and the glorious sunlight I'd enjoyed all morning seeming incongruous after what had happened. I wondered again about the driver: where he was, and what story he'd told himself about our encounter; whether he'd decided that my slapping the side of his vehicle was an act of aggression, as the cabbie had before him, and what his feelings were towards me as a result. I thought about the block of wood, and wondered why he had it. Was it an innocent object that just happened to be lying around in his cab, and that he'd grabbed without thinking in the heat of the moment? Or was he so perpetually enraged by his daily encounters with cyclists that he had taken to carrying a weapon with which to threaten them into submission – or, if he felt they'd got really out of hand, to teach them a proper lesson? (It wouldn't by any means be the first time I'd come across this pedagogical attitude in drivers. 'I was putting you in the cycle lane where you belong', 'You were about to jump the lights – I was stopping you', 'Someone needs to teach you lot a lesson' are all regular justifications for manoeuvres that I strongly suspect are more the result of impatience and aggression than any sense of civic duty.)

Halfway down Red Lion Street, I decided to get back on the bike, feeling as I often do in the immediate aftermath of a crash – suddenly hyper-sensitive to all the threats that I'm usually oblivious to: the treacherous patchwork of potholes and drain covers that could so easily send me flying if a car or pedestrian forced me into them at the wrong angle; how terrifyingly close vehicles are when they pass you; the sharp angles of kerbs and buildings, and how very very hard they are; how very soft my flesh is in comparison, how brittle my bones, how precariously I am balanced on the bike. It felt as if, rather than improving my skill and confidence, all the thousands of hours I'd spent cycling in London had merely heightened my awareness of all the countless things that could go wrong, and how much they would hurt. I stared at the ordinary people barrelling blithely through the traffic on their hybrids and mountain bikes, and envied them their ignorance.

Riding along Holborn, I felt as a swimmer must feel as she loses control, being swept along and buffeted by rapids that she knows will consume her at any moment. Within seconds, someone shouted my name and with a quick flick of my head to check behind me, I hurled myself at the safety of the pavement. It was Nhatt, swinging along in a polka-dot dress with a sketchbook under one tattooed arm, and never had I been so glad to see her. In short order she had convinced me to stop working for the day, and to spend the afternoon drinking pints of cider with her in a quiet pub in Wapping, tucked away next to the river, off a quiet cobbled street where cabs and couriers rarely venture. There was probably no one better I could have talked to. In her days on the road she'd had countless similar experiences, with her big loss of innocence coming fairly innocuously, from a friendly cabbie who'd said, 'You're busy today, ain't you!' and told her the three completely different places he'd seen her, all over the city, just in the last few hours. I remembered how eagerly I'd looked out for Nhatt myself when I first started, and thought about the tendency of most cycling boys to fall in love with her at some point, at least in passing, and then thought about how many people must have noticed her and remembered her and got to know her – and me – without ever saying anything, hidden behind windscreens and under tinted visors, without either of us being aware they were watching.

I took the following day off work, and rode up to Paddington Green to give my statement and hand over the photos I'd taken (nothing came of it, but I was assured that they'd at least keep the information on record, and it would come up if the driver were ever reported for anything else). The journey took me through several of London's biggest interchanges: Vauxhall Cross, where I always eschew the fiddly cycle route through the railway arches for the thrill and speed of riding along with the traffic; round Hyde Park Corner and up Park Lane, and finally, Marble Arch. It was a beautiful ride – mid-morning, so the traffic was heavy, but moving freely, with none of the short tempers and erratic braking and acceleration that congestion breeds, and the channels between the cars seemed perfectly to accommodate me and my bicycle. Indeed, as I sped along among the cars circling Marble Arch, I had the curious sense that they were protecting and escorting me, one on either side, easing round the curves of the junction in perfect synchrony, like figure skaters, or the troops of soldiers who hold up the traffic around Buckingham Palace several times a day. After the rapids that had threatened to engulf me the previous day, I was back in familiar waters, flowing along on the currents I knew of old, as contented as a sea otter, asleep on the waves.

A few days later, I told Andy about the driver with the club. I had taken to starting some mornings in the control room, buying a packet of custard creams at Tesco on my way round Vauxhall Cross, and helping myself to a large mug of instant coffee from the office kitchen, into which I'd dip them as my second breakfast. Andy seemed to appreciate my company as much as I enjoyed his, and would swap stories of his beloved wife and daughter, his biannual holidays and his eight-mile run to work for my tales of London's slowest goods lifts and grumpiest receptionists.

I wasn't sure whether I should tell him about what had happened on Cavendish Square. Although we now spoke regularly and fairly frankly about our jobs and lives, I knew he considered me tough and uncomplaining, remembering his admiration when he found out that, unbeknownst to him, I had spent an afternoon riding around brakeless, after my brake cable snapped with three jobs on board, and I decided it would hold me up too much to stop and replace it. I would occasionally bring out my stories of particular drivers who had terrified or attacked me, but always long after the attendant emotions had died down, so that I could describe how I had felt without actually re-experiencing it. On the other hand, I knew I'd find his paternal outrage comforting.

To my embarrassment, I began to cry again as I told him the story. The other men in the control room sank their necks into their collars and concentrated fiercely on their computer screens, but Andy continued to gaze at me compassionately, and at one point reached over and gave my hand a little pat. I wondered what control room rumours would spiral from *that* piece of intimacy, knowing that Andy (to his sarcastic delight) was regularly suspected of having affairs with half the women in the building, simply because he talked to them about their lives and occasionally went out to lunch with them. In fact, it might also have been rumoured that he was gay (suspicions were already heightened by his daily wheatgrass smoothie and apparent ease in the company of the only *confirmed* gay male employee), were it not for the fact that he was married, and openly and vocally adored his wife. Andy defiantly refused to be affected by any of this, and carried on exactly as he pleased, occasionally mocking the idle accusations of his workmates.

'Today? Going out for lunch with Michelle. Yes, the one I'm having the affair with, yes.'

Once I had finished my story, and dried my tears, and the men in the control room had visibly relaxed, and started eavesdropping again, Andy asked if he could see the photos I'd taken of my aggressor.

'Oh, yes, 'e does look like a nasty piece of work!' he announced, with great satisfaction. ''Ang on – what's it say on the van?'

In the upheavals of the past few days, I had apparently failed to scrutinise the photo, or to realise that most of the van's livery was visible beyond the driver's head:

GHTFLIGHT

ERNATIONAL

'Well, that's got to be something like "nightflight", or "rightflight". Shouldn't be too hard to find out.'

'Try "nightflight",' I suggested, as he turned to his screen, and, sure enough, within seconds, he'd discovered a shipping company called Nightflight International.

'Oh – oh, and 'ave a look at this!' He beckoned me gleefully over to the screen, and I noticed the other controllers pricking up their ears. 'They've got offices in Vauxhall – they're right round the corner.'

For a few minutes, the control room rang with delight as everyone piled in with their revenge plots – the kippers they'd put in his air-conditioning, the potatoes they'd put in his exhaust pipe, the glue they'd put in his central locking system.

Andy waited for the hilarity to die down, then looked me in the eye. 'Seriously, hon, if there's anything you want me to do . . .?'

A couple of days later, he told me that he had phoned up the fleet manager of the other company, and made it very clear that he didn't appreciate his couriers being bullied. I have no idea exactly what it is he'll have said, but I imagine it wasn't pleasant. Andy, for all his sensitive New Age guy present, hints occasionally at a much more hot-headed past, of bar brawls and brushes with the law, and shady associates he'd rather forget. These hints are generally filtered through the pride of a bad boy made good, and the sense of having come a long way from where he started, but occasionally, as now, he would riff for a while on the audaciously violent punishments he might mete out to anyone who raised his ire, or dared to insult his wife and daughter, or upset his riders. Some mornings, after cycling in, he'd recount heated exchanges with drivers that left me feeling both fearful and envious of the fluency of his anger. I was very pleased to have him on my side.

16

'I'll never learn,' I thought to myself a few weeks later, as I launched the bike through a fast-closing gap on Park Lane, trying to get across five lanes of moving traffic in order to turn right into Mayfair, and bracing myself for an earful of abuse from the open window of the white van I'd narrowly missed.

'Oh, what'll it be this time?' I wondered, sifting through the likely insults: 'Stupid fucking bitch? Or perhaps, 'Get out the road, ya fuckin' wanker?' Maybe just a long loud angry blast of the horn.

But instead, the van carried on driving alongside me for a few moments, and the driver leaned out of his window, and very calmly – almost amicably – said, 'There's no repeat button on life, do you know? You don't get it back again. Once it's over, it's over.'

On my way home a few hours later, I stopped off at Brixton Cycles, to replace some part or other and say hi to Nhatt, rehearsed my usual complaints about how quickly everything seemed to wear out, and was gently reminded that my job obliges me to ride more than a thousand miles a month. 'That's the equivalent of crossing several continents a year,' I thought to myself, 'and yet I've barely been out of central London.' Just for a moment, the circuit felt hopelessly small, and I imagined the line I'd drawn through it with my wheels over the past few years, all tangled up like someone's unravelled knitting, and wondered how it might look if I were to stretch it out to its full extent.

I had slid into my second summer on circuit with a confusing mixture of restlessness and contentment. A couple of months previously, as the now familiar storm of plane-tree effluence had assailed my lungs, nose and eyeballs, I had discovered that my (increasingly neglected) plan to return to academia had died off without my even noticing, leaving me with no ambition, and no future plans. I was occasionally plagued by a nebulous anxiety that this really wasn't any way to live one's life, and would wonder if I should retrain as a doctor, or apply to become a firefighter, or look for a 'real' job in an office. The remainder of the time, I rejoiced in the sense of nothing mattering but the present moment; of a lifestyle so all-absorbing that there was no need to seek out anything else.

Not only was couriering sufficient for me – I was now equal to it. Although I knew I was unlikely ever to be as fast as the summer interlopers on their road bikes, or as grace-ful as some of the old-timers, who floated through traffic and over obstacles as if their wheels weren't even touching the road, I was now conversant with the traffic. I knew its many moods; how it will crawl and stall at certain times of day, and flow happily along at others; how to read a driver's mood and intentions from minute clues like the noise of the engine, the angle of his head against the headrest, and countless other little signs that my conscious mind has never fully understood, so that a lot of the time I surprise myself by appearing to predict the future. In fact, I was more gen-erally surprised by just how little I seemed to think when

I was on the road. The busier the traffic, the more readily my mind would sink into a thrall of absolute concentration, reminding me of the loose frown that would settle on Lukasz's face – and probably also my own – when navigating traffic entanglements so complex that no spare energy or attention was available for anything else, let alone a smile.

Riding through busy traffic is, needless to say, a challenging process, and the stakes are high – any small error, on your part or that of a nearby driver or pedestrian, could result in catastrophe, though this will rarely be at the forefront of your mind. Despite the life-or-death context in which the courier operates, the standard manoeuvres of her job (moving across five lanes of fast-moving traffic on Park Lane; accelerating through the handlebar-wide gap between two moving buses on Oxford Street) become as comfortable, habitual and automatic as those of any other occupation. Like learning to use a spreadsheet or operate a till, or typing your password into the system at the beginning of the day, the tricks and habits of riding through traffic start off as something you have to concentrate on, and remind yourself of, but very quickly become second nature – something you'll do without even thinking about it. (How many of us can't remember our password any more, and just rely on our fingers to fall on the right combination of keys?)

It's curious – although I frequently credit my years as a courier with teaching me to think (and to observe, and engage with the world) like never before, much of the satisfaction of the job comes from the irrelevance of thought; the joy of watching your body develop its own intelligence; the satisfaction of subordinating reason to instinct.

Riding through busy traffic requires awesome feats of internal mathematics that my conscious brain could never hope to accomplish. You plot a curve to your right, round that taxi, taking into account the couple of feet it will have moved in relation to the white van next to it by the time you reach it – and then that curve gives way to a leftward curve, across the front of the taxi, and behind the Luton van that a second ago was in a completely different lane. The leftward curve is already coiled in your muscles, all plotted out, before you even start the rightward one, as well as the exact way in which the one will segue into the other. But the traffic is a complex dynamic force – not chaos, by any means, but an order composed of so many discrete and differing parts that it can never, even for one moment, be grasped and understood. The joy of riding along as part of it lies half in the sense of relaxing into the patterns you know so well; half in the hyper-alertness and intense concentration required to anticipate every possible disruption. One vehicle might brake suddenly, halted by an obstacle ahead that you were unable to see from your position behind. An indicator might start to flash. Or the lights ahead might change and the traffic might start to flow more quickly. A pedestrian – or, worse, two or three – might decide to dart between two crawling buses. There might be a pothole that you've forgotten about, or which wasn't there last time you rode this way. So my body writes countless contingencies into the trajectory it's plotted among the vehicles, and with every flicker of my eyes mounts a fresh reconnaissance, taking in the road and the pavements and their contents, calculating all possible movements of each element of the traffic and their interplay with all the others, trying to eliminate all surprises and anticipate all impediments. Most of the time my mind has very little idea of what's going on, and wouldn't be able to keep up even if it tried.

Sometimes – often – I surprise myself. I once found myself slowing down inexplicably as I filtered past a bus on Piccadilly, and a second later a pedestrian stepped out in front of me – if I'd been going at full speed, she'd probably have walked straight into me and knocked me off. I wasn't aware of it, but clearly some part of my mind had registered her crossing the pavement as I approached the bus, and somehow known, or suspected, that she was going to carry on into the road.

It extends to the way I manoeuvre the bike, and the way I navigate from postcode to postcode. Action comes first; thought lags behind. I don't plan my movements, so much as just observe – and analyse, and marvel at – them once I've performed them. Because I spent most of my teens and early twenties sitting at a desk, the processes both of moving physically and of learning *how* to move are still novelties.

Eventually, the Condor Pista Lawrence had sold me that day on the beach was laid to rest. I had never much liked it, and when I found out that I was going to need to replace the headset, the forks, the brake caliper and the handlebars, all in the same week, I decided to cut my losses, and stop spending money on a bike I was sometimes convinced was trying to kill me. I thought about getting a new one from Fullcity. Lawrence had started sending some of his endless jumble of old frames over to Armourtex in Hackney, to be powdercoated in bright, anonymous primary colours, and then rebuilt and resold as 'nearly new'. Somehow this didn't feel quite right to me – it was as if the bike's personality and identity were being effaced along with its chipped paintwork and faded decals. So in the end, I bought an old Joe Waugh frame from a friend, instantly recognisable with its bold font and unsubtle 1980s paint job, and was gratified a couple of years later when an elderly gentleman pulled up next to me at the lights and remarked, 'Joe Waugh – I used to race with him, back in the day!'

The previous owner had called the bike Evelyn, a name I was happy to keep. I built him up with the contents of my bike box and a friend's shed (after a few years, all cyclists will discover that they have the equivalent of a complete extra bicycle sitting around in spare parts), took him to work the following Monday, and quickly became fascinated with the way my body and riding style slowly adjusted to fit the new ride, in tiny and gradual increments.

There were the obvious initial adjustments, like getting used to a new frame size (Evelyn had a shorter top tube, which meant I was far less stretched out than I had been on the Condor) and the brake being in a different place (which led to one or two near misses, but also meant that on one occasion I ended up steering out of what would have been a head-on collision, had I braked). After a couple of days, I thought I'd got the hang of it. But over the next few weeks, I carried on noticing differences in the way I cycled, every now and then becoming aware of some tiny skill I'd recently mastered, which I hadn't even known existed before.

It became apparent to me that the way I balanced the bike (and myself) when going round corners had changed. On

Evelyn, I found that I could corner at a much sharper angle, and could lean the bike much closer to the floor than I'd been able to do on the Condor. Once I'd been doing this for a little while, I started to analyse it as it happened, to try to understand what my body was doing and feeling to be able to pull these new manoeuvres – because I certainly hadn't thought them through, or planned them in advance. My conscious mind had had nothing to do with it.

So, belatedly, I switched on my brain and tried to figure out what I was doing differently. When I pulled one of those tight corners, I'd flick my hips away from the direction I planned to turn, steering the bike from the seat tube rather than the head tube. I'd tighten my inner arm, by pulling my elbow in or back, and dipping my shoulder, making the inside edge of my body much smaller than the outside. I'd tilt my neck slightly to one side, so that I effectively pivoted around the crown of my head. There is more to it than this, but I still haven't fully broken it down. I never quite worked out how it is that I managed to stabilise the bike so much on the outside edge of the curve that I felt comfortable leaning so far over into the centre of it. I suspect my thighs and hips might have something to do with it, but for all I know it could have been my ribcage or my triceps. Nothing surprises me any more. I'm already amazed by what my body comes up with when I leave it to its own devices. After all, who would have thought I'd use the crown of my head to balance?

After my years in academia, where everything I thought and did had to be described, explained, justified, documented, proofread, edited and presented in the correct house style, it was a glorious relief to find an occupation where the need to understand things linguistically was restricted to the most basic necessities – the brusque exchanges over the radio, with their entire vocabulary of fewer than twenty words (not counting street names, which extend it into thousands) and the brief and repetitive encounters with receptionists and security guards, where little more is needed than to ascertain that the package is in the right place, and whether they're willing to sign for it. Even when the conversation becomes friendly or flirtatious, it tends to follow very predictable lines. The job makes few demands beyond the immediate imperatives of getting the package there, of keeping moving. And in between the mostly unremarkable encounters that punctuated the working day, I was free to lose myself in the rhythms of my bike and the road.

Cycling itself is, as far as I'm concerned, probably the purest form of auto-eroticism. There is no exchange or intervention or conquest or surrender; no doubt and no climax – this *jouissance* is perfectly contained and sustained within my own body, which sings and surges as it flies through the streets, consumed in an ecstasy of motion and sensation. My thighs hum with energy as they pump and flex, pushing the bike forward, and my hips roll warmly from side to side, steering it with countless minute adjustments. To turn left, I'll jut my right hip out, press myself into the saddle, and feel my left sit bone pivot cleanly against its firm leather. I notice the individual muscles of my waist flexing as I balance, and every inch of my flesh, from my chest down to my knees, tightening and resettling with every movement, every pedal stroke, every twist and turn. The pores of my skin and the fibres of my muscles are wide,

wide awake, voluptuously drinking in the sensation of the air flowing around me, and responding to the texture of the road beneath me. Never before has my body felt so alive, so supple, so liquid. I have no idea whether this exhilaration might be shared by someone watching me. I sometimes catch a glimpse of it when I watch other cyclists in flight, and know from experience what it is they might be feeling, but for all I know, to the outside observer I am merely a slightly ungainly woman pedalling a battered bicycle slowly along the street. I'd almost prefer it if that were the case, because then the pleasure would be mine and mine alone. It is a beauty without pride, without vanity, without any need for the eye of a beholder. And it was a beauty so all-consuming that, as long as I was on the bike, my periodic qualms about where my life was going were easily disregarded.

17

Sometimes, of course, drowning your sorrows in cycling isn't an option, because there's hardly any work. It was on one such day, not all that long ago, that I spent a good hour sitting outside a cafe on Brewer Street, cursing the August doldrums that seemed to have descended several months early, and trying very hard not to think about a girl who had broken my heart. It was a futile and fairly pathetic effort.

My grief had congealed inside me, hardening in my torso and tightening in my throat, and my nostrils flared frantically as I tried to force myself not to cry. I'd concentrate my attention on the article I was trying to read, and for a minute or two the tears would recede – then, as soon as I'd relaxed, the memories of the previous night would surge back into my head and, once again, I'd have to clench my jaw to keep myself from sobbing, tilting my head back to keep the tears in my eyes. It's not that I hadn't been through this sort of thing before. The romantic ups and downs of my twenties had taught me that, no matter how painful a break-up is, your mind will eventually get used to the new state of affairs and the pain will lessen. Indeed, to hasten this process, it can even be useful, though torturous, to go over the pain again and again, revisiting what was said and remembering what was felt, in the hope that, through

constant repetition, what was initially so exquisitely agonis-
ing will become blunt and boring.

But this particular grief was so fresh and still so unbear-
able, that all I could do to keep myself from breaking down
altogether was to seek constant distraction. When I was on
the bike, I rode fast enough to keep myself out of breath,
so that my brain had only enough oxygen to focus on
what was immediately vital – the traffic, the pedestrians,
my destination and how I was going to get there. When
I had company – in receptions and lifts; on the corner –
I'd immerse myself in conversation, talking frantically and
listening eagerly to hold undesirable thoughts at bay with
innocuous ones. But now I was stationary, and alone. The
article I was trying to read on James Salter's use of free
indirect speech wasn't sufficiently absorbing to distract
me for more than a few seconds at a time, and forgetting
momentarily was almost worse, because what scant relief
I gained was destroyed almost instantly by the horror of
remembrance that followed.

The smartly dressed woman to my right lit up a cigarette,
and as the inaugural wisp of smoke and sulphur drifted past
me, I turned and falteringly asked her if I might have one
too. My voice sounded faint and strangled, but she'd never
spoken to me before, so probably wouldn't guess that this
was anything out of the ordinary. For a second, she looked
startled, and I braced myself to apologise, thinking about
how expensive cigarettes must be these days, and how rude
it is to demand one from a complete stranger outside a cafe.
But then she reopened the box and handed me one, with an
entirely neutral expression.

'Thank you very much,' I said, trying to convey as much gratitude and sincerity as possible.

I don't usually smoke, and haven't regularly bought cigarettes since I was fifteen, so God only knows why I'd suddenly wanted one so much. It was probably just a desperate urge to do something – anything – to displace the horror that was still continually spooling through my head, especially since my rigid throat and chest meant that thus far I hadn't been able to comfort-eat my way through my sorrow. Whatever damage the tobacco wreaked on my lungs, if this helped calm my mind down, it would be worth it.

Sure enough, my tears began to ebb and the sense of dizzying horror receded. I inhaled deeply on three consecutive breaths, and then relaxed, gazing absently at the opposite shopfront as though it were any other day, and I were any other person, and it wasn't the end of the world.

'Do you play the lottery?' asked the woman next to me, out of the blue.

I turned and smiled at her, determined to make up with friendliness for my audacious demands on her tobacco.

'No, I don't. Do you?'

'No.' She smiled back, slightly shyly, as though admitting to some sort of innocence. 'I don't gamble. I can't see the point.'

Her accent wasn't English, but I couldn't place it any more accurately than somewhere in Europe. I told her the story of how my father had put me off gambling for life, when I was very young, by giving me 5p, then offering to double it if I tossed heads. If it landed on tails he'd take it back, and of course this was what happened. We still sometimes wonder how differently my life might have turned out if I'd won the toss. In the event, I was so upset that he eventually relented and gave me back the coin. I haven't gambled since.

'Exactly!' agreed the woman. 'It hurts too much to lose.' I ruefully agreed, and said that I suspected gamblers to be more excited by the sense of risk than whether they win or lose.

'Yes,' she mused. 'We all have a different thrill. What's your thrill?'

'I ride my bike.' I said, gesturing behind her to where it was parked. She smirked slightly, and I thought that she might be about to say that riding a bike in London traffic was far too much of a risk for her, and that I must be crazy, but instead, she told me that she missed her own bike, back in Amsterdam.

'It's only been two days!'

'How long are you in London?'

'Only four days. It's just a forty-five-minute flight, so why not?'

Why not indeed.

'I had a date,' she continued, with the comfortable intimacy one sometimes feels with an acquaintance you both know will be fleeting.

'Oh? Did it go well?' I asked, in faintly conspiratorial tones.

'It's . . . still going on!' she beamed. 'It went . . . very, very well.'

I congratulated her, and she told me about her plans, later that day, to get a tattoo, not commemorating the successful date (to my secret relief), but celebrating her birthday, which was in three days' time.

'Happy birthday,' I said. 'What will the tattoo be?'

She measured out a couple of inches on the inside of her right wrist, with thumb and forefinger.

'It will be . . . Hebrew writing. A word meaning "mother love". Because . . . I work with lots of children and . . . that's what it feels like. It's something very important to me.'

She showed me a flyer for the tattoo parlour she was on her way to, and told me how much she admired the work of the tattooist she had chosen.

'I'm sorry,' she continued. 'I haven't asked your name.'

'Emily. And yours?'

'Desi.'

We smiled at each other again, and she offered me another cigarette.

'It's strange,' she said, hesitantly, 'to make a confession to someone when you've only just been introduced.'

'Not at all,' I assured her, remembering similar confidences from brief encounters in guesthouses and roadside cafes all across Asia. 'I think it's easier sometimes, when it's someone you don't know.'

She continued.

'I did something very bad, a few days ago. Very very bad.' She stopped for a moment, as if reluctant to tell me any more, again caught up in the memory of whatever it was she had done. 'And this man – that I am on the date with – he said that now I have bad karma, and I need to do something good, to, to –'

'To make up for it?' She nodded. I felt a wave of gratitude; a sense of the world slipping into its groove again, of being back in tune after long discord, like the new chain and sprocket I'd just fitted to my bike. 'Desi, I've . . . someone just broke my heart, last night.' My voice sounded tight and croaky again, as my throat stiffened and solidified with the memory. 'And I've been sitting here trying not to cry. And you've given me a cigarette, and talked to me, and now I'm smiling and I feel so much better, and I can't tell you what a difference you've made to my day. Really.' I wanted to tell her that, no matter what terrible things she might have done to other people, in my eyes she would always be an angel.

She rubbed my shoulder, warmly and sympathetically, and although neither of us said it, I suspected she shared my sense of both of us being, at this moment, at opposite ends of the seesaw: her hope and excitement in her new relationship balanced – and possibly foreshadowed – by my grief. She assured me that it would all be OK, and I said that I knew that it would, that it's always just a matter of waiting, and staying alive, and the pain will eventually fade.

We both stared out into the street for a minute. The conversation seemed to have drawn itself to a close at this quiet climax. Eventually, I heard her take a deep breath, as though coming to a decision.

'I hope you won't be offended . . . I want to give you something.' She started to open her handbag, and I wondered what it might be that she was about to offer me. 'I have this lady's face –' Out came a smooth twenty-pound note, with the Queen's placid purple smile uppermost. '– and I don't . . . I can't . . . will you take it, please?'

I couldn't imagine what she must have done for the money in her purse to inspire such guilt, but I recognised the need for atonement, and that this was a gesture where my embarrassment at accepting money from a stranger had to be secondary to the peace of mind I'd be giving her in return. I took the note and held it ceremoniously between my two palms as I thanked her. Somehow grasping it with my fingers would have implied too ready a sense of ownership. It was difficult to accept money, I told her, but I understood her need to give it, and I was grateful.

'You can spend it on your thrill,' she said, and we both smiled. 'What should I . . .?' She indicated her cigarette, which had by now burned down to the butt. I pointed at the drain a few feet in front of us, and we both tossed our butts towards it, hers falling through the grating and mine bouncing off the kerb and rolling to a rest in the groove where the metal met the tarmac.

'In Amsterdam, everyone throws them in the canal,' she told me, with a slight grimace.

She checked her reflection in a small handbag mirror, prodded at her lipstick with a painted nail and ran her fingers through her hair a couple of times.

'Good luck,' she said, standing up and straightening her skirt.

'Good luck,' I replied, watching her as she disappeared round the corner towards Piccadilly Circus. A couple of minutes later, she walked past me again, this time arm in arm with a cheerful-looking man slightly older than her, and slightly shorter. She gave me a wink, and I smiled back in spite of myself. Once again, the city had offered me an unexpected solace, and I was glad I had come to work, rather than sequestering myself in my room with my misery.

I thought back to 2010's summer of restlessness and

contentment, during which I had gradually, almost unwittingly, come to the decision that I was going to leave this reliable solace and cycle round the world. It was something of a paradox, I felt, that the constant longing to be elsewhere, which had been so amply satisfied by couriering for so long, had eventually – and inevitably – meant that my ambitions began to overspill the few square miles that made up the London circuit. I couldn't ever have said I was too comfortable – my days as a courier were shaped by a continually evolving friction, with the bicycle, the traffic, the weather, and the city itself – but London was losing some of its ability to surprise me. The urge to be somewhere else had begun to rekindle.

As my decision gathered momentum, and I began to dream of distant horizons, and my taste in books began to slip from the urban narratives of Iain Sinclair and Alan Hollinghurst to the wilder wanderings of Jay Griffiths and Robert Macfarlane, I began to observe elements of the wilderness in the city I now knew so intimately. I recognised myself in Jay Griffiths's descriptions, in *Wild*, of Igloolik hunters communicating the exact whereabouts of their prey by 'describing all the rocks coupled with the wind direction'; of a landscape of ice that you or I would consider effectively featureless, but in which its inhabitants are perfectly at home, and know where they are, where to go, and how to get there. What anyone considers wilderness is really just the unfamiliar, *das Unheimliche*, the strange. One person's home; another person's foreign country.

I recalled how helplessly lost I had been when I first arrived in London, and didn't recognise any landmarks, or know which direction to go in. As far as I knew, Hackney might have been in the south, and Wimbledon the north, and Brixton on the way to Heathrow. Now I know London as intimately as the Igloolik hunter knows the icecap, or as the Native Australians know the songlines. Places and spaces change with knowledge. They shrink, and become habitable and negotiable.

I spent a nervous half-hour after work one evening waiting for a friend outside the Curzon Cinema (my phone had died, so I had no way of confirming our plans), watching the rush-hour traffic with an outsider's eye and marvelling at the chaos I never really notice when I'm in the thick of it. Massive disorderly stampedes of taxis and motorbikes, shoals of cyclists, all crammed onto far too small a road, all going at different rates and in different directions – then just to add to the confusion of it all, flocks of pedestrians going against the flow, trying to cross the erratic stream of traffic, fighting their way through the current, standing indecisively on the islands and playing chicken with the cars. Thousands and thousands of moving objects, all unpredictable. They may know where they're going, but I don't. How could I hope to negotiate that?

In a city, everything has been planned, designed and manufactured, yet at every moment, the arbitrary, the unexpected, the vague, the random, the sudden, slaps us in the face. Everyone in a city is partially bewildered (yes, even the cabbies and the cycle couriers) because of all its different landscapes – the physical, the historical, the personal – which coexist in exactly the same place, yet are disparate and mutually unintelligible. I know my London; I don't know yours. I can beat my own path through the traffic, but from my seat outside the Curzon, I couldn't imagine how anyone else could possibly find theirs.

It's an artificial, plastic, ersatz wilderness, but it's wilderness nonetheless.

I don't often feel lost in London, but every now and then, usually when I'm off the bike, and therefore not in my element, its terror suddenly strikes me afresh and I wonder how I'll ever find a way out of this chaos. Being in an unfamiliar city – even one's own – is like tuning a radio, and now and then hearing a few words of intelligible human speech in between the whistles and buzzes. As I sat and watched Shaftesbury in full flood, the cycle couriers who passed every few minutes stood out like beacons. Running into someone you know gives you the reassurance that the world isn't the strange and daunting place we imagined it to be. One of the joys of London's essential randomness is that the lines we draw through the city sometimes cross unexpectedly, the culmination of thousands of meaningless little coincidences.

Six o'clock came and went. I concluded that my friend must have had other ideas, and so I set off home, deciding to go via Charing Cross and Whitehall rather than Haymarket and Pall Mall, simply because, after watching the rush hour flood past me, I didn't fancy trying to cross Shaftesbury in order to go south. And, as chance would have it, I ran into a fellow Pink rider at Cambridge Circus and stopped to chat. And, as further chance would have it, right at that moment, my friend flew up Charing Cross Road, late as usual, and I stopped her and apologised for my phone almost ruining our plans, and we got back on our bikes, and less than a minute later were locking them side by side around a lamp post in Soho.

I would miss this, when I left, I thought: this comforting coincidence, this sense of the city perpetually resolving its own chaos. But I was also missing the sense of discovery from my earlier days on the road; the feeling of striking out into darkness; the nebulous and fearful savour of direction without destination. I was ready for a new circuit.

At the east end of Warren Street, near the junction with Tottenham Court, just before it plunges into the enormous intersection where it meets Euston Road and Hampstead Road above the Euston Underpass, there's a small wholefood shop, run by an Indian family, which sells hearty vegetarian curries in Styrofoam boxes to a habitual queue of office workers, and cheap homemade samosas and vegan cakes to hungry cycle couriers. I'm not a regular enough customer for the proprietors to know me, but I know them, and am always pleased when I have the chance to drop by, dithering for slightly longer than I need to over the cake cabinet, carving out a few more seconds in which to exchange our pleasantries.

The wholefood shop is a remnant of a community of South Asian immigrants that planted itself in the smoky and undesirable streets around Euston and King's Cross in the 1960s, thrived for a few decades, and is now being inexorably and insistently edged out by developers. Until recently, there was a ramshackle Indian bookshop a few doors down, where I'd often pass my standby time browsing dusty sunbleached tomes published by Seagull and Rupa, which were like hands reaching out of my past in Delhi and into my present in London. Across the Euston Road to the north east lies Drummond Street, lined with Indian restaurants, grocery stores and sweet shops, and it's a mild shock to realise that these two streets are by rights part of the same district, existing, as they now do, on either side of the yawning continental divide of the Euston Underpass.

One sunny afternoon (in hindsight, probably sometime in August, since I'd invested in a coffee, clearly assuming there was unlikely to be any work for a while), I found myself sitting at one of the stainless-steel tables outside this cafe, eavesdropping on a conversation between two slightly self-absorbed actors at the next table. It was very easy to tell exactly who they were and what they did for a living, because they were showing off to each other or sizing each other up (or both), describing auditions they'd had, parts they'd played, and people they'd worked with in a level of detail that seemed slightly artificial – as if they knew they were being listened to. The man in particular, I noticed, had a tendency to explain and illustrate his every point as if talking to someone who was totally new to the subject, a habit that would normally annoy me, but which as an eavesdropper I was finding rather useful.

'Oh, yes, I studied method with him in New York,' he bragged, referring to someone the other actor had just tentatively namedropped, and then waded into a lengthy discourse on techniques of method acting, which I suspect she found intensely frustrating (since she probably knew it all anyway), and which I found fascinating, since I was completely new to the subject.

It all seemed to revolve around meticulously identifying elements of the actor's own experience and memory that corresponded to those of the character he was playing, and then finding ways of splicing these 'real' emotions with the artificial situation he was enacting on the stage. Predictably, this actor had spent a lot of time exploring his own emotional landscape with the help of a therapist.

'So I spent a lot of time going back into my early twenties, and just . . . being with all the stuff that was going on for me back then. And I found eventually I was able to inhabit that feeling of anger, and helplessness, and being kind of on edge about it all, you know, and then I had to find ways of bringing that in, you know, in rehearsals. So he had me do all these very intense exercises – I mean, on my own, in my apartment – so that I had a way of recalling that stuff. So like, once, I was getting something out of the refrigerator, and for some reason it all hit me right then – and so I ended up going back and doing that again and again. Literally, I'd stand up, walk to the refrigerator and open the door, and I'd be right there, right in that emotion. So I'd be doing this over and over again, stand up, walk to the fridge and open the door, and it would all come back – so in the end I could access that emotion whenever I needed to.'

There was more to it, but I found myself drifting off at that point, captivated by the idea of pinning one's emotions (intentionally or otherwise) to physical actions and places, since that's what I do all the time. Of all my many maps of London, the emotional one is the most elusive, but also the most powerful. The unlikeliest street corners will have some tattered threads of memory fluttering from them like a flag, because of something I did there once, or someone I spoke to, or simply because of something I happened to be thinking as I rode past one day, which then popped back into my mind as I rode past again a few hours later, and after that was forever lying in wait for me on that particular corner, like a swarm of insects, or the gust of hot fragrant air that I savour every time I ride past the bakery on Brockley Road.

It's almost as if the memories have overflowed from my head and scattered themselves about the city – or as if London itself has become an extension of my consciousness. Some parts of my life I can recall simply by thinking of them; others I think I'd remember better if I went back to a certain part of London and plucked them up from the tree I'd hung them from, or retraced them from the park bench I'd scratched them on, or snatched them up as they blew around in circles in an alleyway like a discarded carrier bag. I once spontaneously burst into tears as I bumped up onto the pavement on Albany Road and wiggled in between the bollards at the entrance to Burgess Park. It was a few months since that awful heartbreak, my encounter with Desi on the bench on Brewer Street, and the ensuing weeks when I'd ride home each evening in helpless tears, always by this same route. The grief abated eventually, as I knew it would, but a few strands of it were still strung across the entrance to the park like cobwebs on an autumn morning, and that evening I forgot to duck, and rode straight into them.

But by the time I'd reached the other side of the park, I was smiling. Here on the right were the bushes where I'd once stopped for a wee, late one Friday night in the middle of that glorious summer of 2010, on my way home after a riotous post-work party outside the Foundry. Someone had turned up with speakers mounted on a bicycle trailer, and we'd all danced, exuberantly and goofily, grinning at each other, through the long summer evening and into the night. It was a couple of months after I'd abandoned my PhD plans, a week or two before I realised I wanted to cycle round the world, and I was embracing the heady sensation of leaping off into a completely open future, with nothing to my name but the present moment. I know I was frightened at times, but what lingers from that summer is the roaring sense of freedom, of having no plans and therefore few obligations, of being aware that wonderful things were going to happen, but not yet knowing what they might be. I remember squatting there in the darkness, in the corner of Burgess Park, listening to the hot hiss of my urine and watching the insects floating in the beam my front light was casting over the long grass around it, my sweaty skin caressed by the fresh warm air, and feeling an immense surge of love for all that I was part of (the dancing couriers, the pretty girl I'd met who hadn't been able to take her eyes off me, the delicious sensation of cycling home along quiet roads with the night all around me), and for all the wonders that lay in the wings.

When I cycle through Burgess Park (rarely these days), I revisit that moment as I would the grave of a loved one, simultaneously rejoicing in the past and grieving for it. The girl came and went, as did all my other moments of grief and elation, as did the delicious sensation of not knowing where I was going, and illuminating the future only as I stepped into it.

18

I was sitting outside Fullcity one warm September afternoon, at the tail end of that wonderful summer, dipping custard creams into one of Liam's lattes and gossiping with the man from the handbag stall, when I caught sight of a person who looked amusingly like Roger Ramjet in a suit. As he got closer, I realised that it *was* Roger Ramjet in a suit.

Ramjet was a nickname, of course. His real name was Roger Moore, like the actor – which had more than once aroused the suspicion of policemen, who were convinced he was giving them a false name. He claimed that one of them in particular had it in for him, and was constantly stopping him on one pretext or another, fining him for any possible misdemeanour. Since Ramjet rode without brakes, he was a pretty easy target and, like a few couriers I knew, had a collection of unpaid tickets at home. Some couriers ignored them – others did the rounds of the police road-safety demonstrations, since they would often write off your ticket if you queued up to sit in the cab of a parked truck for a few minutes, and be told things you already knew about blind spots and sightlines.

Ramjet had just come from a job interview. After seven years on the road, it was time to move on.

'Yeah, this is the best job in the world, man! You can spend all day smoking draw, check out the girls in the street, ride your bike around, hang out here – but then it's winter, and it's gonna rain all day, and then it gets really hard . . .'

He told me about an old injury in his right elbow, that gets worse when it's cold, and how his hamstrings hadn't been right for a couple of years.

'So, yeah, maybe it's time to call it a day, you know what I mean?'

Couriering is hard to leave, despite its challenges. The job clings to you like a jealous lover, seducing and sedating you with exhaustion so that you can't even consider any other, and, if you do manage to leave, sucking you back in the moment you falter. It's easy, all too easy, to pick up a day on the road here or there, just to fill in the gaps and make ends meet – and before you know it, one day becomes three, and then you're full time again.

That afternoon, I gazed at Ramjet with mingled delight and dismay. It was good that he was getting out – he'd been hating the job for a while, and was finally attempting to make his escape, rather than letting it grind him down any further. I hoped that it would work out for him. And yet, I'd been having one of my most wonderful days of the year. It was well into September, but London still held just enough of summer for me to be able to ride around in short sleeves. The air was clear and fresh, and the sunlight bright and sparkling, making the whole city gleam and glitter and glisten. There was a slight breeze, which seemed to put everything in motion – the leaves, the clouds, the seasons, and of course me, enjoying the Friday energy, flying and swinging and dancing along, whipping in and out of the traffic, singing loudly to myself, waving at everyone I knew, and even some people I didn't.

Earlier that afternoon, one of my pick-ups had turned out to be a van job – a box the size of a small fridge. But I was feeling energetic, and in the mood for a challenge, so instead of calling Andy to tell him it was a COA (cancelled on arrival), I stuffed one end into my bag, somehow lashed the rest of it down, and headed off up the Col de Waterloo Bridge, over the river and along the Strand towards Soho. And I found that everyone will smile at you when you're riding along with a box the size of a fridge strapped to your back. Even cabbies. Even lorry drivers whose mirror you crash into as you hurtle between two lanes of stationary traffic, remembering that you're slightly wider than usual, but forgetting that you're also taller.

Carrying oversized packages is one of those courier stereotypes that we're all pleased to inhabit from time to time.

'I love it when I've got a poster tube sticking out of my bag,' remarked one of the Creative riders once. 'Makes me feel like I'm a *real* courier.'

Courier bags are intricate works of engineering, capable of expanding to gargantuan proportions, and then flattening down to nothing once they're empty and all the straps are tightened. Even after a couple of years on the road, I was amazed by how many more packages I could squeeze into mine when I thought it was full – and then one more on top, and tie it down with the extension straps, and then one more lashed to the outside with a dead inner tube, and then heave the bag up over my head, so full that I can barely lift it, yet somehow I can still cycle with it.

Our bags are an intrinsic part of our silhouette. Another courier always stands out. Even in a street full of a thousand people, with a second and a half to take them all in before I have to put my eyes back on the road and the bus ahead of me, I'll recognise his telltale shape: an agile figure bent over a bike; bag bulging on his back; radio aerial sticking up over one shoulder. Even now that half the hipsters in London dress the same, I can still spot a courier a mile off. And he'll spot me too, and we'll spare a moment to nod at each other before the road demands our attention once more, or I'll throw one hand up in a flamboyant wave so that he knows I've seen him, even if I can't make eye contact, or we'll shout 'He-e-e-ey!' as we pass. Or sometimes, if we're going the same way, we'll ride alongside each other for a bit; one dodging drain covers in the gutter; the other facing oncoming cars and jaywalking pedestrians as she follows the centre line.

I would miss all of this, I reflected, knowing my days were now numbered, but still wondering whether I really wanted to leave a life I still loved so much. I thought of Ramjet, and every other courier I knew who'd left the circuit, however gladly; of the controllers, many of whom had started off on the streets, and now grew fat at their desks as they listened to the rest of us getting on with it. Already I felt a strong bitter-sweet sorrow at the thought of saying goodbye to them all. Very few people I know ever love the colleagues they share an office with as much as I love those I see racing past me on the road, often acknowledging me for only a split second.

I can't quite explain this excessive affection for people who are, after all, only technically workmates, and in some cases even rivals. To be sure, our delight at running into each other is partly because we never quite get over the coincidence of it. But then it happens so frequently – ride along Old Street and Clerkenwell at about 4 p.m., wave at every courier you see, and you'll never put your hand back on the bars – that it's clearly the normal state of affairs. Maybe what we're really delighted by is this affirmation of our own magic – the way that we're effectively a small, close-knit village stretched across the impersonal wilderness of the city; that, in our constant motion, we traverse and transcend physical space, and somehow arrive at the connections that, in other lives, we'd build only with the small handful of people we live and work and sleep with.

But it was not always thus. Buffalo Bill assures me that, back in the 1980s, most couriers operated without any sense that they were part of a larger group. The first whispers of community were not heard until the early 1990s, when, the first Cycle Messenger World Championships was held, in Berlin. In 1994, London was the host city, and about five hundred messengers attended, from both sides of the Atlantic, arriving at the airport with bikes wrapped in cardboard and tape, scattering themselves among the squats and house shares of their new-found London brethren, and competing in a variety of races, based on the challenges they might face in the course of a day's work. It is difficult to imagine how this happened, in the days before anything and anyone you wanted could be found and contacted within a minute or two of Internet searching.

'How on earth did you manage to stay in touch?' I asked Bill once.

'Faxes,' he replied. 'You know, not many people had fax machines in those days – well, when have they ever, right?

– and a lot of the courier workload was to pick up faxes from the places that did and deliver them to the places that didn't. So we had access to all the machines. And we could phone each other, of course.'

The sarcastic twinkle in his eye suggested that a young thing like me might not believe that phones had existed twenty years ago.

'And we used to post flyers out to people. Hard to imagine, isn't it? You'd have this flyer in your hand, just this home-made thing, for a race that was happening over in Boston or Toronto, and it would be like this precious artefact.'

But how had they found each other in the first place? It took me a little more digging to find out. As it turns out, a few pioneers had visited other cities, discovered there were couriers there too, and recognised them as kindred spirits. The CMWC had been conceived when a Berlin courier called Achim Beier travelled to New York, and talked to the bike messengers hanging around in Washington Square Park.

And, through one of Bill's articles on Moving Target, I became aware of Rebecca Reilly, whose legend loomed large over my years as a courier. Sometime back in the hazy days of pre-Internet rumour and hearsay, Bill had caught wind of 'a female messenger who was making a journey across the United States, visiting cities where there were messengers, living and working in each city in turn. She was writing a book, a collection of messenger experiences. She was reputed to be hard and fast.'

Bill and Rebecca didn't meet until the San Francisco CMWC in 1996, when she came careering down a hill towards him, arms and legs bare, riding with no brakes. As she drew closer, he saw that she was missing front teeth, and knew exactly who he was about to encounter.

'And then', he recalls, 'I heard this horrible rattling noise, and I looked at her front wheel, and thought – oh, my God, she's got spokey-dokes!'

Her wheels were strung with the brightly coloured plastic beads so beloved of kids in the 1980s.

Rebecca comes across as a compelling personality, 'A mixture of vulnerability and bravado,' recalls Bill, 'forever tilting at windmills, real or imagined.' What really captured my imagination was her role as a modern-day Columbus, voyaging out from the familiar world of Washington, DC, where she did her rookie year, to the unknown horizons of Chicago and San Francisco, never entirely sure of whether she'd find messengers there, or how different they'd be from those she already knew.

'She brought the international messenger community onto the streets of every city, large and small, that she visited. She embodied the messenger community, she was its messenger,' wrote Bill.

She self-published her book, *Nerves of Steel*, and it's a lengthy, sprawling, meandering, under-edited tome that, to my mind, perfectly reflects the people on which it is based. It contains a decade's worth of interviews and life stories, and reading it is the equivalent of sitting on a street corner for a year or two, listening to the stories of all the couriers that pass, and learning your way around their endlessly different, endlessly repetitive, endlessly moving world. And then, in the aftermath of 9/11, she joined the US Marine Corps, and left the courier industry entirely behind.

She seemed to have emerged from nowhere, burned brightly for a decade, and then faded back into obscurity, leaving only her book as legacy. All I found of her on the Internet was a short video from 1995, three years into her messenger career, in which she talks us through the contents of her bag on a sunny San Francisco street corner. She's young-looking, lithe and tanned, with a long, sun-bleached braid and a bare midriff, and seems impossibly distant – two decades ago, and thousands of miles away. (Did Anna Livia, by now halfway through her Berkeley PhD, ever watch her ride past, and remember her own days as a courier, already a decade ago, in a rainy city across a continent and an ocean?) And yet, somehow, she's also beguilingly familiar; instantly recognisable as one of us – the scruffy messenger bag with its faded badges; the earthy chuckle; the homemade bike-chain bracelet, much like the one Nhatt wore sometimes; the crumpled cycling cap; the lock tucked into her belt. If she turned up on Creative Corner next week, she'd fit right in. Her radio is bulkier than the ones we use today, but the banter over the airwaves is just the same.

Nhatt, apparently as restless as I was, had by now tired of working in bike shops, and decided to relaunch herself as an artist. Knowing that she couldn't possibly hope to support herself in London on the paltry earnings this would entail, she broke up with her boyfriend and moved back to the States, after over a decade abroad. I immediately started scraping together excuses to go out and visit her in Brooklyn, and the chance to meet Rebecca Reilly was the icing on the cake.

Someone yelled my name from across the street, and I looked up, momentarily forgetting I was in New York and expecting to see one of my courier friends. Instead, I saw a large car heading straight for me, with a telltale bicycle strapped to the back and an energetic blond woman waving at me from the driver's seat.

'I'm going to go park – I'll be right back!' she hollered, and disappeared around the corner onto 4th Street. Two minutes later, she was back, weaving expertly and brakelessly through the traffic and skidding to a stop in front of me, her spokey-dokes clanking to a standstill and then ringing out again as we wheeled our bikes across the street. She was no longer missing front teeth, and she had grown softer and sleeker than the scruffy young thing in the video; otherwise she seemed exactly as Bill had described her.

'This is on me,' she announced as she led me into the restaurant, ordered a beer, and proceeded to spend the next three hours regaling me with gossip and legends from her courier years, tales from her time in the military, and everything she'd been up to since. Far from the superior, standoffish figure I'd somehow envisaged, she was friendly, frank, effervescently talkative, frequently obscene, and often laugh-out-loud funny.

She began at the end, telling me how the US courier industry had contracted abruptly after 9/11.

'And then anthrax happened right after that. The *Washington Times* called me and said, "Hey, are you guys afraid of anthrax?" and I said, "We're afraid of losing our livelihoods, let's put it into perspective here."'

During the anthrax scare, Americans became

understandably afraid to send or receive anything by mail. It accelerated the growing trend of doing business online.

'Y'know, emails got faster, attachments were like – boom! Once you got that there's like Internet speed, and then you got online signatures, and then Capitol Hill put a bunch of stuff online. That was it.'

The work dried up. Courier companies folded, and many couriers had to leave the business. Some found that, after a decade or so on the road, there was nowhere else they could go.

'I consider myself lucky that I got out when I did, cause I know a lot of people that hit bottom and had absolutely no options. There were like a rash of suicides in San Francisco because people just couldn't deal with it. All over the place actually.'

I thought of couriers I had known who committed suicide – three to date, though there might be others I didn't hear about. In comparison, only one rider has died in traffic during my time on the road. I remembered the spring of 2010, when Eyjafjallajökull erupted in Iceland and all of European airspace was closed because of the ash cloud it emitted. Although we hadn't quite expected it to (how could a distant volcano possibly affect the daily envelopes going from Soho to the City?), the courier circuit also ground to a halt, and we spent day after day sitting in parks, gazing up at the clear blue sky above us (whatever ash cloud was there, it certainly wasn't visible to the naked eye), stomachs churning with anxiety over how little we were earning, and what we were going to do about paying the rent, and buying new tyres.

I remember the conversations I had with other couriers that bright, peaceful, uneasy week – there were a lot of them, because we had little else to do, and no other way of making ourselves feel better.

I spoke to one who had made £85 for four days' work that week, and £125 for five days' work the week before.

I spoke to another who said he was budgeting £100 a week for rent and food, hoping to afford a couple of beers on Friday night, and praying nothing went wrong with his bike.

And another, who was selling all his bikes, and just about everything else he owned, just to make ends meet.

And another, who was two months behind on her rent, had run out of things to sell, and had to borrow a tenner from me to buy cat food.

We were embarrassed, I remember that. And furious, that here we were – young and fit and strong and willing, yet not being given any work, and not making any money. It's not as easy as all that, just to step into another career, even if you do decide to leave, even if you do start going to interviews right away, though many did quit the circuit during that period. Most of them were the people who'd only intended couriering to be a temporary thing anyway, who had other options, somewhere else to be, something else to do. The longer-term couriers just hung grimly on, in the belief that work would pick up again, which it eventually did, and we all breathed a sigh of relief and got back to work, ignoring the trauma of those few terrifying weeks when it looked like we weren't going to make it, and forgetting the fact that this could happen again at any moment.

In 2001, after going into debt publishing her book,

Rebecca moved back to DC and got a job with her old friend Bega, who tried to look after his couriers when the industry nosedived, by keeping their $500 guarantees, even though they were making nowhere near that amount of money in real terms. But eventually, the couriers talked him out of it – 'Dude. No. You're going to bankrupt yourself, bankrolling us, doing nothing.' – and came to the agreement that they'd take on some of the long-distance car jobs, to make up the shortfall. Rebecca got a part-time job at Starbucks, to make ends meet, but even working seventy-hour weeks, she found she couldn't keep up with her basic living expenses, and was sinking further and further into debt. Nobody was buying the book.

''Cos I can't market it – I'm doing the best I . . . I didn't even want to explain, so I just, I became . . .'

She faltered, and I recognised the embarrassment of confessing weakness, of admitting that things had got so bad that her habitual toughness and optimism had failed her, of having been in a tight spot that she couldn't talk or ride her way out of.

'I actually became – uh – pretty, uh – honestly, I was pretty low. I was drinking all the time, getting in really violent arguments, and after a while, I just stopped going out, would just sit home and drink until I fell asleep. I thought about killing myself . . . And here I was with a college education – I'd look at it, like, yeah, I have a college education, but I don't have a wardrobe, I can't even go for an interview. None of my skills are current. I'm kinda stuck! So in a fit of desperation, whining about my life to my sister, who'd been in the air force, she said – well, shit, just join the military! You know, because they'll pay for your clothes, they'll give you an education – you get the GI bill, you get out, you go back to school. I thought – that sounds pretty good. I could get food, get my teeth fixed. I hadn't been to a dentist in more than fifteen years, I had no health insurance.'

So that was it. She hadn't joined up to avenge 9/11 and protect the 'American way of life' – she had become a marine because she simply found no other option.

She was, however, an instant hit at the recruiting office, having turned up in a blizzard, on a bicycle.

'They asked me if I'd ever been arrested for something and I said, 'Yeah.'

'What, pot?'

And I was like, 'No, I don't smoke pot at all.'

'Well, what?'

'Assault and battery.'

'Really?'

'Yeah.'

'Tony! Wilbur! Come over here, you gotta hear this story!'

'So they all came up. I told them my story about the fight with the cabbie, how I put him in hospital, and they just thought that was the most wonderful thing. They're like, "Oh' my God, you're gonna make a great marine!" And I thought, "Oh, finally! Someone comes to kill me and I can kill 'em back! That's awesome!"'

But the respect Rebecca had earned as one of the hardest and fastest couriers of her day – female or male – didn't follow her into the military.

'Marines are like the last bastion of the military. A lot of guys get in because – well, they want to be a man. To have a woman do stuff as well as they do was like the biggest insult. They *hated* us.'

Nothing like the courier world then. I wondered – was it because couriers were so accustomed to being hated simply on the basis of being a courier, without anyone bothering to find out whether they were a good one or a bad one, a fast one or a slow one, that they themselves were so keen to focus on people's merit and character. If you're on a bike, and wearing a radio, then you're in – it doesn't matter whether you're female, or black, or gay, or foreign, or riding a cheap mountain bike. And this is an active and necessary solidarity – because if we don't celebrate each other's talents and differences, no one else will, and we'll all be lumped together under the dreary and fallacious umbrella of the Dangerous Hooligan Courier.

By the time she finished, Rebecca had had it with these assumptions.

'You know, maybe I'm kinda stuck up but I consider myself educated and I really didn't like people treating me like trash. I learn Chinese in my free time, and I have a degree, and you treat me like gutter trash? Or worst of all, my pet peeve, is being equated with a prostitute. So it just got really old.'

I remembered Anna Livia's Lizzy, smiling grimly at the women jiggling 'in hot pants and goose pimples' in the doorways of Soho 'knowing that's where she'd end up if she failed at the fifteen a day'. I have been mistaken for a tramp, and am more and more often taken for a man, but as far as I know, no one's ever thought I was a prostitute.

'The thing about courier women is . . . they're so visible,' mused Rebecca. 'We changed the world. We were notice-able. We had sex appeal. We were fast, we were bitchy, we raised hell. We got in fights – well, not all of us. Mostly me. But you know, we didn't back down.'

So perhaps the early 1990s weren't the golden years that I had imagined. Maybe the golden years are now, when a female courier is afforded the same begrudging recognition as her male colleagues, and is aware of the vast international network of camaraderie and mythology at her back.

'Oh, yes, when I started, they were talking about the "good old days" being the late eighties. They made a lot of money back then,' said Rebecca. 'There were wisps – wisps of the courier mythology out there, but nobody really knew. Before I was travelling I only knew of two guys that travelled somewhere, in a year of messing in DC. One of them was a legend. To me, he might as well have been Zeus. The other guy, I actually talked to, and he had gone to Chicago, and he was kind of a dork and had ended up there by accident and said there were messengers there – and it was like: the world was flat until he got back from Chicago.'

I realised that Rebecca was in some sense just like me – enthralled by the tales of titans past, of the legends that had gone before, and of time lost. The muscular men and baggy T-shirted girls of her countless photos are all twenty years older now. Some are dead. Most have left the industry far behind them, built careers, bought houses, raised families. Only a few remain. She told me of one courier – Scrooge – who has worked in DC for over thirty years, and whose son has been on the circuit more than a decade himself.

The following summer, Creative Couriers, for whom I was by then working, celebrated their thirtieth year of business, and Lisa and Tim hired out the top floor of a Soho club and invited along a couple of hundred of their current and former employees. Afterwards, I was no longer quite as in awe of Lisa as I had been, remembering her laughter as she tipsily introduced herself to me at the door, having completely failed to recognise me out of my cycling gear. I asked her if she'd be willing to tell me about the earliest days of the industry, as far as she could remember them, and a week or so later, I found myself sitting in a sunny bar on St John's Street, sharing a bottle of white wine that she'd insisted on paying for and listening as she threw herself back into the past.

She had been a courier for two years, before setting up her own company in 1984.

'So, I met my business partner – hold on, let me think. No, that's the "official" version. The real version is, my lover-at-the-time also didn't have a job, and so she started on the sales side.' She caught sight of my smirk – we've all been there, editing a girlfriend into or out of the story, depending on who we're talking to. 'Oh, you know how it is – you tell the story in different guises to different people. But that's the truth. So we started Creative together.'

The company spent its first year in a poky office above Wardour Street ('We rented from a musician, who was completely stoned all the time'), with three telephones, two chairs, and, after placing an ad in the *Evening Standard* from the phone box in St Anne's Court, three cycle couriers. Radios were far too expensive in the early days, so most couriers would ask to use a receptionist's phone to call POB before they left a pick-up, and carry a stash of 10p pieces so that they could use a payphone if the receptionist said no. Work picked up fast.

'It's the mid-eighties. Everything is booming. Everything is couriered. And everything is Soho-based, or West End; EC1 does not exist, in the media world. So the job was about the quickest way through Soho. And I could still navigate you from any point in Soho to any other point in Soho and walk you through the way that I would ride. Because that's what you had to do. Because it was so fast, and the circuit was so small. You needed the plan in your head because there was so much work – because you wanted it to be that efficient, you didn't want them going there, over there and then back there, no.'

'So it's almost as if the courier wouldn't have to think so much?' I mused. 'Because nowadays, a run might take me from, I don't know, W2 out to E1 or something. So you've got the big decisions, like, for instance, do you go Clerkenwell or Holborn? Whereas, I guess, if it was all within Soho, there are no options really.'

It hadn't occurred to me before to think about it this way – that my job had been made more interesting by the declining workload. Back in Lisa's day, the couriers would have been on the go all the time, but Soho's a tiny place, and there are only so many ways through it. It must have felt, often, like a never-ending merry-go-round: up Wardour, left on Noel, down Berwick, right on Broadwick, Lexington, Great Pulteney, Brewer, and then back onto Wardour. The controllers would have been the ones who found the job exciting, constantly racking their brains trying to plot each courier's route to take in as many pick-ups and drops as possible, while at the same time keeping half an eye on all the new dockets that were pouring in.

'It's like a moving jigsaw,' Lisa told me. 'So it starts off with one scenario, and then it moves, and you have to intellectually move with it, and you have to have the sort of geographical brain that does that. I find it excruciatingly painful to control now.'

'Really?'

'Yeah, I do. I can't control because there's not the volume. And without the volume, I can't move people around, and keep the fluidity. You know, if I've got people everywhere, everything's a possibility. But if I've got people constantly moving, it gets so much more interesting, you know what I mean? I love it when you can just keep people moving. In fact, regardless of volume of work, there are some people who can cope with flow and some people who can't. Some can just trust the flow, and go with it. I work better with that sort of rider. All I ask is just move with me, move, keep moving, and let me do the thinking.'

'It's a bit like dancing,' I suggested, 'with someone who can lead really well.'

I wondered if any of Lisa's young female couriers had *particularly* enjoyed being propelled around Soho by the firm hand of a capable woman, and realised I must be speaking to a close contemporary of Anna Livia's Kit.

It seemed that more of the controllers had been female, in the early days. As well as Lisa, there had been Claire, Auntie Claire, one of those legends whose name ripples through the conversations of old-timers, yet whom no one seems to have kept up with. Lisa described her as 'a legend' and 'a ferocious smoker', and thought the last time she'd heard of her she'd been working as a night controller for a minicab company somewhere on Old Street. Bill remembers her as 'an imposing woman with a fearsome reputation, a sixty-per-day fag habit and the sexiest radio voice I have ever heard'. Not all that different from Kit, really. I was just wondering whether the character could have been based on Claire, when Lisa remembered another female controller.

'There was a woman called Andrea that I didn't ever meet. Now, she was a friend of my mate Robin's, and she started – now what was the company? Quite an important one, can't remember what it was called. If it wasn't Chain Gang . . .'

'Was it Hand'n'Deliver?' I asked, excitedly.

'Hand'n'Deliver! There. Andrea. Never met her. Had a bit of a reputation.'

'What sort of reputation?'

'Well, for being quite hard, quite . . . no nonsense. She had a bit of a scary reputation. I think she might have worked for Robin, very early days – and she might have been one of the first break-offs, actually, because he was quite bitter about her, and I never quite got it.'

This was Zero's Anthea, Anna Livia's Kit. She was quite possibly still alive somewhere, in her seventies, but I knew I'd never meet her.

Glancing at her watch, Lisa finished off her second glass of wine and warmly began taking her leave, on her way back to the office to pick up her wife. I thought of Anna Livia, raising her family in far-off Berkeley, of Rebecca, deploring the lack of datable men on a US military base in Okinawa, and of Ash, now back in Dublin with a car, a house, a steady girlfriend and a desk job, wondering, through the amiable haze of wine and sunshine, whether in a few years' time, I'd find myself somewhere equally unimaginable. Perhaps in another country and another career; planning a family with a woman I hadn't yet met; looking back at my years on the road and marvelling at where I'd been, and how far I'd come, and how long ago it all seemed. But not yet, please not yet, I begged myself, as I tightened the strap of my bag, swung my leg over the bike, felt my muscles settle as my feet clicked into the pedals and pushed happily off into the gathering evening traffic. There was still a long way to go.

19

It's been ten years now since I graduated and, unlike me, most of my peers have been steadily bettering themselves, and are several promotions into a good career, mated and mortgaged, and inviting me to ever-more sophisticated dinner parties. I feel both hopelessly out of place and curiously in my element at these affairs – much as I do, in fact, scrambling my way round London as a cycle courier, fitting in nowhere and therefore everywhere. I spent enough time hobnobbing with the gentry and the meritocracy at Cambridge to speak their language, even if I'll never quite be one of them, and often I'll find I have more to say to these people than they do to each other.

'So what is it you do?' says the TV producer to the accountant.

'I'm an accountant,' says the accountant.

'Oh . . . that's interesting,' says the TV producer, and wonders what to ask next. I can at least ask them which accountancy firm they work for, and then surprise them by knowing which street it's on, where their loading bay is, and sometimes even the name of their receptionist.

People seem relieved when they find out I'm a cycle courier rather than a lawyer or an accountant. Some have never heard of such a job, and ask me to explain exactly what it consists of, what I carry, who I deliver to, and how much money I make. Some ask whether it isn't terribly dangerous, whether I wear a helmet, or how often I've been doored. Some get all excited and tell me how they've always thought couriers are the coolest human beings alive, and secretly want to be one, and have a bicycle of their own, but only get to ride it at weekends. Once in a blue moon, someone will actually have worked as a courier themselves, long ago in another life, like the Australian diplomat whose barbeque I once attended on a roof terrace in Hong Kong, or the photojournalist I met at a friend's birthday drinks in Chiswick.

But by far the most frequent reaction is to ask me whether I stop at red lights, with a tone of schoolmarmish scepticism that suggests they won't believe me unless I admit that I don't. So I insist that I always do, assure them that I consider the rules of the road sacred. Seeing that they're losing the argument they thought they'd already won, my interrogators then change gear, sniffily tell me that I must be one in a million, and start asking me why all the *other* couriers never stop at the lights. Wearily (because I've had this conversation countless times before, and know exactly where it's going), I tell them that couriers vary in their adherence to the rules, that quite a few of them actually pride themselves on keeping to the law, and that those who don't are probably less of a risk than you'd think, because their high level of cycling experience and intimate knowledge of the light sequence and traffic flow of any given junction, combined with a finely tuned self-preservation instinct and the need to get to wherever they're going as quickly and with as few mishaps as possible, mean that they won't jump a light without having carefully assessed the consequences. The person I'm talking to then easily wins the argument by telling me, with a certain amount of indignant relish, that a courier *did* in fact knock them down once, while jumping the lights, and was utterly and insolently unrepentant. All I can do is concede defeat, apologise on behalf of my errant colleague (and all other couriers, just for good measure), and change the subject as quickly as possible. I'm tired of this conversation. It's like a fight between two spouses, always the same, the conclusion foregone even as the first shots are fired.

An old university friend of mine, who now works for an investment bank in the city whose loading bay smells like someone was sick there a long time ago and didn't clear it up properly, tries to have this argument with me almost every time we meet, or asks me why it is that couriers always have tattoos, dreadlocks and piercings. I try to explain that, while a lot of them do, you'll never notice the ones that don't if you're so fixated on one stereotype, but I realised long ago that this conversation is really a polemic masquerading as a discussion – sometimes people just want to share their opinions with you regardless of what you have to say in return, and couriers seem to be a subject on which people have strong opinions.

A man got talking to me outside a law firm on High Holborn once, very pleased with himself for spotting that I was a courier, as he'd evidently read or watched something about our industry recently, and knew all about it.

'So I've heard you can go and work as a courier in any city in the world?'

'Well, it's not really as simple as that – I mean, there's the language barrier, and obviously work permits and –'

'Yes, I've heard you can work in any city in the world,' he interrupted, clearly not wanting to let something as irrelevant as a real courier get in the way of his careful research. 'And look' – he gestured towards one-six Tomasz, a fellow Pink rider, who was at that moment cutting through the tangled traffic in front of us, heading towards the junction with Kingsway – 'apparently they cut their bars right down so they can get through gaps in the traffic.'

I started to explain that, again, that wasn't strictly true, that a rider's shoulders are always the widest part of his body, so adopting a riding position that keeps your hands roughly shoulder width apart is a more effective way of judging gaps, as a cat does with its whiskers, and also keeps the bike more stable than it would be if you kept your fists crammed up together on each side of the stem, as was briefly the fashion among hipsters a few years ago, but after just a few words I realised he'd stopped listening.

'Yes, they have very narrow bars so they can cut through the traffic,' he mused, taking a final deep drag on his cigarette. 'Great talking to you!' he said, with warmth and sincerity, as though our conversation had been genuinely enlightening.

Whether they're convinced I'm a lawless hooligan or the epitome of urban cool, my efforts to persuade people otherwise usually fall on deaf ears. One notable exception would be my father, who was sceptical when I announced, fresh out of my second degree, that I'd found my true calling as a cycle courier – but who then joined me for a morning on the road, spent the whole time virtually squealing with delight, and ever since has been regaling friends and relatives with tales of his daughter's amazing job at every opportunity. But most of the time, people already know what they think of you, and aren't prepared to have their minds changed.

Despite their own misplaced fears, pedestrians are in fact the most frequent and visible hazard of my job. On certain streets, and at certain times of day, I feel under almost constant barrage from people stepping off the pavement without looking, crossing against the lights, running into my path, or, most confusingly of all, starting to cross, looking up halfway and noticing a fast-approaching cyclist, then diving back towards the pavement when I'd already aimed my bike to pass behind them – or changing their mind yet again and rushing forward, or just stopping exactly where they are and standing stock still in the centre of the lane, waiting for me to go round them. No matter how many years you've been doing this, and how much pedestrian psychology you have hardwired into your nervous system, you can never quite predict which way they're going to jump, whether they'll fearfully try to scuttle out of your way, or stand firm, chin out, expecting you to get out of their way.

In the early days, I did a lot of raucous shouting in situations like this. But as the years pass, and so (mostly) do the pedestrians, my attitude towards them has changed. It didn't take me long to work up the courage to yell at them, but it was a good few months before I'd settled on the correct vocabulary and embedded it deeply enough in my brain that it was always at the tip of my tongue when I needed it, rather than coming to me half a minute later, with the junction far behind and the pedestrian long gone. At first I favoured wordless shouts, like 'Oi!' and 'Hey!', which tended to get people's attention, and sometimes surprised them enough that they'd freeze where I wanted them to, and not walk into my path.

Everyone has their own story of the time that they were almost killed by a light-jumping courier, just like the guests at my friends' dinner parties, and just like the characters of Sebastian Faulks's *A Week in December*, a novel that attempts to represent London's bustle and diversity by amassing a disparate and thinly drawn cast, just about their only uniting feature being that they are all, at one point or another, set upon by a speeding cyclist. For Faulks, and for many others, this is clearly a defining experience of London life. *Telegraph* reviewer Tibor Fisher confesses, 'I find it hard to be objective about Sebastian Faulks's new novel because I now consider him to be no less than a blood brother, solely on the strength of the hatred he displays for those delinquent cyclists who bring terror to the pavements and streets of London.' Considering that the novel's other characters include an aspiring suicide bomber and a crooked hedge-fund manager, these are strong words. And worrying ones too, since these blood brothers in hatred seem never to consider that the cyclist might occasionally be in the right, let alone to think more rationally about the comparative risks posed to human life and limb by motor vehicles (let alone bankers and terrorists), which are responsible for thousands of injuries and deaths every year – or to consider the strong incentive a cyclist has *not* to ride into people. Hit someone with your car, and they will probably bounce off, leaving you with nothing more inconvenient than a dented bonnet or a cracked windscreen. Ride into them on your bicycle (if your self-preservation instinct doesn't force you to swerve aside at the last moment), and there's a strong likelihood you'll come off worse, possibly even breaking a bone or two, since it's much more difficult to balance on two wheels than on two feet, and the road is very hard when you hit it at speed. I've collided with three pedestrians in my time on the road: none of these incidents was my fault, and in each case I ended up sprawled painfully on the tarmac, while they stood over me, berating me for riding too fast. The conviction that the cyclist is wrong seems to be a difficult one to let go of.

I've been told that the London police receive more complaints about cyclists breaking the law than they do regarding any other crime – including vandalism, drink driving and domestic violence. People clearly find light-jumping and pavement-cycling intolerably annoying, which, for me, is reason enough to abstain from doing it (regardless of whether I think the complainers might be over-reacting, just slightly). So, as my personal pedestrian policy evolved, I became an ever-more scrupulous adherent to the Rules. I took to carrying a copy of the Highway Code in my bag, hoping for an opportunity one day to wave it sanctimoniously at a fuming driver or pedestrian, and glibly absolve myself by quoting the relevant regulation. I smugly parked myself in front of taxis desperate to edge past red lights (drivers tend to ignore them above a certain traffic density), and militantly gave way to people at zebra crossings, even when they gestured to me to go through ahead of them.

But all of this just made me feel more and more that I was in an abusive relationship with the rest of the city. No matter how hard I tried to win people over, no matter how polite, pleasant, considerate and ostentatiously law-abiding I was, I was still yelled at several times a day, for breaking rules I hadn't broken, for jumping lights I hadn't jumped, and for riding too fast when in fact I'd been hovering almost at a standstill, waiting for someone to get out of my way. I began to rein in my 'Oi!'s and 'Hey!'s, knowing that people would interpret them as mere aggression if they didn't realise they were the one at fault, and began to develop a carefully inoffensive collection of ripostes, designed to warn and mildly admonish pedestrians who strayed or leapt into my path, while also making it clear to them that the misdemeanor was theirs, and not mine.

'Careful!' I'd call, in a gentle sing-song, if I just wanted them to look up and move out of my way, raising the volume or injecting a note of urgency if they'd done something particularly stupid or dangerous, or were in danger of knocking me off.

'Look where you're going!' became another favourite, sometimes fluted in a 'Whoops, silly you!' melody, sometimes stern and disapproving.

'Ever heard of traffic lights?' was the strongest response I'd allow myself, varying my tone from playfulness to mordant sarcasm. Every now and again, as I rode away from the junction, I'd hear someone remark on the irony of a cyclist telling them not to jump the lights.

One afternoon, I soared up Moorgate onto Goswell Road, crossed the junction with Clerkenwell and Old Street on a green light, and found myself barrelling towards a gentleman who'd just stepped out into Goswell Road, north of the junction, crossing against the lights. As I came closer,

I saw that he was watching me approach, and that the red man was still showing on the traffic lights behind him (so presumably also those in front of him), and made a split-second decision to hold my line, assuming, without really thinking about it consciously, that since he didn't have right of way, and could see me coming, he'd slow down to let me by, and say, 'Oops – sorry!' as I passed. He seemed to have other ideas though, and for another split second we stared each other down, his face blossoming with contempt; mine, I suspect, constricted with alarm and confusion. He was around ten years older than me, and pleasant-looking, with a full head of hair, dark-rimmed glasses and a smart woollen overcoat. He probably worked for one of the design studios or architecture firms that Clerkenwell is peppered with. If I'd met him at a dinner party, I'm sure we'd have found we had a lot in common (provided he didn't ask me what I did for a living).

Each of us seemed surprised that the other wasn't giving way. Eventually, I managed to jerk and twist the bike slightly further to the right than I'd been planning to go, and he reluctantly modified his steps, staring at me all the while with unrestrained hatred.

'Fucking *prick*,' he spat, clearly and venomously, as I passed him, pronouncing each word firmly and carefully, with an actor's projection, as if it were a conclusion for which he'd had much more time to reason and rehearse than the second or so for which we'd known each other. We were close enough to shake hands, and it felt obscene, and also puzzlingly intimate, to be insulted so graphically by someone whose face was momentarily only a few inches from my own.

I don't think I'd been called a prick before, though I've been called just about everything else over the years. Under other circumstances, I might even have laughed at his choice of insult, as I did once before, without even meaning to, when a van driver I'd displeased pulled up alongside me, wound down his window, and called me a 'fucking lesbian'. But something about this man, about the certainty with which he'd faced me down, his utter conviction that I was in the wrong, and the chilling intensity of his hatred, sent me instead to the verge of tears.

I was on my way to the Creative control room, around the corner on Northburgh Street and, typing in the code for the door, I could feel my fingers twitching and trembling with shock. As I fumbled the package out of my bag and flung it towards the overnights desk, I tried to channel my looming sobs into anger, raging at the controllers about the injustice of it all, fooling no one. They were sympathetic, of course, but with the resignation and hollow reassurances of people who've seen too much of this sort of thing, and know that it will never change.

I was given another batch of overnights to ferry over to Saffron Hill (which is still technically in Clerkenwell and only a couple of minutes' ride away, but lies across the topographical hinge of Farringdon and the old Fleet river, so somehow feels further off than it actually is), where I'd meet a van driver from another company who'd take them from me and drop them off at Heathrow. I stood astride the bike, among the cars parked along the narrow street, waiting for another car to pass so that I could pull out, and wondering why it was slowing down rather than speeding up as it approached the point where the road widened. All became clear when the driver rolled down his window, and I saw that, impossibly, it was the same man who'd shouted at me at the crossing, just a few minutes ago.

'You!' he exclaimed, in a voice that brooked no interruption or disagreement, stabbing at the air near my face with one erect forefinger, his face tight with fury. 'You went through a red light. You went through a *fucking* red light!' And he sped off, the words 'I didn't . . .' dribbling feebly out of my mouth in his wake.

The incident sat heavily on my mind for the rest of the week, like the residue of a nightmare, long after I had convinced myself that I was definitely in the right (I even went back and checked the sequence of lights at the junction), and that my assailant was probably just a pathetic individual who was having a bad day and looking for someone to strike out at; long after I had told myself that it really didn't matter, and that there was no point in letting myself get worked up about a situation I couldn't hope to change.

It was more than this, I realised. It wasn't just this man's irrational aggression that had polluted my mood – it was the fact that I was having to have this conversation with myself over and over again, every time something like this happened. I had assumed, I think, that the longer I spent couriering the better I would get at letting these things go; that eventually, I would be as calm and good-humoured as Gertie, who seemed to float above the chaos and friction of the city with his unfailing smile. But I might just as easily become as grumpy as Lukasz, as paranoid as Kris, as jaded as Ramjet. I couldn't win, I realised, no matter how impeccably

I behaved, no matter how many lights I stopped at, no matter how many pedestrians I bowed and scraped to.

'Maybe it is an abusive relationship,' I thought to myself. You stay for the good parts, trying to ignore the fact that you will never be able to change the bad parts. And a few days later, I was happy again, surging along with all the joy and urgency of a sunny day and a tailwind and a good night's sleep and four jobs on board, feeling like I could go on for ever. But I knew now that I wouldn't. That the road is a hard place, and that eventually, I'd grow tired of being a lightning rod for everyone else's rage – that one day, who knows when, one particular angry pedestrian or murderous driver, no more remarkable than all the others, would tip me over the edge, and I'd end up leaving for good.

I turned this thought over in my mind for a couple of hours, both safe and sad in the knowledge that this was now finite, that I wouldn't be around for ever. Then the work picked up and the traffic quickened, and I left the thought on that corner of Goswell Road, knowing that it would be there for me to pick up the next time I rode past.

Epilogue

'Old couriers don't die – they just wait and return,' I'd heard Gertie say once. Apparently, I had become one of those serial quitters – always trying to haul myself out of the pit of couriering, but all too regularly being sucked back in. But I returned to London from Tokyo without the sense of desperation and resignation I'd always imagined they must feel, and slotted back into the machine with the same surety of clipping my feet into the pedals, and feeling the bag I had now carried for almost five years mould tightly against my back. I was still dividing myself and my scant belongings between friends' couches and spare rooms, and just like the summer I'd decided to cycle round the world, just like the fateful autumn of 2008 when I had first strapped the radio to my bag, I had no clear sense of where the future might take me. The perpetual exhaustion and busyness of couriering was a welcome relief, as it took the edge off the vertiginous fear I sometimes felt on Sunday afternoons, when two good nights' sleep and a few square meals had given me the energy to start fretting about my lack of direction in life.

Not much had changed, despite my fears that London would be a very different place from the city I'd left behind me eighteen months previously. A few more patches of sky had been colonised by buildings, but now and again I would round a corner and come across an unexpected burst of air and light, where one had been torn down and not yet rebuilt. My body remembered all my old routes and short-cuts, and within a couple of days my mind had caught up and I remembered the names of the streets as well. Pink Express was no more, having been merged with Reuter Brooks in my absence, so I couldn't go back to my old routine of gossiping with Andy over my morning coffee and custard creams, since he was now, to widespread outrage, the most junior member of someone else's control room, only on the box a couple of hours a day.

Every now and then, as I worked my way up Clerkenwell Road, I'd hear someone mutter 'one-four' from the pavement, and instantly know that it was Andy, wandering down to Leather Lane or Holborn to buy his lunch, catching a glimpse of me as I sped past. Sometimes I'd have time to stop and chat; other times I'd shout 'one-four, one-four' back at him and carry on with a wave. I was sad not to be working with him again. But someone had put in a good word for me at Creative, and Bill had said he'd be happy to have me on his fleet.

It was a pretty good fleet, I thought, as I cast my eye over the corner one sunny morning. It was a slowish, stop–start sort of a day, and the rumble and roar of the old Broadwick Street police station being demolished across the road was loud enough to discourage most conversation, even though it had quickly become part of our usual background noise and we noticed it only when the drilling became so loud that the ground shook. To my left, Gertie was immersed in the crossword, a cigarette hanging from his lips, and to my right, Dazzler was staring at the sky as he mouthed directions to himself, occasionally glancing down at the Blue Book in his lap. After over a decade on circuit, he had recently decided that becoming a cabbie was his most viable escape route, and begun the nerve-rackingly long process of memorising every street, landmark and one-way system of the six-mile radius around Charing Cross. Occasionally, I would test him on his runs, and I had already memorised one or two myself – particularly Manor House to Gibson Square, which took the driver past some of my (and Alex's) old haunts in North London and, as the very first run of the 320 they had to learn, enjoyed iconic status among students of the Knowledge. I had run into Alex herself just a few days earlier, excitedly calling my name from the pavement as I sped past her on Bermondsey Street. I screeched to a halt, and we were halfway through hugging each other before it occurred to either of us that we shouldn't be friends, by which time it was far too late not to be.

Over at the pump sat the jovial Sax, sweating lightly after a run over from Hoxton, which he had almost certainly completed faster than I could, despite the fact that his cargo bike was twice as long as my track bike, and equipped with a large aluminium trunk that meant he could shift the sort of loads usually movable only by van. Sax was a strong, clumsy-looking rider – but appearances were deceptive, as he was actually capable of throwing himself (and a couple of hundred kilos of loaded cargo bike) in and out of traffic, up and down kerbs and through crowded junctions with extraordinary grace, and a nonchalance that was both beautiful and distinctly alarming to watch. Alongside him sat Jon, whom I'd first met at a Mayfair squat years ago, and who was now waiting for his DPhil viva to roll around before finally moving on to lecture in modernist fiction at King's College.

Around us the streets started to fill with bustling bodies as the lunchtime rush began, and a bright yellow Ferrari appeared from Lexington Street and crawled hesitantly over the cobbles towards us, the driver very clearly lost, before disappearing up Poland Street. Just before the car rolled out of sight, the nearside window opened a few inches and a manicured female hand flicked cigarette ash out into the gutter.

'Eight-four, eight-four,' said Bill's voice over the radio. We all looked up momentarily, and Jon jumped to attention.

'Eight-four?'

'Details for you, Lower John.'

'Roger-rodge,' said Jon, standing up, tightening his bag, stepping over to the nearby lamp post and politely edging his bike out from behind Dazzler's. As he disappeared stage right, Homer pulled up from the other end of Broadwick Street, parked his bike on top of Dazzler's, with an almost imperceptible nod passing between the two of them to confirm that this was OK, and squeezed himself in between Gertie and me on the wall. Unlike the rest of us, he had something to get off his chest, and launched into a gentle tirade about a last-minute visa emergency he was having to sort out before a trip home to Malaysia the following week. I listened with half an ear, the rest of my attention sedated by the warm sunshine and the comforting blur of people passing before my eyes. The yellow Ferrari reappeared, this time from the eastern end of Broadwick Street, the invisible driver languidly flicked ash out of the open window again, and the car hesitated once more and then purred off back up Poland Street.

One-seven Emi drew up and the energy of the corner shifted once again, as she was clearly in a hyperactive mood, and did a couple of circuits of the pump, growling like a motorbike and giggling at our feigned alarm as she finally pulled up inches from our toes. And then the work picked up, for some unknown, unseen reason (or several), and one by one we all flew the coop.

I was sent across Regent Street into Mayfair, to pick up an overnight from an investment firm on Bruton Street, who always left their packages ready for us to collect in their unmanned waiting room on the fifth floor, which probably saved a bit of time, but also gave me the faintest sense that my presence was unwelcome, and that the cufflinked denizens of the office preferred not to have their harmonious environment polluted by my sweaty self. The envelope, propped delicately against a vase in the book-lined hallway, was addressed to some other financial firm on Queen's Road in Hong Kong, and as I held it in my hands I was suddenly overwhelmed by a sense of the world opening up inside me. Six months ago, I had been in Hong Kong. I had walked along Queen's Road, feeling the way the humid air was occasionally cooled by the breezes filtering through the skyscrapers from the harbour, and remembering the ferry that had carried me across from Tsim Sha Tsui; how I'd revelled in the salty succulence of the sea air, and the groaning of the ancient wooden piers as the waves came and went and the tall buildings and taller peaks reared up ahead of me. What other worlds, I wondered, were contained within the prosaic addresses on all the packages I carried, behind the doors I cycled past, and in the minds and memories of the people

I met every day? The person who wrote 'Queen's Road' on the envelope probably had no idea of where it would end up, no memory of the scent of the breeze and the sounds of the Hong Kong traffic. Was it ridiculous, I thought, or was it entirely reasonable, that every mile I travelled, every city I visited, would some day bring me back to this tiny, endless London circuit, throwing me out in great arcs into the world, and pulling me back to contain all of it within the same city, within my same mind?

The lift took me downwards, opening to let someone in from the second floor, and for a second I looked out into a busy office, the receptionist gazing down at her keyboard, and a group of people shaking hands as they wrapped up a meeting and took their leave of each other. Through a window at the far end, I could see a window-cleaner, bathed in sunlight, clinging to the building like a spider, one hand on the rope and one at work on the glass, before which a man glanced from keyboard to screen, oblivious to the very different operation being performed just a few inches to his right. I thought of all the times I've raced along Marylebone Road or the Highway, momentarily keeping pace with the open window of a cab, and become aware of the person within, gazing at the road ahead or fiddling with their BlackBerry, their crisp collar and their coiffed hair, effectively sitting side by side with me for a few seconds, our two worlds adjacent, even though one of us is at rest and one is in constant motion, before the traffic quickens or slows, or I turn off towards my next loading bay.

I craned my neck as the lift doors closed again, wondering if the window-cleaner was Jack from Fullcity, but before

I could be sure, the metal slid in front of my face and all I could see was my own gleaming reflection. I had seen Jack on his bike several times since I got back, our faces lighting up in the split second between recognising and passing each other, but we hadn't had a chance to stop and catch up. Fullcity, I knew from the grapevine, had changed hands in my absence, and was now being run by a cheerful crowd of former couriers. No one seemed willing to say what had become of Lawrence, though I was told that some people's suspicions that he had been fencing stolen bikes had turned out not to be entirely unfounded. A few weeks ago, I had run into him at the newly opened Rapha cafe on Brewer Street, and been faintly disturbed when after a couple of minutes he had thrust his face towards mine with a theatrical double-take, and said, 'I never realised you had such beautiful eyes.' His own were glassy and unusually wide, and during the course of our conversation, I edged further and further down the bench I was sitting on, while he edged closer and closer to me, until just as I was about to slip off the end, Bill called me on the radio and I had an excuse to ride away.

Lukasz, on the other hand, had greeted me with an ear-to-ear grin when our paths crossed on Clerkenwell one day, and shortly afterwards tracked me down in Soho to welcome me home, and tell me a dark story of how he had spent the last couple of years back in Poland, dealing with the aftermath of a family death and his own unravelling, before knitting himself together again and returning to London. He suggested a post-work drink, and this time we succeeded, meeting in the Bunhill Fields Cemetery a week or so later. I spotted him, long before he spotted me, sitting motionless under the drifting shadows of the plane trees, a bag of almonds in one hand, and a single nut in the other, outstretched towards an anxious grey squirrel poised at the other end of the bench. I got the impression he had been there some time.

As I stepped out onto Bruton Street, my stomach told me that it was almost lunchtime, and I wondered if I'd get the chance to sit in Bunhill Fields for a while myself, once I'd dropped the overnight off at the Creative offices over in Clerkenwell. I pushed off from the kerb, clicked my left foot into the pedal, edged my way through a line of shoppers absent-mindedly trailing across Bruton Street against the lights, and set off on one of my favourite routes through the West End – the one that takes me down Savile Row, out of Mayfair on Vigo Street, slices straight through Soho on Brewer and Old Compton, and then a quick wiggle across Cambridge Circus and into Covent Garden via Litchfield Street, so that I can be crossing Kingsway within a minute or so of leaving Berkeley Square. It's not that far, of course, but moving so swiftly between such very different neighbourhoods gives the sense of a much greater distance travelled, and I enjoy the fluency with which I can dance along winding streets that visibly confound tourists, and even most Londoners.

'So, yeah,' said a voice at my shoulder as I rode into Lincoln's Inn, and, as I turned to see who it was, Homer picked up the thread of his embassy saga, exactly where he'd left it as I rode away from the corner, just as if we were still sitting there. I had been planning to follow my usual short-cut along Whetstone Park and out onto High Holborn, but for the sake of camaraderie, idle interest and a scenic detour, I followed him round towards Fleet Street to hear the end of the story, eventually waving goodbye as I reached the gateway to New Square.

I thought of Ash briefly as I bumped over the cobbles, the memory of her loss still haunting that corner, although the pain had washed away over the years, like a bloodstain on an old pillowcase, so faded and pummelled and familiar that now its presence was almost comforting. I thought of the scars on my body that contained small pieces of London, and thought that here was a corner of London that would always contain some small pieces of me, and that I could come back here if I ever needed to revisit and remember them.

Half a minute later, I turned off Chancery Lane onto Holborn, Ash left behind me in New Square, Homer charging along Fleet Street or Tudor Street somewhere to the south of me, a sliver of Hong Kong in my bag, and the filth and sunshine of London settling on my skin. The traffic sped up and thinned out as I swung left onto Gray's Inn Road, and I tucked myself in among the cabs and buses, following the lines of the road, my destination no longer in mind, but still in body, lost in the ebb and flow of the city.

Acknowledgements

Before anyone else, I have to thank my wonderful agent, Rachel Mills, without whom *What Goes Around* most definitely would not have been written. Thank you also to Laura Hassan, my editor, for her thoughtful and inspired work on the manuscript, and to all at Faber, and Peters, Fraser & Dunlop who have helped me bring this book to fruition, especially Marilia Savvides, and Jemma Pascoe, who was never quite sure, when I arrived in reception, whether I was there on my own behalf or to deliver a package for someone else.

Many of the courier family have given me their stories for this book, willingly and unwittingly, with and without their names, and I'd like both to thank them for their generosity, and to apologise for the errors and distortions I know I have made.

Thanks especially to Rebecca Reilly, Bill Chidley, Lisa Byrne, Andy Ellis, Alex Cat, Stephanie Bartczak, Titta Laattala, Selim Korycki, Gertie, Zero, Tim Pickering, Winnie Chang, everyone at Pink and Creative, and the memory of Anna Livia.

I must also thank all the people who have, in their various and wonderful ways, believed in me, encouraged me, and given me the backbone I needed to bring this book to fruition. I'm particularly grateful to Susie Alexander, Raymond

Miles-Kingston, Matthias Wjst and Chris Morris for their generous and often unexpected support, and to my parents, for having me.

Thank you to Imogen Rhia Herrad, for a decade of inspiration; thank you to Lucy Fry, for showing me how it was done; thank you to Nhatt Attack, for all of our friendship and mutual admiration; thank you to Peter Fremlin, for your constant and enjoyable interrogation; thank you to Lee Craigie, who came up with the title.

I'd also like to thank former flatmates Florence Chappell and Anne Elkins, who suffered my stress and untidiness while this was being written; Mimi and Jamie Alaghband-Zadeh, whose house I was living in when it was conceived; Susie and Iain Ross, for making sure I ate properly; Hannah Darvill, Andrew Ormerod, Katie Birkwood, Sarah Outen, Chloe Alaghband-Zadeh and Zan Kaufman, Vicki Rainsley, Hazel Pearson, and Mel Wright, who told me I was a writer long before I believed it myself.

And, finally: Aisling Mathews – thank you for your love, your patience, your forgiveness, and above all your friendship. Without you it would all have been very different.

Glossary

alleycat – an unofficial urban race, often with a scavenger hunt element, using the riding skills couriers develop as part of their job

COA – 'cancelled on arrival', usually when the courier arrives to find the client has changed their mind, or that they've been sent to the wrong address; in most cases the courier will still be paid part of the fee for their trouble

coaster brake – a brake integrated into the bicycle's rear wheel that allows the rider to stop herself by backpedalling, while still being able to freewheel

disc brake – a metal disc attached to the hub; the brake pads squeeze the disc rather than the rim of the wheel, extending the life of the rim and greatly improving the rider's stopping power

empty – what the courier says to the controller to indicate that they've delivered all the packages in their bag and are ready for more

fakengers – urban cyclists who adopt the supposed style and attitude of cycle couriers without ever having worked as one; a portmanteau of 'fake' and 'messenger'

fixie – (fixed gear; track bike) a bicycle on which there is no freewheel, so the rider pedals constantly, and can control and stop the bike merely by altering their cadence; often preferred by couriers because of the increased control over the bike, and because there are fewer moving parts to go wrong

groupset – usually refers to the collection of mechanical parts with which a bicycle is built up: typically comprising gear shifters, brake levers, brakes, derailleurs, a chainset and a cassette

head tube – the part of a bicycle frame that runs between the handlebars and the fork, and holds the headset

headset – a set of components mounted in the head tube, containing bearings that allow the rider to steer

on/off the plot – 'the plot' is a list, real or imaginary, by which the controller keeps track of which couriers are currently mobile and available for work. A courier might occasionally ask to go off the plot if she needs a break for some reason, or enquire politely, after a two-hour wait on a park bench, whether she is still on the plot, or has been forgotten

POB – 'package on board'; indicates that the package has been successfully collected from the client and is (ideally) in the courier's bag

POD – 'proof of delivery'; in the old days, a paper docket signed by the recipient of the package; nowadays an electronic signature on the courier's Xda, which is instantaneously transmitted to the control room

pre-book – a job booked in advance for a certain time (sometimes on a daily basis), rather than the client simply phoning the courier company whenever they have something to collect

seat tube – the part of a bicycle frame that runs between the seat and the pedals

stem – the part of a bicycle that connects the handlebars to the fork, via the headset

tourer – (touring bike) a bicycle designed for long-distance travel; typically more robust than the average, and capable of carrying heavy loads

trackstand – something you'll often see couriers doing at the lights: balancing at a standstill, without putting a foot down

Xda – the palm-top computer (increasingly smartphones are used) on which the courier receives her electric dockets, updates their status to POB and eventually receives the signature from the client